Practical Softwa Project Management

Design and track execution models, and manage dependencies, changes, and project issues

Abhi Basu Thakur

First Edition 2025

Copyright © BPB Publications, India

ISBN: 978-93-65891-911

LIMITS OF LIABILITY AND DISCLAIMER OF WARRANTY

To View Complete
BPB Publications Catalogue
Scan the QR Code:

www.bpbonline.com

Dedicated to

I dedicate this book to my beloved family, friends, and colleagues. Your unwavering love, support, and belief in me have been a constant source of strength. Without your encouragement and collaboration, this endeavor would not have been possible. You have stood by me through thick and thin, and for that, I am deeply grateful.

About the Author

Abhi Basu Thakur is currently working as a Director of Software Engineering at NetApp India Ltd. Prior to that, Abhi has worked in Philips India Ltd and Wipro Technologies in various software development roles. He has around 27 years of experience in software development and has led many projects in embedded software development, mobile software development, and enterprise infrastructure management software. He has led teams of 50+ engineers and has developed products from the ground up. He has worked with teams across the globe. Also he has directly interacted with many fortune 500 customers who use the products and helped in building solution for their environments. He has completed his Bachelor's in Electronics and Telecommunications Engineering from Jadavpur University, followed by a Master's in Computer Science from BITs Pilani and an Executive General Management Program from IIM Bangalore. He has a passion towards working on new technologies and have 15 plus years of experience in project management.

About the Reviewers

❖ **Sangeetha Govindarajan** is a seasoned product management leader with a strong focus on digital transformation, innovation, and enterprise tools. She has over 14 years of experience working with global tech companies such as Walmart, Amazon, T-Mobile, and Microsoft. Sangeetha specializes in product strategy and scaling solutions, utilizing platforms like Atlassian, JIRA, Confluence, and GenAI. As a technical reviewer, Sangeetha has contributed her expertise to journals, research papers, and books in the technical and product management space. Her passion lies in refining content that covers cutting-edge developments in digital products and enterprise solutions. An avid reader and mentor, she is deeply involved in the product management community, supporting the next generation of product leaders through her reviews and mentorship efforts.

❖ **Shalini** is a Senior Technical Product Manager with over a decade of experience delivering enterprise-scale technology solutions across Logistics, SaaS, and e-commerce. Her professional journey spans entrepreneurial ventures, mid-sized tech firms, and industry giants like Amazon and Walmart. She has led high-impact initiatives in supply chain automation, platform modernization, in-cab technologies, and digital transformation, driving innovation through a strong blend of technical expertise and product strategy. Her core competencies include API design, systems thinking, stakeholder alignment, development of scalable products, and go-to-market strategy that improve operational efficiency and customer experience.

Her ability to navigate complex ecosystems and align cross-functional teams has made her a trusted product leader in both agile startup environments and structured enterprise settings. Beyond her corporate contributions, she is a published author, keynote speaker, and dedicated mentor, passionate about enabling the next generation of product professionals. She actively contributes to the product management community and serves as a technical reviewer for books related to technology, leadership, and product development.

❖ **Dinesh Dakshinamoorthy** is a Senior Technical Product Manager with a strong background in building innovative, scalable solutions across supply chain, logistics, and data-driven product domains. At Amazon, he has led end-to-end product development initiatives, from vision and roadmap definition to go-to-market strategy, while working closely with engineering, operations, and business stakeholders. He combines deep technical understanding with a passion for simplifying complex workflows, driving automation, and enabling data-informed decision-making. He is known for his strategic mindset, collaborative approach, and customer-obsessed problem-solving. In addition to his core role, Dinesh actively mentors aspiring product managers and enjoys contributing to thought leadership through technical writing and industry engagement.

Acknowledgement

I would like to express my sincere gratitude to all those who contributed to the completion of this book.

First and foremost, I extend my heartfelt appreciation to my family and friends for their unwavering support and encouragement throughout this journey. Their love and encouragement have been a constant source of motivation.

I am immensely grateful to BPB Publications for their guidance and expertise in bringing this book to fruition. Their support and assistance were invaluable in navigating the complexities of the publishing process.

I would also like to acknowledge the reviewers, technical experts, and editors who provided valuable feedback and contributed to the refinement of this manuscript. Their insights and suggestions have significantly enhanced the quality of the book.

Last but not least, I want to express my gratitude to the readers who have shown interest in our book. Your support and encouragement have been deeply appreciated.

Thank you to everyone who has played a part in making this book a reality.

Preface

Software project management is a challenging job. To deliver a software project requires good project management skills, understanding the technicalities of what is being developed, managing a team of individuals and motivating them for project success.

Comprising nineteen insightful chapters, this book covers a wide range of topics essential for understanding the intricacies of project management for a software development project. We start with how the teams in a software organization are organized. From there, we delve into how a project is initiated, how estimation and planning is managed, how the team has to be organized in order to execute the projects.

Chapter 5, Requirement Analysis, focuses on requirement analysis, followed by project kickoff and how to manage the architecture and design phase.

Chapter 9, Tracking Execution, talks about how the projects are tracked when execution is going on. Dependency and change management in projects are discussed in Chapter 10, Dependency and Change Management.

Issues raised in the project, and how to track those are discussed in Chapter 11, Issue Tracking: Probably the easiest of the things for a project manager. This is followed by security compliance, CI/CD delivery. Also, in the later chapters, it is discussed which reports project managers should be aware of. This will be followed by post-project reviews. Another important aspect which is discussed in the last chapter is appraisals for the team. How appraisal needs to be done, and how the team needs to be kept motivated, is discussed in this chapter.

This book is designed to cater to all software developers, would be software project managers and program managers, people who project managers and program managers. If the person is related to a software development project and wants to know how project management works, then this book will help in that purpose. Software developers will understand how project management works and can orient their work accordingly.

Through practical examples, comprehensive explanations, and a structured approach, this book aims to equip readers with a solid understanding of project management. Whether you are a novice or an experienced learner, I hope this book will serve as a valuable resource in your journey of exploring the foundations of software project management.

Chapter 1:Overview of Software Project Management- we'll be discussing in the upcoming chapter. We will delve into the various types of software development projects, exploring the differences and unique aspects of each. Additionally, we'll compare program management to project management, highlighting the distinct roles and responsibilities within these areas.

We will also cover organizational hierarchies and how they impact roles and responsibilities, as well as the variations that can occur within different teams and projects. This chapter will provide a comprehensive understanding of these critical aspects, which will be essential for our project's success.

Chapter 2: Initiating a Software Project- This introductory chapter provides an overview. Firstly, we will discuss the initiation of the project, outlining the fundamental steps required to get things started on the right foot. Next, we will explore the various gates in software development, which serve as crucial checkpoints to ensure our progress aligns with our goals and standards. Finally, we will focus on resource planning and allocation, a vital aspect that will help us manage our resources efficiently and effectively.

Chapter 3: Estimations and Planning- This chapter will focus on the ways to estimate and plan for a project. Estimations are most of the time approximate; in that case, how to use the estimates has been discussed. Also, how to use the data to plan for projects and what tools are available at hand to plan have been discussed in the chapter.

Chapter 4: Team Management, Organizing Your Team- Team Management: This chapter will discuss about how to organize the team, what are the different skill sets needed, how to organize the team. What should a manager look out for, what are the dos and don'ts? How to keep the team motivated.

Chapter 5: Requirement Analysis- This chapter will describe the requirements and the role of the project manager in requirement analysis. What to one be careful about in requirement analysis? What is the role of the project manager in requirement analysis? What are the different tools that can be used for requirement analysis?

Chapter 6: Architecture and Design Phase- This chapter describes how to manage the architecture and design phase in a software development project. What are the templates for architecture and design documents, and what is the role of the project manager in the architecture and design phase is discussed in this chapter.

Chapter 7: Project Kickoffs- How to do the project Kickoff. What are the topics to cover for Project Kickoff? Managers need to set targets for the team that are realistic and should help the team to reach those targets in a finite amount of time. The team will not be aware of the time. What should be the goal of the team that should be set during project kickoffs?

Chapter 8: Designing Execution- Design the project for successful execution. This is about how the execution model should be designed in order to be successful. Be ready to analyze at every point of the project and ready to change.

Chapter 9: Tracking Execution- How to track a project's progress. When the project starts running, it becomes hard to track. By the time, we understand, probably crucial moments have passed, and we will be setup for disasters. So it is very important to track the progress and do the analysis.

Chapter 10: Dependency and Change Management- How to track dependencies. What tools to use? Dependencies will most likely not come on time. It is not the ideal situation always. Also changes will come almost come all the time because of customer requirements or something urgent. It is important to park the current work and handle these changes.

Chapter 11: Issue Tracking - How to track the issues which has been filed in the project internally by the team. How to track the issues which has been filed by the customers and other teams within the organization.

Chapter 12: Documentation- One of the key aspects of a product or service is good documentation. A product may not be able explain everything thru the UI, Some features may be difficult to understand. Limitations, configurations are best explained via the documentation. Customers will question the feature if something is missing.

Chapter 13: Delivery- Post-project is done, delivery is the last milestone of the development cycle. This chapter will describe what are the different ways to deliver the project. How on device software delivery, on prem software delivery, how saas delivery will have to be managed.

Chapter 14: Security of the Product- Security is a very important aspect of the product nowadays. With the increasing ability to share data via wi-fi, Bluetooth products are vulnerable to hackers attacking the system. Hence it is very important to plan, estimate and execute for security issues.

Chapter 15: QA and Automation- QA and automation are one of the most important factors in a software development project. They ensure that the product developed is of very good quality. If the product is not of good quality, customers will not use the product for a long time. QA and automation team should ensure consistent quality in terms of functionality, better usability of the product.

Chapter 16: Continuous Integration and Delivery- Continuous integration and delivery is the process of continuously integrating and delivering. Not all products are delivered like this. In cases where it is not possible to deliver like this, the process prepares the builds continuously and keeps them ready. In cases where it is possible to deliver the builds continuously, the CI/CD process can be quite handy along with QA automation.

Chapter 17: Metrics to Gather and Tools- Different metrics to gather and tools. Metrics provide insight into the projects. The chapter provides a list of metrics that can be gathered at different stages of the project. If these metrics are gathered, then it will help to provide visibility into the project at any stage.

Chapter 18: Post Project Review- Continuous improvement for the team, technology needs to be harnessed.. How do trainings need to be planned? How do the technical trainings need to be planned? Teams are initially immature. Maturity improves with time, but does not increase in a day

Chapter 19: Appraisals- Appraisals are an integral process of software development teams which normally happens at the end of the year. The team members are appraised based on their performance. Managers play the most important role for their team members. Gathering metrics for decision making, and how to come to a conclusion regarding the rating of the person is discussed in the chapter.

Coloured Images

Please follow the link to download the
Coloured Images of the book:

https://rebrand.ly/vux4hiv

We have code bundles from our rich catalogue of books and videos available at **https://github.com/bpbpublications**. Check them out!

Errata

We take immense pride in our work at BPB Publications and follow best practices to ensure the accuracy of our content to provide with an indulging reading experience to our subscribers. Our readers are our mirrors, and we use their inputs to reflect and improve upon human errors, if any, that may have occurred during the publishing processes involved. To let us maintain the quality and help us reach out to any readers who might be having difficulties due to any unforeseen errors, please write to us at :

errata@bpbonline.com

Your support, suggestions and feedbacks are highly appreciated by the BPB Publications' Family.

Did you know that BPB offers eBook versions of every book published, with PDF and ePub files available? You can upgrade to the eBook version at www.bpbonline. com and as a print book customer, you are entitled to a discount on the eBook copy. Get in touch with us at :

business@bpbonline.com for more details.

At **www.bpbonline.com**, you can also read a collection of free technical articles, sign up for a range of free newsletters, and receive exclusive discounts and offers on BPB books and eBooks.

Piracy

If you come across any illegal copies of our works in any form on the internet, we would be grateful if you would provide us with the location address or website name. Please contact us at **business@bpbonline.com** with a link to the material.

If you are interested in becoming an author

If there is a topic that you have expertise in, and you are interested in either writing or contributing to a book, please visit **www.bpbonline.com**. We have worked with thousands of developers and tech professionals, just like you, to help them share their insights with the global tech community. You can make a general application, apply for a specific hot topic that we are recruiting an author for, or submit your own idea.

Reviews

Please leave a review. Once you have read and used this book, why not leave a review on the site that you purchased it from? Potential readers can then see and use your unbiased opinion to make purchase decisions. We at BPB can understand what you think about our products, and our authors can see your feedback on their book. Thank you!

For more information about BPB, please visit **www.bpbonline.com**.

Join our book's Discord space

Join the book's Discord Workspace for Latest updates, Offers, Tech happenings around the world, New Release and Sessions with the Authors:

https://discord.bpbonline.com

Table of Contents

Overview of Software Project Management

Introduction

One of the key reasons for successfully executing a software project is software project management. Good management can lead to better execution, quality, timely delivery, and motivated team members. On the other hand, mismanagement can lead to delays in delivery, demotivated team members, attrition of team members, etc. There are many variables while executing a project. This is similar to a mathematical equation having many variables. If these variables are not managed well, the project can run out of control. Also, there has to be continuous feedback through different reports, like test cases run, percentage of test cases, number of user stories done, and velocity of the team, to understand the state of the project. Without proper monitoring, managers will not know where the project stands. This chapter gives an overview of the different types of projects that a project manager can encounter, the hierarchies of an organization, and the roles and responsibilities of different people. Many organizations will have different names for these roles, but they can be mapped to the roles described here from the responsibilities they execute. Many organizations do not have these roles, and some people play multiple roles. This way, sometimes things may get done, and sometimes they may not. Also, what happens if that person playing multiple roles leaves the organization? It is extremely difficult to get people on the team who will pull everything through. The idea is that everyone plays a small part in the project and gets it done. Everything that needs to be done for the project is in this book.

Structure

In this chapter, we will discuss the following topics:

- Types of software development projects
- Program vs. project
- Roles and responsibilities
- Importance of the SDLC process

Objectives

After studying this unit, you should be able to understand how different project teams are organized and how they synchronize amongst themselves for the smooth execution of the project.

There are many aspects of project management that a manager needs to take care of. Some of these are defined via the **software development lifecycle (SDLC)** process for software development. Requirement analysis, estimation, planning, architecture and design, testing, automation, documentation, release, and post-release support are the different aspects of the SDLC. In the subsequent chapters, the topics mentioned in the previous chapters will be discussed. Managers will get an overview of what to expect and how to take care of various situations while the project is being executed. It will help to improve the overall execution of the project.

It has to be remembered that people are executing the project. These ambitious sets of people in the team have growth in mind: making more than their current remuneration, getting tasks challenging their skills, having a benign work culture, job safety, and good management. As we have heard, employees leave because of their managers, it is paramount that employees are cared for well. In countries like the USA and Japan, employees tend to stick to a company for a long time, while in countries like India, employees tend to have much less stickiness to a particular organization and are always on the move. The reason is that India has seen rapid growth in software development jobs, presenting new opportunities with a concentration of software jobs, mainly in Bengaluru, Gurgaon, and Hyderabad. Thus, it does not require relocating to a different location. Also, talented individuals do not guarantee a successful project execution since these engineers can work differently. A good project manager binds all the engineers and cross-functional teams to a common goal, which is the project's success.

Types of software development projects

There can be different types of software development projects; it can be either done in-house or outsourced to other companies.

Software development happens in two different types of organizations:

- Services organizations
- Product development organizations

Some of the domains of software development projects are as follows:

- ERP software development
- IT infrastructure
- Embedded software development
- Automotive software development
- Aerospace software development
- Mobile application software development

The ways these projects can be executed are as follows:

- In-house development with its own set of engineering
- In-house development with the contractor. Project management is done in-house.
- In-house co-development with a contracting team.
- Outsourcing the entire development to a contracting team.
- Outsourcing part of the development and keeping the core part of the development in-house.

The model of development depends on what is suitable for the organization. The following factors determine which model to follow:

- Cost is a major factor for decision-making.
- Expertise is not always available in-house.
- Time available for development.
- Maintenance versus development from the ground up.

Program vs. project

Each program can be very large, and it may not be possible to execute the program by a single monolithic team. Normally, the program is broken down into smaller components, each managed by a team. This team is fully responsible for delivering the program. A project manager's scope is limited to the part of the program the individual executes. However, a shrewd project manager normally has a high level of knowledge of what is happening in the program. This is to anticipate any risks and upcoming challenges in the program. A program comprises many teams, and the roles and responsibilities of the managers are discussed in the next section.

For example, let us say an e-commerce website development project is getting done. The entire program of website development can be managed by a program manager. Now, the e-commerce website has many components. For example, shopping cart, catalogue management, supplier onboarding, billing, inventory, and many more. Each of these can be handled by different project managers. Or maybe 2-3 projects are handled by a single manager. The program manager helps to coordinate and synchronize different project managers and teams.

Roles and responsibilities

The roles and responsibilities of a team are as follows:

- **Project manager:** A project manager is responsible for executing the project within time and with quality. They should be able to keep their motivation high. A project manager may be managing a software or a hardware team.

- **Program manager:** A program manager executes the overall program. Normally, they coordinate across different teams and make sure the program succeeds. They have weekly team meetings and send signals to the higher management regarding the program's health.

- **IT manager:** IT managers make sure that the systems running the software components are available and running. They ensure that the systems are being monitored and take corrective actions.

- **QA manager:** A manager who is responsible for testing the system. There can be one or many QA managers in the system. They ensure that the product delivered is of good quality.

- **Documentation:** Documentation is primarily for products that are external and consumer-facing. If the product is made for another team, the development team can create the documentation and pass it on to the other team.

- **Support:** The project manager can take on the role of a support manager, or the support manager can be someone from the support team.

Refer to the following figure:

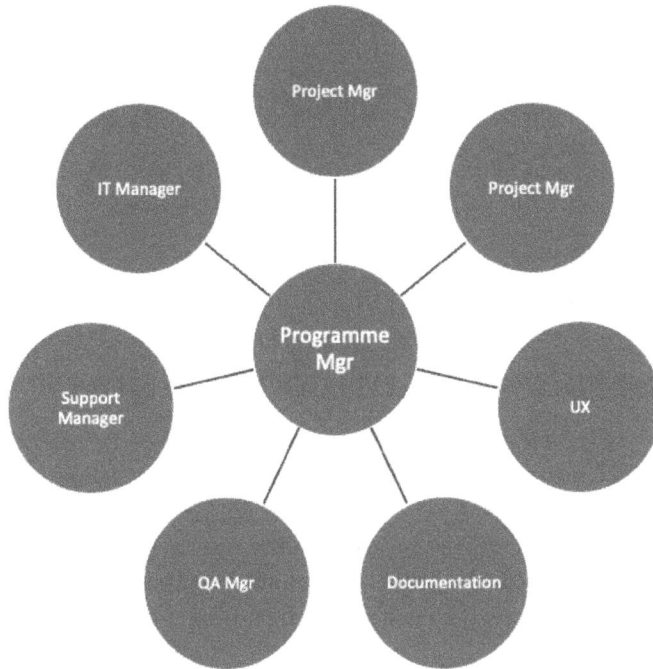

Figure 1.1: *Functional team composition*

The formula for reporting hierarchy in engineering is shown in *Table 1.1*:

Roles	Number of people	Role
Manager	8-10	Project execution, engineering team management
Senior manager	16-20	Project execution, managing 1 or 2 managers. Engineering team management
Director/ Deputy General Manager/ Program Manager	40-50	Project execution, managing 2 or more senior managers, resource balancing across multiple teams, setting priorities for the team.
Sr. Director/ General Manager/ Sr. Program Manager	80-100	Coordination across different directors, moving teams across, resourcing, visualizing future priorities.
Associate VP/BU Head/Group Manager	200-300	Typically, a business unit owner. Owns P&L of that particular unit. Usually works with the CFO
VP/ Organization Head/ Group Head	400-600	An organization head. Typically an organization looking into a particular domain.

Roles	Number of people	Role
Head of Engineering	1000-2000	Manages multiple organization heads.
CEO	1000-Any number	Head of the company. Engineering sales
Board of Director	CEO and team	Directing the CEO about what to do. These 5-8 wise men have seen all and done all. They guide the CEO of a company.

Table 1.1: Reporting hierarchy in engineering

Variation in roles and responsibilities

The above roles as specified in the table may be applicable for a development organization, but it may not be true for support, product management or sales organizations. They may have different structures. The grade of a product manager may depend on the number of products that the person is handling, but not on the number of engineers reporting. Also, whatever has been described in the table is a framework; this is not a hard rule. A director or senior director may have a lesser number of individuals reporting.

Many startups have CEOs who manage the projects. The layers in between are absent. It is not mandatory to have these layers in between, but as the company grows bigger, these layers need to be there to scale the project execution better.

A project manager's scope is limited to the particular project being executed. However, this is one of the pillars of the program. Anything wrong in the project can destabilize the entire program.

For example, in the e-commerce website development discussed before, one manager may be handling the billing module of the project. If the billing module is not good in terms of quality, then the entire project may be derailed.

The management chain above the project manager is responsible for overseeing the execution of the project. They seek reports to see if everything is running smoothly in the project. If things are not running smoothly, then they intervene and make the project execution smoother.

If there is a recurrent problem, then the organization may do something depending on the problems they are seeing in the program.

Recurrent problems in the program may originate from the following:

- Repeated problems, like bugs in the product. Even after multiple rounds of testing, the product is not getting stabilized. That means one part of the change is impacting the other part. This may be because of the wrong design.

- Some problems, like scale and performance, are not getting solved, and spending more time is not going to solve the issue. For example, the product is unable to scale even after repeated cycles and is not designed to run in a clustered environment. Converting from a standalone system to a clustered environment is not trivial and requires a lot of knowledge and effort. Senior managers provide guidance on how to solve these problems.

- Recurrent team issues, for example, the team is getting into conflicts frequently within the team, as well as with the dependent teams. The morale of the team is low, and it is very difficult to motivate the team to get things done.

- Missing dates, low return on investment. For example, consumer electronic devices need to be on the shelves by mid-November in many markets across the world. Otherwise, the devices miss the holiday season. Now, if management feels that the product launch will miss the date because of the software development missing the dates, then they might as well stop the project. This may eventually save more money rather than wasting it.

- Customer preferences and market needs have evolved over time. For instance, features that customers once found essential might have changed during the project's development. For example, the way customers search for products on an e-commerce website might have shifted, requiring a more intuitive search functionality. Additionally, advancements in technology can influence customer expectations. When new technologies emerge, such as ChatGPT in 2023, which revolutionized the software industry, customers may prefer solutions that incorporate the latest innovations, leaving behind older methods.

To illustrate how preferences have shifted over time, consider the example of customer service in the e-commerce industry. Previously, many companies relied on traditional customer service methods such as call centers and email support. Customers would reach out to these support channels, wait for a response, and then get their issues resolved. This process could be time-consuming and often frustrating for customers.

However, with the advent of ChatGPT and similar AI-driven technologies, there has been a significant change in how customer service is approached. ChatGPT, an artificial intelligence developed by OpenAI, provides instant and accurate responses to customer queries. By incorporating natural language processing capabilities, it can understand and respond to a wide range of customer questions, often providing more efficient and satisfactory interactions compared to traditional methods.

For instance, a customer facing an issue with their order on an e-commerce platform can now engage with a chatbot powered by ChatGPT. AI can quickly analyze the customer's query, access relevant data, and provide a solution almost instantaneously. This shift has led to a decrease in the reliance on human customer service representatives for routine queries, allowing them to focus on more complex issues.

As a result, customers have grown to expect immediate assistance and resolution, making the old ways of waiting for email responses or spending long minutes on hold seem outdated. This change in preference highlights the growing demand for speed, efficiency, and technology-driven solutions in the modern marketplace.

The management chain sitting on top of the managers is analyzing these aspects on a recurring basis every month and every quarter. They analyze the projects and are responsible for making critical decisions about the program. Some of the decisions could be:

- Adding more people to the program.

- Suggesting ways through which some of the issues can be resolved.

- Making decisions on stopping or proceeding with the product.

Importance of the SDLC process

The primary role of the project manager is to take the project through an SDLC model and deliver the product. The following are the SDLC steps, which should be followed while developing software:

- **Requirement analysis**: Understanding what the customer wants. For example, if developing an e-commerce website, identifying features like user login, product search, and checkout process.

- **Estimation of the project**: Determining the time and resources needed. For example, it is estimated that developing the e-commerce website will require six months and a team of five developers.

- **Delivery of the requirements via architecture, design, implementation, and testing**: Creating the system's structure, building it, and ensuring it works correctly. For example, designing the database schema, coding the login functionality, and testing the site's performance under heavy traffic.

- **Continuous integration/continuous deployment**: Regularly merging code changes and deploying them to production. For example, Jenkins is used to automatically test and deploy new features to the e-commerce website daily.

- **Security**: Ensuring the software is protected from threats. For example, implementing SSL certificates for secure data transmission and performing regular vulnerability scans on the e-commerce website.

The subsequent chapters will discuss in more detail each of these topics and what a project manager should be aware of, and what reports to look for to understand the progress of the project.

Often, project managers behave as if they know all and do not have to learn anything new. However, that is the wrong kind of thinking to have. Technologies are evolving, and so are the ways to achieve the projects. It is important to listen to others and assimilate the best practices in the projects.

Conclusion

In conclusion, effective project management is crucial for the successful execution of software projects. It plays a vital role in ensuring timely delivery, high quality, and motivated team members. This chapter covered various aspects of project management, including different types of software development projects, execution models, and the distinction between program and project management.

It also emphasized the significance of people aspects in project management, highlighting the importance of taking care of team members' growth, motivation, and job satisfaction. A skilled project manager plays a crucial role in aligning the team toward a common goal and ensuring project success. Furthermore, the chapter discussed the roles and responsibilities of different team members, such as project managers, program managers, IT managers, QA managers, and support managers. The hierarchical structure within engineering organizations was also explored, providing insights into reporting hierarchies and variations based on the organization's size and growth stage.

Lastly, the chapter touched upon the decision-making process at higher management levels, where recurring problems, customer preferences, and market forces are analyzed to make critical decisions for the program's success.

In the next chapter, how a new project is initiated will be covered. Projects go through an initiation process, and a proper initiation process helps in the smooth running of the project, lesser miscommunication, and properly mapping of the deliverables to the requirements.

Points to remember

- Good software project management is essential for successful project execution, quality, timely delivery, and team motivation.

- Software development projects can be executed in-house or outsourced to other companies.

- Different types of software development projects include ERP software development, IT infrastructure, embedded software development, automotive software development, aerospace software development, and mobile application software development.

- Execution models for software development projects include in-house development with own engineering team, in-house development with contractors, in-house co-development with a contracting team, outsourcing the entire development, or outsourcing part of the development while keeping the core part in-house.

- Program management involves breaking down a large program into smaller components managed by different teams, while project management focuses on executing a specific part of the program.

- The key roles and responsibilities in a software project team include project manager, program manager, IT manager, QA manager, documentation specialist, and support manager.

- The reporting hierarchy in engineering organizations typically includes managers, senior managers, directors, and higher-level positions overseeing project execution and resource management.

- Recurrent problems in a program require analysis and decision-making by the management chain to address issues, make necessary adjustments, and ensure program success.

- Effective project management involves understanding the software development life cycle, managing people, choosing the right execution model, and differentiating between program and project management.

Multiple choice questions

1. **Which of the following is a key reason for the successful execution of a software project?**
   a. Management
   b. Timely delivery
   c. Lack of team motivation
   d. Poor quality

2. **Which of the following is not a phase of the SDLC?**
   a. Requirement analysis
   b. Testing
   c. Marketing
   d. Release and post-release support

3. **Which of the following is a type of software development project?**
   a. Financial planning
   b. Industrial manufacturing
   c. ERP software development
   d. Agricultural farming

4. **Which execution model involves outsourcing the entire development to a contracting team?**

    a. In-house development with own engineering team

    b. In-house development with contractors

    c. In-house co-development with a contracting team

    d. Outsourcing the entire development

5. **Who is responsible for executing the overall program in software project management?**

    a. Project manager

    b. IT manager

    c. Program manager

    d. QA manager

6. **Which role is responsible for testing the system in software project management?**

    a. Project manager

    b. IT manager

    c. Program manager

    d. QA manager

7. **Which role is responsible for ensuring that the systems running the software components are available and running?**

    a. Project Manager

    b. IT Manager

    c. Program Manager

    d. QA Manager

8. **What is the purpose of documentation in software project management?**

    a. For customers to know product usage

    b. Internal team consumption

    c. Resource balancing

    d. Both a and b

9. **Which position is responsible for overseeing the execution of the software development project and intervening if issues arise?**

    a. Project Manager

    b. Senior Project Manager

    c. Program Manager

    d. Both a and b

10. **What is the primary responsibility of a project manager in software project management?**

    a. Resource balancing

    b. Quality assurance

    c. Timely project execution

    d. All of the above

Answer key

1. b
2. c
3. c
4. d
5. c
6. d
7. b
8. d
9. d
10. d

Exercises

1. Explain the importance of effective project management in software development projects. Provide examples to support your answer.

2. Describe the different types of software development projects and provide an example for each type. Discuss the unique challenges associated with each type.

3. Discuss the factors that influence the choice of execution model for software development projects. Explain how cost, expertise, time, and maintenance considerations impact the decision-making process.

4. Explain the roles and responsibilities of a project manager in software project management. Discuss the key skills and qualities that make a project manager effective in leading a team.

5. Describe the reporting hierarchy in engineering organizations for software project management. Discuss the roles and responsibilities of managers at different levels and explain how they contribute to the success of the projects.

CHAPTER 2
Initiating a Software Project

Introduction

The successful initiation and management of a software project are crucial for organizations aiming to solve problems or develop software products. Whether operating as a product-based company focused on software development and sales or a service-based company catering to customer requirements, the process of initiating a software project requires careful planning, collaboration, and adherence to defined stages.

This chapter looks into the intricacies of initiating and progressing through the stages of a software project. It explores the roles of key stakeholders, such as product managers, in defining project objectives and translating customer needs into product requirements.

Structure

In this chapter, we will discuss the following topics:

- Project initiation
- Stage gates in software development
- Resource planning and allocation
- Checklist for project initiation

Objectives

This chapter aims to provide an understanding of the initiation and stages of a software project within an organization. It aims to explain the process of starting a software project, defining project objectives and scope, and obtaining requirements. The chapter also highlights the importance of collaboration among different stakeholders and teams, as well as effective resource planning and allocation.

It gives readers insights into the key steps and considerations involved in initiating and managing a software project while emphasizing the importance of stakeholder collaboration, requirement analysis, and continuous improvement.

Project initiation

A software project is initiated by the organization to address specific issues or a set of challenges.

For example, a **fast-moving consumer goods company** (**FMCG**) may initiate a software project to solve some of the issues related to its operations. The FMCG company may not have in-house technical expertise. They may get a software services company to implement a solution for them.

In the case of a product-based company, the primary aim is to develop and market software products to customers. These customers may be enterprises looking for tailored solutions to optimize their operations or individual users seeking simple, user-friendly applications for personal use. For example, Oracle is a software product company whose main aim is to sell the products developed in-house, like the MySQL database.

If it is a software services company whose main job is to develop software on a turn-key basis, then the requirements are obtained from the customer. The main job of the service company is to deliver the software according to the requirements. For example, organizations like *Wipro*, *Infosys*, and *Tata Consultancy Services* are primarily service companies that develop and maintain software on a turn-key basis.

In all the above cases, there is either a product manager or a business analyst who is providing the requirements.

The role of a product manager is multifaceted and central to the success of a software project. At the onset, the product manager is responsible for defining the project's objectives and scope. They work closely with stakeholders to understand the overall vision and ensure that the project aligns with the organization's strategic goals. One of the critical tasks of a product manager is to gather and articulate requirements, ensuring they are clearly documented and communicated to the development team.

A product manager must have a deep understanding of the market and customer needs. They are tasked with translating customer sentiment and feedback into actionable product features and enhancements. This requires continuous engagement with end-users and stakeholders to ensure that the product meets or exceeds their expectations. Additionally, the product manager is responsible for prioritizing features and setting the roadmap, balancing various demands and constraints.

Effective communication is a cornerstone of the product manager's role. They act as a bridge between the technical team and non-technical stakeholders, ensuring that everyone is aligned and working toward common goals. They also facilitate collaboration among different teams, fostering an environment where ideas can be freely exchanged and challenges can be addressed collectively.

Moreover, the product manager needs to keep an eye on the competition and industry trends, making strategic decisions to maintain a competitive edge. They analyze data and metrics to assess the product's performance and make informed decisions about future developments.

In essence, the product manager is the custodian of the product's vision, ensuring that it is realized through meticulous planning, effective communication, and continuous iteration. Their ability to align the project's objectives with customer needs and organizational goals is pivotal in driving the project's success.

The role of the product manager can be defined as follows:

- Defines project objectives and scope
- Gathers and articulates requirements from stakeholders
- Translates customer feedback into product features
- Prioritizes features and sets the product roadmap
- Facilitates communication and collaboration between technical and non-technical teams
- Monitors competition and industry trends
- Assesses product performance using data and metrics

The role of a **business analyst** (**BA**) can be defined as follows:

A BA plays a crucial role in bridging the gap between the business and technical sides of a project. They work to understand the needs and challenges of the business, gathering and analyzing data to identify solutions and improvements. Their responsibilities include:

- Gathering and documenting business requirements from stakeholders
- Analyzing and validating data to understand business needs and trends
- Creating detailed project plans and specifications
- Facilitating communication and collaboration between business and technical teams
- Ensuring that solutions meet business objectives and requirements

- Conducting impact analysis and risk assessment to support decision-making
- Providing ongoing support and recommendations for process improvements

In essence, the BA is a vital intermediary who ensures that the project delivers value to the organization by aligning technical solutions with business goals.

At the onset of the project, the **project objectives** and **scope** are defined by the product manager of the project. A product manager's role is ensuring the requirements are correctly spelled out. The product manager chalks the product's vision and is responsible for understanding customer sentiment and translating those to product requirements.

Stage gates in software development

Normally, gates are defined while software is being developed. The first phase is Gate 1, where the requirements are defined. The BU head is convinced about the project and is willing to fund the project. Based on a rough estimate, the team is sized, and then the project is manned by the project manager and some individuals.

Then comes Gate 2, where the project's feasibility is determined, whether it is technically feasible to do this project. Organizations make decisions based on the results of the feasibility study and forecast the return on investment of the project. For example, some consumer durable projects are shelved if they cannot hit the shelves of retail stores by the December holiday season. The project can also be shelved if the competition has better technology than what the consumer durable company is preparing. There can be two reasons for this: management may decide to buy a company that has better technology, or they may buy the underlying product from an **Original Equipment Manufacturer** (**OEM**) and then rebrand it as their own. While it may be disheartening for the entire software development team, it makes sense to the organization in terms of return on investment.

Activities in each Stage Gate

The following table provides a summary of the activities accomplished at each Stage Gate of the project:

Stage	Stage number	What to do in this stage?	Responsibility	Who should approve?
Ideation	Stage Gate 0	Capturing, Voice of customer, Customer Interviews, What problems customers are facing? Asking them probing questions to get more details about the problems.	Business Analyst, Product Manager	BA, PM, Engineering, Sales, Marketing, Support

Stage	Stage number	What to do in this stage?	Responsibility	Who should approve?
Requirements	Stage Gate 1	Coming up with a common set of problems to address from the Stage Gate 0 stage. The requirement is still on paper without any visualization of the same. However, the team is able to articulate how the product will be like in text.	Business Analyst, Product Manager	BA, PM, Engineering, Sales, Marketing, Support
Scoping, Architecture	Stage Gate 2	Whether it is technically feasible, Study of the architecture by all the teams.	Principle Architect, Architect, Engineering Organization	PM, Engineering, Support
Design, Implementation	Stage Gate 3	Actual product design and implementation.	Engineering Organization	PM, Engineering, Support
Ready to release. All artifacts ready, Marketing announcement	Stage Gate 4	All the artifacts of the product are ready. Go to Market announcement has been done. All statutory legal clearances, security clearances have been obtained.	Engineering Organization, Documentation, Support Organization, Marketing	PM, Engineering, Support, Release Management
Release, Release the product.	Stage Gate 5	Finally, the product is released.	Engineering Organization, Release Mgmt organization	PM, Engineering, Support, Release Mgmt

Table 2.1: Stage gates

Software development companies should adhere to Stage Gate processes. After the software is released, key stakeholders include the marketing, sales, and customer support teams. Customer support organizations play a vital role in assisting customers with any software-related issues. If the customer support team is unable to resolve the issue, it is then escalated to the engineering department for further resolution.

In stage 0 and stage 1, the key stakeholders include product management, BAs, engineering, sales, marketing, and support teams. These stakeholders collaborate to analyze and clarify project requirements, ensuring alignment with business objectives and market needs.

Product management or BA gets involved from the very beginning of the project, starting at Stage Gate 1. During this stage, product management collaborates with other key stakeholders such as BAs, engineering, sales, marketing, and support to analyze and clarify the project requirements. This ensures that the product aligns with the overall business objectives and market needs.

Throughout the project lifecycle, product management continues to play a critical role in incorporating feedback from various departments, including marketing, sales, and customer service. This iterative process helps refine the product, ensuring it meets user expectations and business goals. By engaging with all relevant departments and stakeholders, product management ensures that the product is well-positioned to succeed in the market and generate revenue for the organization.

Stage Gate 2 is the scoping and architecture phase of the project. During this stage, the key stakeholders involved include product management, engineering, and architecture teams. These stakeholders collaborate to define the scope of the project, establish the overall system architecture, and ensure that the technical framework aligns with the project's objectives and requirements. The involvement of these teams is critical in this stage to ensure that the project is technically feasible and scalable. This phase is typically initiated once Stage Gate 1 is completed and approved by the relevant stakeholders. The bifurcation is as follows:

- **Product management**: This team plays a pivotal role in defining the project scope and ensuring that it aligns with business objectives and market needs. They should be involved from the start of Stage Gate 2 to articulate the vision, gather requirements, and prioritize features.

- **Engineering team**: The engineering team's involvement is crucial for assessing the feasibility of the project and determining the technical requirements. They should join the discussions early in Stage Gate 2 to provide input on system design, resource needs, and potential constraints.

- **Architecture team**: The architecture team is responsible for establishing the overall system architecture and ensuring that the project's technical framework is robust and scalable. Their participation is essential throughout Stage Gate 2 to create a solid foundation for the subsequent design and implementation phases.

By involving these key stakeholders from the outset of Stage Gate 2, the project can ensure a technically feasible, well-scoped, and strategically aligned development process.

Stage Gate 3 encompasses the actual design and implementation of the product. During this critical phase, the engineering and design teams collaborate closely to transform the defined requirements and architectural plans into a functional product. This stage involves detailed design work, coding, and the integration of various system components. The engineering team is mainly responsible for Stage Gate 3.

It is crucial to ensure that the design aligns with the established architecture and that the implementation adheres to best practices and coding standards. Regular design reviews and code audits may be conducted to maintain quality and consistency throughout the development process. By the end of Stage Gate 3, a working prototype or initial version of the product should be available for testing and further refinement.

Stage Gate 4 marks the final preparation and transition to the release phase. At this stage, it is crucial to ensure that all artifacts, such as documentation, training materials, and support resources, are ready and complete. Marketing teams should prepare an announcement strategy to create buzz around the product launch and coordinate with sales to ensure a smooth rollout. The engineering and quality assurance teams should conduct final testing to catch any last-minute issues and confirm that the product is ready for distribution. The engineering team is mainly responsible for Stage Gate 4.

Stage Gate 5 is the actual release phase, where the product is officially launched into the market. During this stage, all teams work in unison to ensure a successful product launch. Marketing teams execute the announcement strategy and launch campaigns, while sales teams gear up to promote and sell the product. The customer support team stands ready to assist new users, addressing any initial questions or issues that may arise.

It is crucial to gather feedback from end-users and stakeholders after the release to monitor the product's performance and user satisfaction. This feedback is invaluable for planning future updates and improvements. This also helps to gain the confidence of the people who are responsible for selling and using the product. A software product can be great, but unless it is marketed or sold well, it will not generate much revenue.

Resource planning and allocation

All the major stakeholders will be required to provide manpower for the project. Different business units should commit manpower to the product. They should also be aware of the timelines of the product deliveries to plan their activities accordingly.

Other organizations should plan their tasks well so that if they must train the team to prepare to handle this new product, training should be planned. If CapEx has to be planned for running the product, then it has to be done. If any hiring has to be done, this has to be planned, and a budget has to be allocated. For example, if a project has to be done in Golang, the team has to be trained in this programming language. If this is not possible, then new people should be hired who are knowledgeable in Golang. If any hardware is required, it should be ordered, and the budget should be allotted for that.

Software is often sold standalone. However, it is sometimes embedded inside hardware, and then the hardware is sold, for example, automotive or mobile software. So, the engineering team should comprise all the stakeholders. The engineering team may have counterparts from mechanical, electrical, and electronics engineering. All the teams must align and agree when the stages are passed.

Before initiating resource allocation, it is essential to have a clear understanding of the project requirements. This includes:

- Defining project scope and objectives
- Identifying key stakeholders and their roles
- Estimating project timelines and milestones
- Determining the required skills and competencies

The success of a software project largely depends on assembling a competent project team. The team should include:

- **Business analysts**: To understand and document business requirements
- **Program managers**: To facilitate synchronization across multiple project teams.
- **Project managers**: To oversee project execution and ensure alignment with objectives
- **Software engineers**: For coding, integration, and testing
- **Quality assurance specialists**: To ensure the product meets quality standards
- **Marketing and sales teams**: To plan and execute the product launch
- **Support teams**: To provide customer assistance post-launch

Effective resource allocation requires meticulous budgeting and financial planning. Key considerations include:

- Estimating total project costs
- Allocating budget for manpower, software licenses, and hardware
- Planning for contingency funds to address unforeseen expenses

Depending on the project requirements, procurement of hardware and software may be necessary. This involves:

- Identifying the necessary hardware components (e.g., servers, workstations)
- Procuring software licenses and development tools
- Ensuring compatibility and integration with existing systems

Resource allocation is not a one-time activity; it requires continuous monitoring and adjustments. Key practices include:

- Regularly reviewing project progress and resource utilization
- Conducting design reviews and code audits to maintain quality
- Adjusting resource allocation based on project milestones and feedback

Effective resource allocation is vital for the success of any software project. By understanding project requirements, assembling a competent team, budgeting wisely, procuring the necessary tools, and continuously monitoring progress, organizations can ensure efficient and effective project execution. Proper resource allocation not only helps in meeting project deadlines but also contributes to the overall quality and success of the software product.

Regardless of the stages, there is always a possibility that the project may not proceed as planned. Situations such as market fluctuations or unforeseen circumstances can lead executives to decide to terminate the project if they deem it unprofitable for the organization. Thus, it is essential for all teams to be prepared for such eventualities.

For instance, imagine a scenario where a tech company is developing a new software product. The engineering team has completed Stage Gate 3, and the product is now in the final testing phase in Stage Gate 4. However, due to a sudden shift in market trends, the demand for this type of software drastically decreased. The executives, after analyzing the potential losses, decide to halt the project to avoid further financial strain. Consequently, the engineering, marketing, and support teams must quickly adapt to this decision, reallocate resources, and refocus their efforts on more viable projects.

Checklist for project initiation

In order to initiate a project, this project initiation checklist can be used:

Check points	Yes/No
Business case is understood by everyone	
Team have been budgeted for the project	
Any hardware/software procurement has been budgeted	
Cross functional teams are on board	
Common meeting has started	
Escalation hierarchy has been established to resolve issues	

Table 2.2: Project initiation checklist

A program manager should check if all the points in the checklist have been met by the team. If yes, then the project is good to start. If anything is not met, the team can agree for a contingent approval. Contingent approval is like a conditional approval. Let us say, one of the line item is not done and it will be done in a few days. Then, the team can agree for a contingent approval even though all the checklist items are not approved. For example, let us say that the "Cross-functional teams are on board" row has not been met by all the teams. Let us know that the project requires five different teams. However, only three teams have fully come on board. 2 teams have not been onboarded completely yet because of current assignment has not been completed. However, the 2 teams have committed to a date for onboarding once the current assignments are wrapped up. The risks has been well understand because of these teams joining late and that have been factored in as a part of the overall project plan.

However, **Business Case understanding** cannot be targeted for contingent approval because it is the most important topic for this phase.

This above checklist is a template and can be customized based on the type of project being executed. For embedded domain projects, there may be some specific checklist which can be added to the checklist. For financial domain projects, there may be some other specific checklist. So depending on the need the checklist can be customized.

Conclusion

The initiation of a software project in an organization involves defining project objectives and scope, typically determined by a product manager or BA. Software development in product-based companies focuses on creating software to sell to customers, while service-based companies develop software based on customer requirements. Stage gates are defined throughout the software development process to ensure feasibility, progress, and alignment with organizational goals. Stakeholders, such as marketing, sales, and customer support, play crucial roles post-release by providing feedback and incorporating it into the product to enhance its marketability and customer satisfaction. Committing resources, planning activities, and aligning teams are essential for successful project execution, and it is important to be prepared for potential changes or project cancellations based on market conditions or organizational considerations.

In the next chapter, we will look into how to estimate and plan for the project. The project may be subject to a go or no-go decision based on the estimates. If the estimate is very high and there is not enough budget, the project may not get the go-ahead.

Points to remember

- Clearly define and document the project requirements to ensure a shared understanding among all stakeholders and mitigate potential misunderstandings or misinterpretations.

- Engage in active communication and collaboration between the BA and engineering teams to address any ambiguities or gaps in the requirements and ensure a solid foundation for the project.

- Allocate sufficient time for thorough requirement analysis, allowing the engineering teams to study and digest the requirements, ask clarifying questions, and seek necessary clarifications before proceeding with development.

- Foster a culture of continuous feedback and iteration by actively involving marketing, sales, and customer support teams throughout the software development process to incorporate their insights and enhance the product's marketability and customer satisfaction.

- Remain flexible and prepared for potential changes or project cancellations, as market conditions or organizational considerations may require adjustments to the project's direction or even discontinuation.

Multiple choice questions

1. **Who is responsible for understanding customer sentiment and translating it into product requirements?**
   a.   Business analyst
   b.   Product manager
   c.   Engineering manager
   d.   Both a. and b.

2. **Which Stage Gate determines the technical feasibility of a software project?**
   a.   Gate 1: Ideation
   b.   Gate 2: Feasibility
   c.   Gate 3: Design
   d.   Gate 4: Release

3. **Which department is responsible for resolving customer issues with the software?**
   a.   Marketing
   b.   Engineering
   c.   Customer support
   d.   Both b. and c.

4. **What is the purpose of incorporating feedback from marketing, sales, and customer service?**
   a.   To gain confidence from stakeholders
   b.   To improve the software product
   c.   To align with market demands
   d.   Both b. and c.

5. **Why is it important to allocate resources and plan activities for a software project?**
   a.   To ensure the timely delivery of the product
   b.   To train the team for handling the new product
   c.   To budget for necessary hardware or hiring needs
   d.   All of the above

Answer key

1. d

2. b

3. d

4. d

5. d

Exercises

1. Describe the role of a product manager in a software project, highlighting their responsibilities and the importance of their involvement.

2. Explain the concept of stage gates in software development and discuss their significance in ensuring project success. Provide examples of different stage gates and their purposes.

3. Discuss the importance of incorporating feedback from marketing, sales, and customer support into the software development process. Explain how this feedback can contribute to the success of the product.

4. Describe the process of requirement analysis in software development. Explain the role of the engineering team in this phase and how they collaborate with the BA to clarify and understand the requirements.

5. Discuss the potential challenges and uncertainties that software projects may face, even after passing through the stage gates. Explain the importance of remaining flexible and adaptable to address these challenges and ensure project success.

Join our book's Discord space

Join the book's Discord Workspace for Latest updates, Offers, Tech happenings around the world, New Release and Sessions with the Authors:

https://discord.bpbonline.com

CHAPTER 3
Estimations and Planning

Introduction

In project management, accurate estimations and effective planning are essential for project success. Estimations provide a gauge, albeit imperfect, of project feasibility and resource requirements, while planning establishes a roadmap for achieving project goals. This chapter will explore various estimation techniques, including exact number of lines calculation, high-level t-shirt sizing, story point-based estimation in agile, effort-based estimation, and similar project-based estimation. Additionally, we will discuss popular project management tools, such as *Microsoft Excel, Microsoft Project, Jira, Confluence, Trello*, and *Smartsheet*, highlighting their features and benefits. By understanding and utilizing these estimation techniques and planning tools, project managers can navigate the complexities of project execution, optimize resource allocation, and enhance the likelihood of project success. Seldom are estimations correct; however, the manager still needs to execute the project.

Structure

In this chapter, we will discuss the following topics:

- Estimation techniques
- Estimations are most often wrong

- Tools for estimation
- Making plans available to all

Objectives

In project management, there are various estimation techniques that play a crucial role in ensuring successful project execution. These techniques allow project managers to estimate the time, effort, and resources required to complete different project tasks. It is important to explore and understand these estimation techniques to make informed decisions throughout the project lifecycle.

Each estimation technique has its own strengths, limitations, and considerations. This chapter will explain the different estimation techniques and tools for estimation.

Also, estimations are seldom correct, so what is the need for estimation? By the end of this chapter, we will learn how to use estimations, since estimations are most often wrong. Furthermore, we will learn how to communicate the plan to the entire team.

Estimation techniques

Once a project kicks off, the first task of a project manager is to get the estimation and planning done for the project. There is no basis for determining whether all that has been asked for can be delivered in the time provided.

Estimation is a big exercise, and most often, estimations are wrong. Therefore, estimations can be used as a gauge and not as exact.

There are many techniques for making estimations. Some of them are as follows:

- High-level t-shirt size calculation
- Effort-based estimation
- Exact number of lines calculation
- Budget-based implementation
- Story point-based estimation in agile
- Similar project-based estimation
- Estimation of maintenance projects

The following figure represents the various estimation techniques:

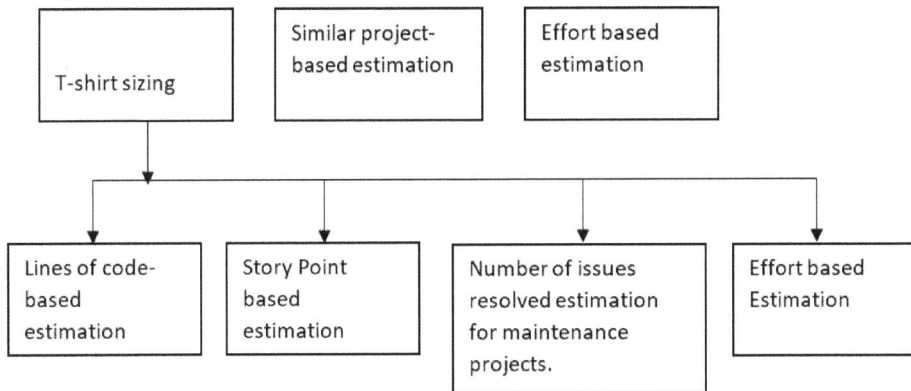

Figure 3.1: *Estimation techniques*

Exact lines of code based estimation

In this method, you need to understand the requirements first. After this, the requirement is broken down into software components. Generally, an architect is responsible for breaking down requirements into smaller software components. This is the first phase, and normally, the components are at a bit higher level. Then, the architect assigns lines of code estimates based on his or her experience and intuition about the project. There is no way to verify whether the estimate is correct or wrong. Managers can cross-question and validate to some extent that the estimations are correct. You can assume that the estimation is wrong by a few X times if the project is multi man year project.

If the project is very small, or if it is in the order of a few man weeks, then most likely, the estimate is going to be correct. However, if the project is more than a multi man year project, then the estimate will definitely be wrong.

It is very difficult to estimate based on the lines of code. The reasons are as follows:

- The language in which the application will be written is not known. Depending on the language, the lines of code will be different.

- It is impossible to know all the different languages used in the project. Some parts of the project can be in C, some parts can be in C++ or Java, and some parts can be in other languages.

- The complexity of the project is not dependent on the language. Any language can be used, but technical complexity cannot always be language-dependent.

- All engineers will not be comfortable in all the languages. The speed of development will be different for different engineers.

- Testing complexity may not be factored in.

- Infrastructure level set up and complexity may not get factored in.

In spite of these limitations, this method should be pursued for the following reasons:

- It gives a first-pass idea to the architect and senior tech leads about the gauge of the project. This gives an idea whether the project is big or medium size and what are the technical complexities which they can face, it is somewhat understandable while doing the estimate.

- If the architect is not confident about the project, then the project manager cannot decide whether to continue with the same architect or to hire a new one for that position.

- Also, the technology and the complexities of the project will be clear. It will be understood whether the team has sufficient expertise to implement this project.

In some companies, there is a database of previous projects executed. Especially in service-based companies, if there is a fixed-price project, then the accuracy of estimation is very important. The estimates can be based on the data available in the database for similar projects. It is seldom true that any new project estimate will be exactly based on a previous project. However, it is still good to see some previous data and then do the estimate. If it can be near about perfect, then it will be a good start.

Normally, the number of lines of code written in a project varies between 10 to 15 lines of code per day. If the total number of lines of code is known, dividing the total lines by the number of lines of code per day will give an idea of the size of the project. It should not be taken as the exact size; this should be used as a gauge. Usually, a Java developer writes between 2000 to 3000 lines of code per year for a development project.

For example, if a team is developing an e-commerce online store for a particular customer, then let us say it takes 90 person-months to set up the same. Now if another customer requests for an almost similar e-commerce online store then the estimate can be almost similar to 90 person-month.

High-level t-shirt sizing

High level t-shirt sizing is used when a quick estimate needs to be given to the upper management. Upper management decides about the project, and quick information is required. Typically, this can be done in one or two days. This technique can be used when the information is requested very quickly.

In the following table, features are listed, and then the t-shirt size estimation is given for each of the features:

Serial number	Feature Name	T-shirt size
1	feature one	small
2	feature two	large

Serial number	Feature Name	T-shirt size
3	feature 3	medium
4	feature 4	XXL

Table 3.1: T-shirt sizing

Small features can be assumed to be either one week or two weeks in size. A medium feature can be twice the size of a small feature. Large features can be twice the size of the medium features, and so on.

At the end, the manager is supposed to convert the sizes to weeks and then to months and then add up the total. The manager needs to account for the development QA and release activities while giving these estimates. T-Shirt based estimation technique can be used as a gauge for the project. It is used to estimate how long the project will take roughly. The error percentage for this type of estimation can be high. This is the first type of estimation that is done when a project is obtained.

This is done to save the team's overall effort from other high-priority activities and for quick decision-making. Granular-level estimation can be the exact number of lines of calculation, story point-based estimation, or effort-based estimation.

For example, a customer requests a high-level estimate for an e-commerce store development. The team receives the requirement and breaks down the e-commerce store into multiple modules, like billing, catalogue, cart, etc. The team then estimates on a high level by assigning T-shirt sizes to the modules as shown in the following table:

Serial Number	High Level Estimate
Billing	XXL
Catalogue	XL
Cart	L

Table 3.2: T-shirt based sizing for an e-commerce website

Story point-based estimation in agile

Story point-wise estimation is a technique used in agile. The features are broken into stories; the entire team brainstorms the stories and then estimates based on story points.

Story point-based estimation in agile is a collaborative technique where features are broken down into user stories. The team collectively brainstorms and assigns story points to each story, representing the effort required. This method is beneficial for quick decision-making, as it provides an initial gauge for project duration without delving into detailed calculations. Although the error margin can be significant, it saves the team from extensive effort on low-priority activities, allowing them to focus on more critical tasks. This initial estimation helps in setting expectations and planning the overall project timeline effectively.

The following table shows an estimation technique based on story points:

User stories	Story points
User story 1	1
user story 2	2
user story 3	3
user story 4	5
user story 5	˙8
user story 6	0

Table 3.3: Story point-based estimation

The story points usually follow the Fibonacci series. While executing the project, if in 2 weeks, 20 user story points have been completed by a team consisting of a fixed set of engineers, the manager can assume that in the next two weeks, around 20 story points will be completed by the same team. Usually, the story point is not estimated beyond 5. If anything goes more than five story points, the story is broken down.

Story point test estimation is particularly used for sprint planning. For more information, please undergo agile training to understand more about story point-based estimation.

Effort-based estimation

Effort-based estimation is estimated on total engineering hours, engineering weeks, or engineering months. This can be done both at higher level estimates as well as lower level estimates. Higher level estimates can be done when a quick turnaround is required for providing estimates. Lower-level estimates can be done when the project execution is in progress.

This estimation can be done by the project manager and the architect combined. The architect may not have an idea of how much time was taken to complete similar projects before. The manager may have a better idea since they have experience executing projects before. Based on the feature, both the manager and the architect can estimate the effort required to deliver the feature. Also, based on a running project, the manager will have a better idea of how long it will take to deliver a particular project. When done at a higher level, the number of hours can be more erroneous than when done at a lower level.

For example, without using Google Maps, if you have to estimate travel to a long distance, the estimation can have more errors. However, if you are travelling a short distance, the probability of correctly estimating the time taken will be higher. The same principle applies to software estimation.

An example of higher-level estimation is shown in the following table:

Serial number	Feature name	Estimation person weeks
1	Feature One	30
2	Feature Two	40
3	Feature Three	50
4	Feature Four	10

Table 3.4: Effort-based estimation

An example of a lower-level estimation for Feature One is as follows:

Serial number	Sub feature name	Estimation person weeks
1	Sub Feature One	2
2	Sub Feature Two	3
3	Sub Feature Three	5
4	Sub Feature Four	1

Table 3.5: Low-level effort-based estimation

To further illustrate, consider the development of a mobile application versus an embedded software project.

For the mobile application:

- **High-level estimation**: The project manager and architect may determine that developing the app will take approximately 40 person weeks in total.

- **Low-level estimation**: Breaking it down, user authentication might take 5 person weeks, UI/UX design might take 10 person weeks, backend integration 15 person weeks, and testing 10 person weeks.

For the embedded software project:

- **High-level estimation:** It might be estimated that the project will require 60 person weeks due to the complexity of working with custom hardware.

- **Low-level estimation**: Specific tasks like hardware interface development might take 20 person weeks, real-time processing algorithms 15 person weeks, integration and testing 20 person weeks, and documentation 5 person weeks.

Providing both high-level and low-level estimates ensures a comprehensive understanding of the project's scope, effort, and timelines.

Similar project-based estimation

This technique is again used for high-level estimation. A similar project is identified, and the current project estimate is based on the previous project.

The actual effort spent on previous projects may be hard to find; however, the lines of code in the projects can be used as a gauge to determine the effort required for the projects.

There are different types of software projects; some of them are as follows:

- Development of embedded software
- Development of standalone applications
- Development of SaaS applications
- Development of mobile applications

Depending on the type of project, the estimations can vary. For example, the velocity of development for an embedded software project is lower than compared to an application server development project. The reasons is as follows:

- Embedded software is dependent on the hardware, and developing the software on this custom hardware takes more time.
- Sometimes, higher-level languages cannot be used in Ford development, and lower-level languages have to be used. So API support is less, which increases the duration of development.
- During development, the hardware may not behave exactly right from the very beginning of the project. Hardware also goes through iterations to make it perfect.
- Embedded software development is a niche skill, and engineers must develop the skills to develop it.

For example, let us say that last year, a mobile application development project was done for a mobile game. Now, let us say a similar project has to be done this year. The team can look into the estimates, learnings from the previous year's project, and apply the same to this year's project.

Budget based estimation

In this method, a certain amount of effort is allocated to each feature, depending on the overall duration of the project. Then, the project is executed.

A budget-based estimation method assigns a specific amount of effort to each feature, considering the overall duration of the project. This approach involves breaking down a larger project into smaller sub-projects, prioritizing requirements based on importance. Features that can be completed within the allocated budget are addressed first, leaving less critical features for future releases. This method helps release the product to the market faster, allowing for user feedback to guide subsequent iterations. It acknowledges that initial features may not always resonate with customers and focuses on minimizing investment risks by adjusting features and timelines as needed.

A bigger project is broken into smaller sub-projects. For each subproject, the requirements are prioritized from highly important to least important. In the budget allocated, whatever features are possible to be completed in order of priority are completed. Remaining features are either dropped or planned for the next release. This type of project is done to release the product to the market and get feedback. Since initially, it is not known which feature will actually click with the customers, if for a long time, all the features go from highly important to least important, then the investment will be very high. This methodology is followed in order to cut down on the duration of the project.

For example, the product manager gives a set of requirements to be completed in 3 months. Let us say the features are F1, F2, and F2. The high-level estimates show that to fully do F1, F2, and F3, the time taken will be more than 3 months. In that case, the features F1, F2, and F3 are further broken down. For example, F1 feature may have sub features SF1, SF2, SF3, SF4 etc. Now, depending on the time available, only SF1 and SF2 can be done. So, for each feature, a budget is allocated. Let us say 1 month for the entire team is allotted for each feature. So the team can only deliver the important sub-features within this 1-month budget.

Estimations are most often wrong

Estimations are most often wrong. Only 1 out of 100 developers can be consistently correct with the optimum estimation. That software engineer should be an outstanding engineer. Some smarter engineers can always overestimate, meaning they intentionally estimate more time than what is required and lazily complete the work as per the timeline. Overzealous engineers normally underestimate and give lesser time estimates than what will be required to complete the task. Most engineers fall into this category. The error percentage of wrong estimates can derail a project completely. By knowing the team through some execution cycles, a project manager can understand which engineer gives what kind of estimates. Performing a continuous estimation is a perfect way to overcome this kind of issue. At the beginning of the sprint, doing estimations is a perfect way to narrow down to correct estimates. However, it is seldom followed in the teams diligently. The project manager needs to factor in the errors and also ensure that the team is following the agile methodology of estimation, which is to estimate at the beginning of the sprint, review it in the retrospective, and get better with it in the subsequent sprints. When the project is ongoing, the manager needs to inform the stakeholders about the wrong estimations so the entire team and management can adjust to the situation. Informing much later is a problem; informing much earlier is always better.

Some managers give an end date of the project or provide an end date that has a lot of buffer. Opinions may vary regarding which is a better method to factor into the effort estimates. However, the preference should be to give optimum estimates and not put too much of a buffer. If the project takes more time than estimated, it is better to drop some low-priority features to meet the timeline. Or if the timeline is flexible, it will be good to extend the timeline.

Too long timelines are also detrimental to the morale of the team. The team needs to see success. So, shorter timelines are better, and removing low-priority features is preferable without moving the timeline. The features that were removed can be done in the next sprint.

Some factors that can affect an estimation are:

- Inexperience or lack of experience in estimation, even if the agile way of estimation is followed.

- Unknowns, which generally pop up in a development project.

- Lack of understanding of the breakdown of the tasks.

- Someone is showing muscle in the team and dominating the estimation process.

- Lack of involvement of the cross-functional development teams, like backend, user interface, and QA, in the estimation process.

- Lack of knowledge about a particular technology that is important for the project.

If there are so many issues with estimations, then why do we need to do estimations? Estimation is a way to gauge the size of the project, meaning whether it is a one-month project or a six-month project. Use it only for gauging. Some idea about the duration is better than nothing at all. Prioritize the important features first and the less important features towards the end. A project manager and product manager need to decide when to call an end to the project and at which feature to stop it.

Tools for estimation

The most popular tool used for estimation is Microsoft Excel.

However, there are other tools also available, for example,

- Microsoft projects
- Jira and Confluence
- Trello
- Smartsheet

Microsoft projects requires expertise and practical experience have shown that managers do not have the skills how to use Microsoft projects. However, if proper training is obtained for planning using Microsoft projects, it is one of the best tools for project planning. Using Microsoft project, any manager can plan the beginning of the project. However, as soon as changes are to be made to the original plan, Microsoft project plan becomes hard to manage. However, it becomes much easier if someone is trained in Microsoft projects. There are tips and tricks with Microsoft projects, using which changes to the plan post the initial plan can be met very easily, and the overall project delivery date can be arrived at easily. Dependency impact can seen in Microsoft projects if the dependent tasks are correctly linked to the parent tasks.

Jira is another tool that is used by teams across the world for project management. This is the most popular tool today. Jira is an easy-to-use tool and is particularly useful when using agile methodology development. It is useful for creating the epics, creating user stories from the epics, and creating the tasks for the teams. If it can be used properly, then it becomes very effective to manage the iterations of an agile project. However, it is difficult to plan for the overall project using Jira. Someone needs to be extremely well trained in Jira to plan for the overall project just using Jira. It is hard to understand how the overall project is panning out through Jira alone. It is also hard to communicate with teammates who can be across the globe. So, it is better to use a combination of Jira and confluence on how to plan for the project. Confluence page can have a high-level breakdown of the product into Epics. In Jira, you can have the epics broken down into user stories. On the confluence page, the high-level project plan can be shown. Confluence also has Kanban plugins that can show Kanban boards of the project. It is recommended to undergo training in Jira to know how to plan for a project using Jira. Most of the project teams do not exploit the power of Jira fully and they use part of it, which is mostly about breaking the tasks and assigning tasks to individuals. The tasks are then tracked to completion. However, if used effectively, Jira can provide the overall end date of the project. It will keep showing the team's velocity and can provide many other metrics, which may be otherwise hard to get.

If the waterfall method of development is followed, it is good to use Microsoft Project. If the agile way of development is followed, using Jira is the best approach.

The key difference between Microsoft Project and Jira is that while Microsoft Project is normally edited by the project manager, Jira is edited by the manager as well as the team on a continuous basis. Since the effort is distributed and managed by the entire team, plans in Jira are much more relevant at any point in time.

Microsoft Excel is another tool used by managers. It is a very rudimentary tool and can be used only for very high-level planning. Due to many limitations, it cannot be used for detailed planning. Microsoft Excel ideally should not be used for project planning.

Comparison of different tools used for project planning is shown in the following table:

	Microsoft project	**Jira and confluence**	**Microsoft Excel**
Usability	Difficult without training	Moderately difficult without training Relatively easy compared to Microsoft project	Easy to use
Can it manage complex project	Yes	Yes	Difficult to manage complex projects with excel
Automatically impacting dependent tasks	Maybe, depending on the way the project is planned	Maybe dependent on the way the project is planned	No

	Microsoft project	**Jira and confluence**	**Microsoft Excel**
Keeping project plan updated	Solely dependent on the manager	Dependent on the entire team	Dependent on the manager
Ability to use by the entire team	Not possible	can be used easily by the entire team	not possible
Easy to see progress	Difficult to see progress. Keeping Microsoft project updated is a challenge.	Easy to see progress. How ever overall project progress is hard to see without proper training	Impossible to see the project progress.
Global transparency	Becomes proprietary to the project manager. no one can see the sheet by default unless and until it is put in SharePoint.	By default it is visible to everyone provided the person has access to the Jira and confluence pages.	Becomes proprietary to the project manager. no one can see the sheet by default unless and until it is put in SharePoint.
Metrics, velocity	Difficult to see in Microsoft project	Easy to see in Jira automatically generates many metrics, for example, velocity, likely closure date of the project etc.	Excel cannot generate metrics by default.

Table 3.6: Comparison of different tools for project planning

Making plans available to all

Make plans available to all; do not hide from team members. They will have a shared goal.

However, do not share the plan when it is in progress. Share the plan only when it has been finalized and not when it is in progress. It causes anxiety to the team members if their name appears against a certain project, and the next day, their name disappears against that particular project. Now, the manager's intent may not be wrong, but it may be difficult to convince an engineer about the same.

Conclusion

In conclusion, this chapter has explored the critical aspects of estimations and planning in project management. We have examined various estimation techniques. Additionally, we have introduced popular project management tools such as Microsoft Excel, Microsoft Project, Jira, Confluence, Trello, and Smartsheet, highlighting their features and benefits in facilitating effective planning. By leveraging these techniques and tools, project managers can make informed decisions, optimize resource allocation, and navigate the complexities of project execution with confidence. Ultimately, everything is dependent on the team which is going to do the work.

The next chapter will focus on ways of building the team. Accurate estimations and effective planning are key contributors to project success, enabling teams to achieve their goals, meet timelines, and deliver successful outcomes. In the next chapter, we will discuss how the team needs to be organized, what help the management hierarchy provides, and how to decide whether work should be done internally or outsourced.

Points to remember

- Estimations are important but challenging, serving as a gauge rather than an exact measure.
- Various techniques exist, including t-shirt sizing, effort-based estimation, lines of code calculation, budget-based implementation, and story point-based estimation.
- Consider limitations when estimating based on lines of code, such as language variations, complexity factors, and individual developer speed.
- Popular tools like Excel, Microsoft Project, Jira, Confluence, Trello, and Smartsheet aid in project planning and estimation.
- Accurate estimations and effective planning are crucial for project success, enabling informed decision-making, optimal resource allocation, and navigating project complexities.
- It seldom happens that estimations are accurate. Teams should strive for it and get as close as possible.

Multiple choice questions

1. **Which estimation technique involves assigning lines of estimates based on an architect's experience and gut feeling about the project?**
    a. High-level t-shirt sizing
    b. Exact number of lines calculation
    c. Story point-based estimation
    d. Similar project-based estimation

2. **Which tool is commonly used for high-level project planning but may become challenging to manage when changes are made to the original plan?**
    a. Microsoft Excel
    b. Microsoft Project
    c. Jira
    d. Confluence

3. **What is the primary purpose of high-level t-shirt sizing estimation?**

   a. To provide an exact estimate of project effort

   b. To determine the technical complexities of the project

   c. To quickly provide an estimate to upper management

   d. To calculate the exact number of lines of code in the project

4. **Which estimation technique is particularly used in agile development and involves assigning story points to user stories?**

   a. Budget-based estimation

   b. Effort-based estimation

   c. Story point-based estimation

   d. Maintenance project estimation

5. **Why are accurate estimations and effective planning important for project success?**

   a. They help minimize the need for project management tools

   b. They ensure that all team members have the same level of expertise

   c. They enable informed decision-making and optimal resource allocation

   d. They eliminate the need for project managers to make any adjustments during project execution

Answer key

1. b
2. b
3. c
4. c
5. c

Exercises

1. Create an estimation based on high level t-shirt based estimation for your project.

2. When will a budget-based estimation be used? Explain with an example.

3. For the same project, create a scrum board in Jira and create a story point-based estimation for a two-week sprint.

4. Which tool is best for project management in your opinion, and why?

5. Elaborate on how the plan will be made available to the team and how it will be shared with the team.

CHAPTER 4

Team Management, Organizing Your Team

Introduction

This chapter will discuss how to organize the team, what the different skill sets needed are, what a manager should look out for, how to keep the team motivated, what we can do, and what we should not. This chapter covers important aspects such as recruitment, assimilation of new employees, external company hiring, vendor selection, in-house team dynamics, planning for attrition, conflict management, goal setting, and the role of management hierarchy. It emphasizes the significance of recruiting the right candidates, creating a supportive environment for new employees, selecting appropriate vendors, and effectively managing teams across different locations and time zones. The chapter provides practical insights and strategies for building successful teams, fostering collaboration, and achieving project goals.

Structure

In this chapter, we will discuss the following topics:

- Recruitment, options to recruit
- Identification of good candidates while interviewing
- Assimilating how to manage egos
- Outsourcing vs. doing by the team

- Planning for attrition
- Making hard decisions
- Management hierarchy and its help
- Define objectives and manage team
- Vocal vs. silent workers
- Remote working

Objectives

This chapter seeks to explore different recruitment options and understand their advantages and considerations, provide strategies for the assimilation of new employees into the team, ensuring a smooth transition and productivity, discuss the factors to consider when hiring external companies and selecting vendors for project execution, highlight the key roles and responsibilities in outsourced projects and the importance of their contributions, address the dynamics of in-house teams, whether local, hybrid, or fully remote, and the tools that facilitate collaboration. These objectives aim to provide practical guidance for effectively organizing and managing teams in software project management, leading to successful project outcomes.

The first process in building a team starts with recruitment. The first section of this chapter focuses on recruitment and the different recruitment options.

Recruitment, options to recruit

Building the team starts with recruitment. Recruitment is the key to project initiation. Recruitment can happen from the following places:

- Internal recruitment
- External recruitment
- Hiring external companies
- Can be local hires
- Can be hybrid hires or remote hires
- Can be a full local team
- Can be a full global team

There are advantages to internal recruitment. Team members will be aware of the processes and the culture of the organization. If the culture of the organization is good, it is beneficial; however, if the culture of the organization is not conducive to the good working environment, then it is terrible to have them on the team. The skills of the team members may not always be appropriate as per the requirements of the project.

External recruitment will be required in case of a new project or to fill attrition for the current team. External recruitment adds new perspectives to the team, people bring new knowledge and culture to the team. However, the key to recruiting good candidates is to have good interviews, which can help identify the right skills and attitudes of the candidates.

Identification of good candidates while interviewing

During recruitment, the following aspects are key to identifying whether the candidate is a good fit for the team:

- Skills of the candidate and whether the skills fit well into the project.

- Attitude of the candidate which is hard to determine, but if you get indicators that their attitude is questionable, then judge carefully.

- Thoroughly discuss the skills mentioned in the resume of a candidate.

- If the candidate has frequently switched companies, it is better not to choose them. They are most likely not fitting anywhere else.

- Interviewers should not try to judge the knowledge of a candidate with respect to their own. Instead, they should focus on the ways in which the candidate can contribute to the project and probe them in that area.

- The hiring process should be done quickly without wasting much time. In an ideal case, the candidate should be chosen within one month of the initiation of interviews. Otherwise, it may adversely impact the project. Sometimes, to look for the perfect candidate, the manager may take a long time. The risks involved in such a case are as follows:

  o An ideal candidate may be hard to find.

  o The requisition to hire the candidate may get closed because of budgetary issues.

  o The ideal candidate selected for the job might choose to join another company.

  o The duration of the project will increase in case of delays.

Managers should strike a balance between skills, attitude, team fitment, and growth opportunities, and then select the right candidate and focus on the project.

Assimilating how to manage egos

Post recruitment, if they are given a level playing field with the existing employees, then the new recruits become productive and start contributing to the project. Post recruitment is the assimilation phase of the new employees once they onboard the team. The following steps can be performed to ensure a smooth assimilation of the new employees:

- Provide an overview of the project.

- Have training sessions to help the new employees understand the intricacies of the project.

- Conduct small coding sessions to ensure that the new employees ramp up.

- Making sure that the existing employees are helpful towards the new employees.

- Create a level playing field for new employees instead of being biased towards the existing employees.

- Team building activities can help break the ice between the existing and new employees.

- Nowadays, some employees work remotely. Getting them to engage and making them comfortable is a challenge. Extra effort has to be put in to ensure that the remote employees are engaging with the new employees as well as with the existing employees.

- A face-to-face meeting goes a long way in making the employee feel confident about themselves and comfortable in their surroundings. When they meet face-to-face, they become familiar with the body language of the managers and team members.

Outsourcing vs. doing by the team

Having external companies is more appropriate when the expertise is not present in-house. Building expertise takes a lot of time, and it is not always easy. It may turn out to be more costly in cases where internal expertise is not available. Also, if it is a project with no development insight in the near future, then outsourcing to an external company can be a good option. The success of the project depends on choosing the appropriate organization that can deliver the project on time and of good quality within the approved cost. The vendors should be chosen carefully after checking their past deliverables, expertise in that particular subject, availability of manpower, and whether they will be able to backfill in case of attrition. It seldom happens that the vendor is able to deliver a project on a turnkey basis. It requires close cooperation between the customer and the vendor to deliver the project. It should be a win-win situation for both the customer and the vendor.

In summary, the following points should be kept in mind while choosing a vendor:

- Check if internal expertise is present.

- If it is a long-duration project or a short-duration project.

- If it will be costlier to do it in-house.

- If there are enough engineers available in-house.

- If it is a one-off project.

The checklist to select the vendor is given as follows:

Criteria	Yes or No
Does vendor have expertise?	
Do they have sufficient manpower to deliver?	
Do they have the ability to replace engineers?	
Have they delivered any projects for your current organization?	
How is the response ark communication from the vendor?	
What is the cost involved?	
Does anyone in your executive chain know any executive in the winter organization? It may help in some situations.	
Does the company have presents in the location where the project has to be executed?	
If not located in that locations can move engineers to that location?	
Do they have authorization to work for that project? For example, U.S. Federal government projects can only be executed by U.S. citizens.	
The vendor be located in another geography and time zone and still deliver the project	

Table 4.1: Checklist to select the vendor

Even if the project is outsourced, the outsourcing company needs to involve its own manpower in order to oversee the project. A couple of people who are absolutely required to ensure the smooth functioning of the project are as follows:

Role	Effort required	Work Involved
Program manager	High, if there are multiple vendors involved. Low to medium, if there is a single vendor.	Coordination and release management. Adhering to the processes.
Project manager	Medium.	To oversee if the project is running on track. Also helps to remove the blockers in the project.
Product manager or business analyst	Medium.	To clarify requirements on a regular basis.

Role	Effort required	Work Involved
Software architect or domain specialist.	Very high.	Making sure that the code written is of good quality, the architecture has been properly thought through and documented and the designs are correct. If this is not ensured, then the product will not be stable. There can be one or many domain specialists in different domains of the product. Particularly important for doing architectural discussion, design reviews, code reviews.
Security specialist.	Medium.	All vendors will not have security expertise. It is better to have a security specialist look into the product for security issues.

Table 4.2: Roles and responsibilities

The in-house team can be local, hybrid, or totally remote. The tools used in the project should be able to help in working across the zones. Tools such as *Jira, GitHub, Bitbucket, Confluence, Microsoft Teams, Zoom*, etc., help in collaborating across the zones. These tools provide a level playing field for all employees, whether local or remote. If the manager is able to synchronize the team and orient these employees to the goal of the project, then achieving the end goal becomes easy.

Planning for attrition

While planning for the project, it will be important to plan for attrition. Keeping the team intact, motivated, and working towards a common goal is a sure-shot recipe for success. A demotivated, loosely associated team will have attrition. Along with planning for attrition, try to understand the root cause and fix the root cause of attrition.

Some attritions hit harder, these are attritions of the key people in the team. Try to protect these key individuals who can solve difficult problems. There is always an 80:20 rule, which says that 80% of the work is done by 20% of the people. Thus, protecting these 20% of the people is of utmost importance. If there is an attrition, backfilling anyone out of this 20% workforce will be a herculean task. The depth of knowledge about different processes and the ability to get things done will be lost.

Making hard decisions

Attrition can also be involuntary if a person is not performing at all because of the following reasons:

- Lack of skills
- Disinterested in work

In this case, it is important to remove the employee from the organization or move them to other teams where these skills are suitable. If the person is present on the team, it will lead to low motivation across the entire team because some people will take the burden of the non-performing employee, and that might cause an issue in the team.

Firing a person from the organization is not an easy task. There are rules and regulations across different countries and even in different regions of a country. Working through the rules and regulations and removing a person from the organization is a daunting task. Thus, the manager should be well aware of the guidelines that have been decided by the human resources team of the organization. Proper documentation needs to be maintained with proof that the employee has failed to perform and is not able to deliver the tasks that have been assigned to them. If there is any legal procedure, then this tool will be used to counter the legal case filed by the employee who has been removed from the job.

Planning for vendor attrition

Vendor attrition can also happen, and it can prove to be a bigger problem. If the vendor quits the project, then getting a replacement is a difficult task. There should be clauses in the agreement with the vendor that they need to give at least a three-month notice in order to quit the project.

In case the vendor has decided to quit without spending any time on the project, the manager should try to hire another vendor within a month. This is to help facilitate the knowledge transfer in two months from the old vendor to the new vendor.

In case the manager feels that the same work can be done by the in-house engineers, then the manager should start the transfer of information process and start ramping up the in-house engineers.

Replacing vendor due to non-performance

In case the vendor is unable to perform and not able to deliver, then it is important to terminate the contract immediately because having them in the team will take a lot of bandwidth from the inhouse engineers. Instead of helping, they might be slowing down the entire team. Vendors cannot deliver immediately what has been given to them in spite of having technical expertise. In-house team members will tell from the beginning that the vendor is incompetent. They are taking too much time and are unable to deliver. However, the vendor also needs some time to ramp up and understand the subject before they start delivering. The manager needs to create a win-win situation for both the vendor and the organization. Otherwise, crucial projects may take longer to deliver and might miss the market time frame.

Management hierarchy and its help

In *Chapter 3, Estimations and Planning,* the management hierarchy has been discussed. Any issues with the project delivery that the manager is not able to solve need to be discussed with the management hierarchy.

However, the manager should try to solve all the issues by themselves. Managerial skills depend on problem-solving. How the manager is able to solve different kinds of problems and different kinds of situations defines how good the manager is. If the manager takes up most of the problems in the management hierarchy to find solutions, then the manager is not doing a good job. Also, though the management hierarchy is there to solve problems, none of them encourage encountering problems., they want the manager to come up with solutions themselves. However, the management hierarchy can be used to validate the solution options. The best solution that needs to be pursued is also suggested by the manager.

Management hierarchy is just to review the solution to the problem. Hence, the bottom line is to try and solve the problem yourself. Do not go to the manager with the problems, but with the solutions and the best solution amongst the many. Complaining does not help; solving problems does.

Define objectives and manage team

For a team to succeed, whether it is an individual or a vendor, the following points should be made clear from the beginning of the project:

- Setting goals for defining roles and responsibilities:

  o Clearly define the roles and responsibilities of each team member based on their skills, expertise, and project requirements.

  o Ensure that everyone understands their roles and the expectations associated with them.

  o Define leads for the projects and make sure that there is no overlap and distinct roles and responsibilities for each individual. If there is an overlap, then the team is too big for the project. Look for other projects instead.

  o Define clear project goals, objectives, and milestones to provide a sense of direction and purpose to the team.

  o Break down the project into smaller tasks and assign them to team members, ensuring that goals are achievable and measurable.

  o Set realistic expectations regarding timelines, quality standards, and deliverables.

- Teamwork for building a collaborative culture:
  - Foster a collaborative and inclusive environment where team members feel comfortable sharing ideas, asking questions, and seeking help.
  - Encourage open communication and establish channels for effective information sharing within the team.
  - Promote teamwork and emphasize the importance of collective accountability.

- Establishing effective communication:
  - Use appropriate communication tools and platforms to facilitate seamless communication among team members, especially in distributed or remote teams.
  - Schedule regular team meetings, both synchronous and asynchronous, to discuss project progress, address concerns, and align goals.
  - Encourage active listening and provide opportunities for everyone to contribute to discussions.
  - Over communicate through emails, messaging systems like Teams, Confluence, Word Documents. Make sure that everyone understands what is going on in the team. Make sure that everyone feels included.

- Managing team dynamics and conflict management:
  - Understand the strengths, weaknesses, and working styles of team members to effectively assign tasks and foster collaboration.
  - Encourage a healthy work-life balance and provide support when team members face challenges or obstacles.
  - Resolve conflicts or disagreements promptly and constructively, promoting a positive team atmosphere.

- Providing support and growth opportunities:
  - Offer training, mentorship, and professional development opportunities to enhance the skills and knowledge of team members.
  - Provide resources and tools necessary for efficient work, such as project management software, version control systems, and collaboration platforms.
  - Recognize and appreciate the achievements and contributions of team members to boost morale and motivation.
  - Regularly evaluate the performance of the team, identify areas for improvement, and implement necessary changes.
  - Encourage feedback from team members regarding processes, workflow, and team dynamics.

o Conduct retrospective meetings to reflect on project outcomes, learn from successes and failures, and implement lessons learned in future projects.

Vocal vs. silent workers

Flamboyant and *silent* workers refer to two different types of employees in the context of team dynamics. Identification of silent workers is important. They move quite a lot of things without publicizing the work. Most of the time, the flamboyant workers try to steal the limelight by talking more and doing less. The people pulling most of the project are going to talk less. It is not that some of the flamboyant team members are not doing the work. But reference can be data-driven, like how many Jiras are fixed and how many checks are made.

The following are the characteristics of a flamboyant worker:

- Flamboyant workers are outgoing, expressive, and tend to draw attention to themselves.

- They are often confident, vocal, and proactive in sharing their ideas and opinions.

- They may possess strong communication and presentation skills, making them effective in team discussions and presentations.

- Flamboyant workers can bring energy and enthusiasm to the team, inspiring others and driving creativity.

- However, they may sometimes dominate conversations, overshadowing quieter team members, and their ideas may not always align with the overall team goals.

The following are the characteristics of a silent worker:

- Silent workers, on the other hand, are more introverted and reserved in nature.

- They tend to listen more and speak less, preferring to observe and reflect before sharing their thoughts.

- Silent workers often possess deep analytical and critical thinking skills, enabling them to provide thoughtful insights and solutions.

- They are typically good listeners and can contribute valuable input when given the opportunity.

- However, their reserved nature may lead to their ideas and contributions being overlooked or undervalued in team discussions.

In summary, flamboyant workers bring energy, confidence, and assertiveness to the team, while silent workers offer thoughtful analysis and insights. Both types of workers have unique strengths and perspectives that, when balanced and properly harnessed, can contribute to a well-rounded and successful team. It is essential for team managers to create an inclusive environment that encourages participation from all team members, regardless of their communication styles.

Remote working

Remote working, often referred to as telecommuting, presents a modern approach to completing tasks outside the traditional office environment. This mode of work offers flexibility, allowing employees to create a personalized and comfortable work setting. It reduces commute time, which not only alleviates stress but also promotes a better work-life balance. Remote working can lead to increased productivity, as employees may face fewer distractions and are able to tailor their schedules to suit their peak performance times. Moreover, it opens opportunities for companies to tap into a global talent pool unbounded by geographical constraints.

Remote working has become the norm nowadays. Software teams are spread across the globe and sync up over Microsoft Teams, Zoom, and various other tools to work with each other.

Teams need to be managed really well in order to get the full potential out of all the individuals. Communication is key to the success of the team. The lack of face-to-face interaction can lead to feelings of isolation and disconnection from the team. Communication may suffer due to the absence of spontaneous in-person conversations, and coordinating across different time zones can be complex. Additionally, remote workers may struggle with setting boundaries between work and personal life, potentially leading to burnout.

In contrast, working from the office fosters a sense of community and teamwork through direct, in-person interactions. It allows for immediate feedback and collaboration, facilitating quicker problem-solving and innovation. The structured environment of an office can help employees maintain a clear distinction between work and personal life, reducing the likelihood of overworking. Furthermore, being physically present in the office can enhance networking opportunities and career growth through informal interactions and visibility.

However, the traditional office setting also has its drawbacks. Daily commutes can be time-consuming and stressful, impacting overall well-being and productivity. The rigid structure of office hours may not cater to all employees' peak productivity times, potentially leading to inefficiencies. Additionally, office environments can sometimes be distracting, with interruptions from colleagues and a constant buzz of activity.

In conclusion, both remote working and working from the office have their distinct advantages and challenges. The choice between the two depends on individual preferences, job roles, and organizational culture. Ideally, a hybrid model that combines elements of both can offer the best of both worlds, promoting flexibility, productivity, and employee satisfaction. Team managers should strive to understand the unique needs of their employees and create a balanced work environment that leverages the strengths of both remote and in-office work.

Here are a few guidelines on how to run a remote team:

- All the team members need to have a sense of inclusivity. No one should feel left out.

- Communication has to be top-notch.

- Use group emails, group video meetings, and group chats to communicate with the team.

- Tools should be in place to facilitate online collaboration. All tools should be remotely accessible.

- Speed of accessibility of the tools needs to be very good.

- IT infrastructure support for the remote team should be excellent. If any issues with the network or laptop, they should be fixed very quickly.

- The speed of access of the remote tools should be excellent.

- Everyone should be judged based on delivery, not in which mode they are working.

- Do as many video calls as possible as allowed by the company and the policies of the region.

- Make sure that everyone's potential is fully utilized to the maximum. Any dip in performance will impact the overall project.

- Remote employees miss out on team-building activities. Have a budget to get the team in the office for team building.

- In the case of laying off employees, do not target only remote employees. If a layoff has to be done, this should not be a criterion.

Conclusion

In this chapter, we have learned that the manager should choose the right balance for the candidate and then choose the candidate quickly. The decision to hire external vendors or whether to get it done internally is based on the tools provided. The team also has to be made productive quickly. Plan for voluntary as well as involuntary attrition. Analyze vendor performance and take steps to improve or replace. The team should have an objective, a goal, which needs to be aided by the management chain. Identify good works, not just the vocal ones.

After team formation, the next stage is to analyze the requirements. In the next chapter, we will discuss the process of analyzing the requirements and what to take care of in this stage. Thorough analysis of the requirements leads to better planning, execution, and qualification of the project. The team formed should be trained to do the requirements review.

Points to remember

Here are a few key points to remember from this chapter on team organization and management in software project management:

- **Recruitment**: Choose the appropriate recruitment option, whether internal or external, to build a skilled team that aligns with project requirements and organizational culture.

- **Assimilation of new employees**: Ensure a smooth assimilation process for new team members by providing project overviews and training sessions and fostering a level playing field for both new and existing employees.

- **Vendor selection**: When outsourcing or hiring external companies, carefully select vendors based on their expertise, past deliverables, communication, and ability to meet project requirements within the approved cost.

- **Planning for attrition**: Plan for attrition and understand the root causes to maintain a motivated and cohesive team. Protect key individuals and address non-performance promptly to minimize the impact on the team.

- **Effective team management**: Establish clear goals, roles, and responsibilities, foster a collaborative culture, communicate effectively, manage conflicts, provide support and growth opportunities, and continuously evaluate and improve team performance.

By considering these key points and implementing appropriate strategies, software project managers can optimize team performance and collaboration and ultimately achieve successful project outcomes.

Multiple choice questions

1. **What are the advantages of internal recruitment in team building?**
   a. Familiarity with organizational processes and culture
   b. Access to a wider pool of talent
   c. Fresh perspectives and new knowledge
   d. Ability to fill skill gaps easily

2. **Which factor is crucial to consider during candidate interviews for recruitment?**
   a. Length of previous job tenures
   b. Interviewer's own knowledge and expertise
   c. Skills alignment with project requirements
   d. Number of previous employers

3. **What is a key consideration when outsourcing to external companies?**

   a. Availability of internal expertise

   b. Cost-effectiveness compared to in-house development

   c. Ability to completely delegate project responsibilities

   d. All of the above

4. **Which role is responsible for overseeing project progress and removing blockers?**

   a. Program manager

   b. Project manager

   c. Product manager

   d. Security specialist

5. **What is an essential aspect of team dynamics in a distributed or remote team?**

   a. Frequent face-to-face meetings

   b. Exclusive focus on local hires

   c. Use of collaboration tools for communication

   d. Avoiding team-building activities

6. **What should be considered when planning for attrition in a project?**

   a. Identifying root causes and addressing them

   b. Ignoring the impact of attrition on team dynamics

   c. Reducing team motivation and cohesion

   d. Delaying the search for replacements

7. **How can conflicts within the team be effectively managed?**

   a. Ignoring conflicts and hoping they resolve on their own

   b. Promptly addressing conflicts and promoting constructive resolutions

   c. Encouraging flamboyant workers to dominate discussions

   d. Avoiding open communication and collaboration

Answer key

1. a

2. c

3. d

4. b

5. c

6. a

7. b

Exercises

1. Imagine you are starting a new software project in your organization. Which recruitment option would you choose and why? Provide a brief explanation of your decision.

2. Develop a plan for assimilating new team members into your software project team. Outline the key steps and activities you would include to ensure a smooth integration and productivity of the new employees.

3. You are tasked with selecting a vendor for an outsourced project. Create a checklist of criteria that you would consider during the vendor selection process. Include at least five important factors to assess potential vendors.

4. Identify a potential conflict scenario within a software project team and propose a strategy for effectively managing and resolving the conflict. Describe the steps you would take as a project manager to address the conflict and promote a positive team atmosphere.

5. As a project manager, define three specific project goals for your software project and outline the communication plan you would implement to ensure that all team members are aware of the goals, understand their roles, and can contribute effectively.

Join our book's Discord space

Join the book's Discord Workspace for Latest updates, Offers, Tech happenings around the world, New Release and Sessions with the Authors:

https://discord.bpbonline.com

CHAPTER 5
Requirement Analysis

Introduction

This chapter focuses on understanding and analyzing requirements in software development projects. Having the right requirements helps to deliver better products of good quality. It emphasizes the need for careful analysis by the project manager and team once the requirements are provided by the business analyst or product manager. The chapter highlights the significance of brainstorming and clarifying requirements from the beginning to uncover hidden aspects. How to do these will be discussed in the subsequent paragraphs.

The content emphasizes that larger projects with more complexity and requirements should be broken down into smaller projects for better analysis. It mentions tools like *Jira, Confluence, Jama, Rational Doors,* and *Microsoft Excel* that can be used for requirements management, with Jira being a popular choice. The chapter also highlights the pitfalls of requirements analysis, such as misunderstandings, lack of clarification, partial understanding, over-analysis, and inadequate documentation.

Structure

In this chapter, we will discuss the following topics:

- Role of project manager in requirement analysis
- Other planning aspects

Objectives

By the end of this chapter, the reader will be able to recognize the importance of understanding and analyzing requirements in software development projects. Understanding and analyzing requirements play a crucial role in software development projects. It is essential to highlight their importance as they lay the foundation for the entire development process. Careful analysis and brainstorming are necessary to uncover hidden requirements and ensure a clear understanding from the beginning. However, requirements analysis also comes with its challenges and pitfalls. Misunderstandings, lack of clarification, and over-analysis can hinder the progress of a project. Moreover, changing requirements can have a significant impact on project alignment, schedules, dependent teams, integration, and business processes. In this regard, program managers and project managers have the responsibility to align teams and educate them about changes in requirements. It is important to differentiate between functional and non-functional requirements, with the latter being equally significant. Example of functional requirement is, developing a shopping cart for an ecommerce website while high availability of the shopping cart is a non-functional requirement. Assigning unique numbers for tracking purposes helps in managing and organizing requirements effectively. To capture and document requirements in a structured manner, a document such as a **Software Requirements Specification** (**SRS**) can be used. By focusing on these objectives, we can gain a comprehensive understanding of requirement analysis and its impact on successful software development projects.

Role of project manager in requirement analysis

Understanding the requirements is key to executing the project. Once the business analyst or product manager provides the requirements, the manager and the team should carefully analyze them. Brainstorming will help uncover many hidden requirements, and it is important to clarify from the beginning.

They should read the requirements and try to brainstorm the details. Understanding is a slow process, so plan for enough time to understand the requirements. How much is enough? 1 to 2 weeks should be enough to understand the requirements, brainstorm, and provide feedback. Do not boil the ocean, meaning do not try to perfect everything in the first go, and spend a month's time to understand everything. There is every possibility, after a few sprints, that the requirements may change. So, getting into implementation after a short requirement analysis phase should be the target.

A bigger project will have more complexity and requirements, while a smaller project will have fewer. So, it is prudent to break down the bigger projects into smaller projects and analyze the smaller requirements.

Jira, Confluence, Jama, and Rational Doors can be used as tools for requirements management. Jira provides a single tool from which requirements can be broken down into Epics. An Epic is a large body of work that can be broken down into smaller tasks or user stories. It serves as a high-level description of a project or feature, encompassing multiple aspects that need to be addressed. By breaking down an Epic into smaller, manageable user stories, teams can focus on incremental progress, ensuring that each piece aligns with the overall goals and delivers value to the end-users. This structured approach enhances traceability and collaboration, making it easier to track progress and adapt to changes throughout the development process.

Effective brainstorming for requirement analysis involves several key steps to ensure that all aspects of the project are thoroughly considered and documented.

Conduct workshops and focus group sessions with the engineers to facilitate open discussions and gather diverse perspectives on the project requirements. These sessions can reveal nuances that might be overlooked in individual interviews or surveys.

Develop detailed use case scenarios to illustrate how the end product will be used in real-life situations. This helps in identifying functional and non-functional requirements and ensures that the final product meets the users' needs. These will be the software requirement specifications.

Create prototypes or mock-ups of the proposed solution. These visual aids can help stakeholders better understand the requirements and provide useful feedback early in the development process, reducing the risk of costly changes later.

Utilize mind mapping techniques to visually organize and connect requirements. This can help in identifying relationships between different requirements and ensure that all aspects of the project are covered.

Documenting the requirements, doing proper reviews, responding to review comments, and conducting meetings to close these quickly are some of the tools that can be used to complete this phase.

The pitfalls of the requirements analysis are as follows:

- The requirement is not understood correctly
- The requirement is not clarified with a business analyst or product manager
- The requirement is partially understood. One or two requirements are understood, but the rest are not clarified
- The requirement is not understood fully by the team leads
- Over-analysis of the requirements can lead to unnecessary delay
- Requirements are not captured in a document and are discussed verbally or in emails

- Participation from all the teams is required; whether it is hardware or software, backend, frontend, or QA, the entire team should understand the requirements

The manager needs to guard against all the above and needs to keep the project moving to the next milestones.

Changing requirements

Once defined and understood, it does not mean requirements will not change over the duration of the project. Requirements change because the markets change, customer preferences change, the company's direction changes, and feedback from proof of concepts is obtained. If the project duration is longer, then the initial requirements will most likely undergo a lot of change. Shorter projects will most likely undergo small changes with respect to the initial requirements.

Changing requirements is one of the reasons why projects are likely to be misaligned. If the requirements change, the existing work may not be relevant. In some cases, engineers may have to stop working on the existing work, and new work has to be assigned. The work planned for the subsequent sprints may have to change, or alterations have to be made to the work that has been planned. Capturing the changes with respect to the initial requirements is a challenge, and misalignment can happen because of these. For example, let us say that a product manager had given a requirement for search functionality in an e-commerce application.

In case multiple teams are involved, it is the project manager's responsibility to align the teams' understanding with the changing requirements. The project manager also has the responsibility to further educate the team about the changes and realign the project according to the new requirements.

Any change in requirements may have an impact on the following:

- Software schedule
- Hardware schedule
- Dependent teams' schedules
- Integration schedules
- Marketing, sales, or business process improvement

The manager should conduct meetings, update the documentation, update Jiras, and pass on the requirement change information to the team. The information should be spread across to everyone and not to a few people. Including all will reduce the information gap, and it will improve the quality of the product.

In a smaller team, it will be the responsibility of the project manager to factor in the changes because of changes in requirements.

The intricate relationship between various teams in a larger project is crucial to understand. Each team, whether it be software, hardware, or marketing, functions like a cog in a larger machine. When one team experiences a change in requirements, it can set off a domino effect that impacts the schedules and deliverables of all dependent teams. By clearly defining and communicating these interdependencies, project managers can enhance the overall scheduling process. This involves mapping out how each team's work influences others and ensuring that any changes are quickly and comprehensively conveyed across all involved parties.

For instance, if the software team needs additional time to implement a new feature, the hardware team may need to adjust its integration schedule to accommodate the delay. Similarly, marketing and sales teams will need to realign their strategies and timelines to ensure a cohesive product launch. By fostering open communication and regular updates, project managers can minimize disruptions and ensure that all teams remain synchronized. This proactive approach not only mitigates risks but also enhances the efficiency and quality of the end product, as all teams can anticipate and plan for changes well in advance.

In some organizations, there are **Change Control Boards** (**CCB**), where a team of people sit together, analyze the requirements, and decide on a Go or No-Go decision. A Go decision is taken depending on the feasibility of the proposal, time taken, complexity, and customer benefit.

The CCB board decides how important the requirements are. Is this an absolute must-have, or can it wait? The team also analyzes whether the requirement is feasible to deliver. For example, technically, if the requirement is feasible to be delivered. Does the team have the requisite knowledge, are the tools present, and can the dependent modules be prepared? If the supplier is involved, can the supplier provide the tools? All these contribute to the complexity and the time taken to deliver. The more the unknowns, the complexity of the projects increases, and the time taken to deliver will also increase. Now, if the time taken increases, then the customer benefit needs to be evaluated. If, because of the delay, the customer benefit diminishes, then the team can decide against implementing the change requirements.

Types of requirements

There are two types of requirements:

- Functional requirements
- Non-functional requirements

Functional requirements specify how a feature should behave. Meaning how the user is supposed to interact with the system. What functionality can the user get from the system while interacting with the system. Functional requirements define the specific behavior or functions of a system, detailing what the system should do. These requirements are typically action-oriented and describe the tasks the system must perform to meet user needs. For instance, in a banking application, a functional requirement could specify that when a user clicks on the **Transfer Funds** button, the application should prompt the user to enter the amount to be transferred, select the source and destination accounts, and confirm the transaction. Similarly, in an e-commerce platform, a functional requirement might state that clicking the **Add to Cart** button should add the selected product to the user's shopping cart. The shopping cart will be updated, and the updated item list should be shown in the shopping cart. Also, the total amount to be paid should be updated. Any discount available on the updated amount should also be reflected in the cart. These requirements are essential for ensuring that the software performs the necessary operations to fulfill its intended purpose.

A nonfunctional requirement is a requirement that specifies some other requirements than the functionality. The following are some of the nonfunctional requirements:

- Timing requirements, for example
- Performance requirements
- Scale requirements
- Color reference requirements
- Deployment requirements
- High availability requirements
- Disaster recovery requirements
- International languages to be supported
- Browsers
- Operating systems
- Power saving
- Memory & CPU requirements
- Security requirements

For example, for a shopping cart, it may be specified that when clicking the **Add to Cart** button, the product should be added to the shopping cart in one second. The color theme of the shopping cart should be green. The title of each page should be in red color.

Each requirement should have a number. Requirements, if referred through numbers, are much easier to track.

Some of the requirements will change as the project moves along. Project managers should constantly demonstrate the progress to the business analysts or product managers and to the dependent teams to show how the feature is progressing. At least one demonstration every two months is recommended to ensure that everyone is updated on the progress and how the feature is shaping up.

The demonstration helps to understand the following:

- Get immediate feedback about the implementation and features
- If any changes have to be made, it can be assessed by the product manager quite early
- Assess the progress of implementation
- Assess the quality of the product to a certain extent

The project manager can maintain transparency of implementation this way instead of showing power point presentations.

A business analyst or a product manager can provide a descriptive requirement or a one-line requirement. In case it is a one-liner, the manager is responsible for expanding the requirements and then validating them with the project manager. For example, the one-liner requirement can be to *design a shopping cart for a grocery store*.

It is a well-known problem, and it may seem very obvious, and the team may start developing the architecture without discussing the requirements. However, the business analyst will have something in mind that may not be spelled out in the one-liner. So, it is important to expand the requirement in a document. It can be termed as SRS, which specifies all the details of the requirements. The SRS documents form the reference or the baseline to the subsequent development of the product. In the absence of a good SRS document, the implementation may not proceed along the intended path and may lose focus.

Software requirement specifications

Recommended documents should be written in a specific format, and that document is known as an SRS document. The following table describes what the software's recommended specifications should cover. This document, once available from the product manager/business analyst, has to be reviewed thoroughly by the project manager and the software development team. However, the requirements will mostly change over a period when the project is ongoing. This may change because of user feedback, market shifts, or technological advancements. Not everything will change, but some parts of it will change. There are two ways in which these changes can be captured. One is to update this document, and the second is to submit change requirements for Jiras. These Jiras will have separate categories and should not be mixed with the implementation Jiras.

The SRS document format is as follows:

Section	Description
System description	What is the system supposed to do?
	For example, if a Video Player is being developed, explain the objective of the same.

Section	Description
Functional requirements	Break down in details the functional requirements of the system. Break down the functional requirements into smaller requirements and number the same. Example, for a Video Player, break down the functional requirements. SRS_REQ_1: Should be able to play video in .mpeg format. SRS_REQ_2: Should have play, pause, fast forward, rewind buttons. SRS_REQ_3: Should be able to recognize the character present in the screen.(One innovative requirement)
API requirements	If there are any API requirements, then describe the same.
UI requirements	If there are any UI requirements, then describe the same.
Non-functional requirements	Non-functional requirements as has been discussed above.
Hardware specifications	What are the hardware requirements to run the software. For example, what are the hardware requirements for running the video player.
Delivery timeline	Which requirements needs to be delivered when. Product management wishlist needs to provide the wishlist dates for the project.

Table 5.1: SRS document format

Checklist for requirements phase completion

In this phase the requirements are understood, and it marks the completion of a stage of the project. The projects are divided into multiple stages and requirements understanding is the first phase of the project. The checklist for requirements phase completion is as follows:

- Requirements are understood and approved by all stakeholders.
- Stakeholders are the engineer project teams, documentation team, support teams, technical program managers.
- A review meeting is organized to review the checklist.
- A Flexibility Matrix has been identified, for example, amongst features to be developed, the number of engineers, and time, which are flexible needs to be determined:
  - o Feature: Less/high/medium flexible

- o Number of engineers: Can it be increased or decreased on demand
- o Time: Can the timeline of the project be lengthened or shortened
- Has the timeline been established for the delivery of the project.

The checklist is not there for the program manager to drive, but rather to ensure that all the stakeholders approve all the requirements. If there is a single team, then it is the project manager's responsibility to ensure the approval of the requirements document.

Other planning aspects

In this section, other subtle aspects of planning are covered. The project manager needs to ensure that the project is kept rolling and is not stuck in one stage. Overanalysis prevention, planning upfront, breaking down the project into smaller components, and prioritization can go a long way in improving the deliverables of the project.

Guarding against overanalysis

Once the requirements are obtained and the analysis starts, the manager should guard against over-analysis. Overanalysis leads to paralysis, and it needs to be watched out for from the requirement stage.

Some of the symptoms of overanalysis are that people will be unwilling to proceed unless some parts of the requirements are made exactly clear. The team wants those parts to be exactly written down so that they can proceed. The team declines to proceed with the rest of the requirement analysis until these are sorted out. If this is done, then the team needs to understand that they are losing time.

For example, let us say that a product manager has asked for an online shopping website to be defined. Now, let us say the team has some concerns about some of the requirements, regarding maintaining the duration of order history, what are all the billing mechanisms which can be integrated into the product, what is the maximum number of items which can be added to the cart, what are the color schemes to be used in the shopping cart etc. The team can go onto over analysis and not proceed on the implementation. The team may lose precious time doing so and may delay the project implementation.

The team starts analyzing the requirements and goes very deep into them. They did a good job of shredding the requirements into sub-feature level requirements, and they continue to do so. The project may not require all the sub-features, but the team is excited to break them down further and perform the analysis. The manager needs to draw a line to the extent to which the analysis needs to be done and should call for a stop at a certain point.

The manager should define timelines for completion and should ensure that the team proceeds to the next stage after the time is over. Some requirements will always be open and can be clarified as the project progresses. Some of these requirements will eventually change as well, so there is no point in looking into it.

Planning from the requirement analysis

As soon as the product manager provides the requirements, the manager should start planning the project.

The requirements may include purchasing hardware or software. Organizations have complex procedures for buying equipment or software from other companies, which take a lot of time. The manager should foresee these requirements and start planning the project.

Also, buying equipment or software requires a budget, which may not be readily available unless it is preplanned. So, getting the budget will be a big hurdle prior to placing orders for the equipment. This is generally the hardest part unless something has been kept aside for unforeseen circumstances.

The project manager should prepare a good proposal to secure funding in that case. The highlight of the proposal should be why the software or hardware is necessary for the project. It should also specify if any alternatives have been considered. Without the software or hardware, how the project may get impacted needs to be specified.

Additionally, the team's skills may need to be augmented to meet some requirements. The manager should plan to upgrade the engineers' skills. Planning training also requires a lot of time. It must go through a complex buying process. It is complex because all of the following require effort, like vendor identification, identification of a good trainer, tuning the content of the training to the needs of the team and the project, availability of the trainer. If there an in-house training division, then this process becomes a lot easier. The trainer's time may not be available immediately because the trainer is also booked. At least one month of lead time is required before the trainer is available.

Space availability needs to be planned so that the team can sit together. In an office environment, sitting next to each other can help collaborate with the other team members. Getting seats next to each other may not be possible quickly. The team needs to coordinate with the space management team in the organization to get seats in the same place for the entire team.

There could be many more such things, which may be project context-specific. So, the manager needs to plan for this after seeing the requirements. If everything is available early in the project cycle, this will help in the execution. If it is delayed, the project may also be delayed.

Smaller projects will have lesser complexity

Smaller projects are less complex than larger projects. Often, people who are working on maintenance projects, where some bugs have to be fixed within a certain time, do much better than other team members who are working on large feature development.

This is because bugs are defined finitely. The project is relatively small compared to feature development, so it may seem that the individual is doing a better job in bug fixing than in feature development.

Smaller projects will also have a smaller timeline and will likely be completed within time. A delay of two weeks for a one-month project may not seem like too much of a delay, but the percentage delay is 50%. It took 50% more time than the estimated time.

For a larger project, let us say a 10-month project, a 50% delay will mean a delay of five months. Five months seems like a long time and may be more than two weeks, though the percentage delay is the same.

Hence, from the beginning, the project manager should try to break down the requirements into smaller chunks and should plan to deliver the smaller chunks. Larger chunks will mean trouble. People will lose patience. Team members will lose motivation if projects are ending. Timelines will go haywire. Overall, it will impact the manager.

Methods of prioritization

Prioritization is very important for project execution. It should be done at each stage of the project. It starts with requirements prioritization. Also, prioritizing sub-features in a feature. To prioritize and plan your work, apply the Japanese principle of 5S. There are plenty of YouTube videos on 5s. A brief about the 5s principle is as follows:

The Japanese principle of 5S stands for Seiri (Sort), Seiton (Set in order), Seiso (Shine), Seiketsu (Standardize), and Shitsuke (Sustain). This methodology aims to create and maintain an organized, clean, and efficient workplace. The first step, Seiri, involves removing unnecessary items from the work area. Seiton ensures everything is properly arranged and easily accessible. Seiso focuses on cleanliness, while Seiketsu standardizes the best practices across the organization. Finally, Shitsuke instills discipline to sustain these practices over time. By applying 5S, teams can improve productivity, reduce waste, and create a safer work environment.

Prioritization should be done at the requirements level and then at the sub-requirements level of that specific requirement. The requirements are as follows:

- Requirement 1:
  - Sub requirement 1.1 – priority 1 – High priority
  - Sub requirement 1.2 – priority 2 – Medium priority
  - Sub requirement 1.3 – priority 3 – Low priority
- Requirement 2:
  - Sub requirement 2.1 – priority 1 – High priority
  - Sub requirement 2.2 – priority 2 – High priority
  - Sub requirement 2.3 – priority 3 – Low priority

- Requirement3:
  - Sub requirement 3.1 – priority 1 – High priority
  - Sub requirement 3.2 – priority 2 – Low priority
  - Sub requirement 3.3 – priority 3 – Low priority

While understanding the requirement, try to prioritize it. That way, the execution can be focused on high- and medium-priority requirements. Low-priority requirements need not be done immediately or may not be done at all.

This is also a way to contain the scope of the implementation. Otherwise, if low-priority requirements are implemented, the implementation will become huge with very low returns. Also, once requirements are implemented in the product, they become a maintenance nightmare throughout the product's lifecycle.

So, focused requirements are the need of the hour for any project. There should be a razor-sharp focus on the requirements to be implemented.

Conclusion

Effective requirement analysis is crucial for successful software development projects, ensuring a thorough understanding of the project's goals and constraints. The project manager plays a pivotal role in requirement analysis by carefully analyzing and clarifying the requirements provided by the business analyst or product manager. Tools like Jira, Confluence, Jama, Rational Doors, and Microsoft Excel can aid in requirements management and traceability, with Jira being a popular choice. Pitfalls of requirements analysis include misunderstandings, lack of clarification, over-analysis, and inadequate documentation, which can lead to delays and misalignment. Changing requirements are common and require effective change management by the program manager and the project manager to align teams and realign the project accordingly. Requirements are categorized into functional and non-functional requirements, each with its own significance in specifying the behavior and other aspects of the software system. Planning, prioritization, and effective communication are key factors in successful requirement analysis and project execution.

By following best practices in requirement analysis, project teams can ensure a comprehensive understanding of the requirements, minimize risks, and deliver software solutions that meet stakeholder expectations.

In the next chapter, the next phase of project execution, the architecture and design phase, will be discussed. After the requirement study is done, the architecture of the product needs to be created. Then, the designs for individual components need to be created. The designs should fit into the architecture.

Points to remember

- Requirement analysis is crucial for successful software development projects.

- Carefully analyze and clarify requirements provided by the business analyst or product manager.

- Use tools like Jira, Confluence, or Excel for requirements management.

- Beware of pitfalls such as misunderstandings, over-analysis, and inadequate documentation.

- Changing requirements are common; manage them effectively.

- Prioritize requirements and focus on high and medium-priority items.

- Plan, communicate, and align teams throughout the requirement analysis process.

Multiple choice questions

1. **What is the purpose of requirement analysis in software development?**
   a) To design the user interface of the software
   b) To identify and document the goals, needs, and constraints of the project
   c) To perform a code review and ensure code quality
   d) To conduct user acceptance testing

2. **Which of the following is a common pitfall in requirement analysis?**
   a) Over-analysis of requirements
   b) A clear understanding of requirements by all team members
   c) Capturing requirements verbally or through emails
   d) Minimal participation from team members

3. **Which tool is commonly used for requirements management and traceability?**
   a) Jira
   b) Microsoft Excel
   c) Confluence
   d) Rational Doors

4. **What are functional requirements?**
   a) Requirements that specify how a feature should behave
   b) Requirements related to hardware specifications

c) Requirements for user interface design

d) Requirements for performance and scalability

5. **Who is responsible for aligning teams with changing requirements in a project involving multiple teams?**

   a) Business Analyst

   b) Program Manager

   c) Project Manager

   d) Software Developer

6. **What is the purpose of an SRS document?**

   a) To capture and document all the details of the requirements

   b) To track project progress and milestones

   c) To provide user instructions for the software

   d) To manage the project budget and resources

7. **Why is prioritization important in requirement analysis?**

   a) To ensure all requirements are implemented

   b) To minimize the complexity of the project

   c) To allocate resources and budget effectively

   d) To document requirements in a structured format

Answers

1. b
2. a
3. a
4. a
5. b
6. a
7. c

Exercises

1. Take a sample software project scenario and identify the key requirements that need to be analyzed. Create a list of functional and non-functional requirements based on the scenario.

2. Given a set of requirements, practice breaking them down into smaller, more manageable requirements. Number each requirement and identify any dependencies or relationships between them.

3. Select a popular requirements management tool such as Jira or Confluence. Create a sample project and input the requirements into the tool, organizing them into epics, user stories, or other suitable categories.

4. Choose a real-world project case study or scenario. Conduct a brainstorming session to uncover potential hidden requirements that may not have been explicitly stated. Document these additional requirements and discuss their impact on the project.

5. Take a set of requirements and evaluate them for clarity and completeness. Identify any ambiguities or missing information and propose clarifications or additions to ensure a comprehensive understanding of the requirements.

Join our book's Discord space

Join the book's Discord Workspace for Latest updates, Offers, Tech happenings around the world, New Release and Sessions with the Authors:

https://discord.bpbonline.com

CHAPTER 6

Architecture and Design Phase

Introduction

The chapter aims to provide a comprehensive understanding of the critical phases of software architecture and design. The chapter will look at software architecture as the blueprint for an application and highlight the architect's role in guiding the development process. Additionally, it will explore key topics such as scalability, maintainability, and testability, which are essential considerations when designing a robust architecture. The chapter aims to empower readers to make informed decisions during the architecture and design phases, ensuring the successful development of high-quality software systems.

Structure

The topics to be covered in the chapter are as follows:

- Architecture phase
- Design phase
- Test design
- Scaling vs. toy application
- 24x7 running
- Power saving, memory optimization
- Post-sales, support, maintenance, and augmentation plan

Objectives

By the end of the chapter, the reader will be able to understand the fundamental principles and concepts of software architecture, establishing a solid foundation for designing robust software systems. They will have explored the process of designing a software architecture, including identifying requirements, analyzing constraints, and making informed architectural decisions. Additionally, they will have gained knowledge of common architectural patterns and styles, understanding their characteristics, benefits, and trade-offs for effective architectural design. The reader will also have learned how to consider factors such as performance, scalability, security, and maintainability during the architecture design process. Furthermore, they will understand the importance of documentation and communication in software architecture and will have acquired effective techniques for documenting and communicating architectural designs. Ultimately, the chapter aims to equip the reader with the knowledge and skills to create well-designed software architectures that align with project goals and facilitate successful software development.

Architecture phase

After the requirement phase starts, the architecture and design phase follows. First, the higher-level architecture for the product is designed. Next, the lower-level architecture is designed.

High-level design (HLD) focuses on defining the system's overall structure and identifying the main components and their interactions. During this phase, architects create an abstract representation of the software system, outlining the major modules, subsystems, and their relationships. The goal is to establish a clear roadmap that guides the development team in building a coherent and well-organized system. HLD involves analyzing the system requirements, considering constraints, and making strategic decisions about the architectural patterns, styles, and technologies to be used. This phase sets the foundation for detailed design and implementation, ensuring that the system meets performance, scalability, security, and maintainability requirements.

In HLD, architects provide a comprehensive overview of the system's architecture, including high-level diagrams, component descriptions, and interaction models. These artifacts serve as a blueprint for the development team, helping them understand the system's structure and guiding their work. HLD also involves identifying key interfaces, defining data flows, and specifying the system's integration points with external systems or components. By focusing on the big picture, HLD ensures that the system is designed to accommodate future changes and enhancements, reducing the risk of costly modifications later in the development process. Effective HLD requires collaboration with domain experts, stakeholders, and other team members to ensure that all perspectives are considered and that the design aligns with the project's goals and objectives.

Low-level design (**LLD**) looks further into the specifics of the HLD, translating the broad architectural blueprint into detailed design specifications. This phase involves defining the internal structure of each component and specifying the algorithms, data structures, and interfaces required for implementation. LLD focuses on creating detailed module designs, including class diagrams, sequence diagrams, and state diagrams, which provide a clear and precise understanding of how individual components will function and interact. By addressing the finer aspects of the system, LLD ensures that each component is designed with precision and clarity, allowing developers to implement the system effectively and efficiently.

During LLD, architects and developers collaborate closely to identify potential issues and validate design decisions, ensuring that the system meets the specified requirements and constraints. This phase also involves selecting appropriate design patterns, optimizing performance, and considering factors such as error handling, security, and maintainability. By providing a granular view of the system's design, LLD helps mitigate risks, enhance code quality, and facilitate seamless integration between components. Ultimately, LLD serves as a critical bridge between HLD and actual implementation, ensuring that the software system is robust, scalable, and aligned with project objectives.

While building a house good architecture is necessary to build a good house. Architects design houses depending on customer needs and provide all the drawings to the builders, who are responsible for construction.

Various domain experts, such as electricians, plumbers, and interior designers, are responsible for their respective roles.

A software project is almost like designing a house. Initially, an architect designs the project's architecture. Respective domain experts, such as device driver specialists, server specialists, database specialists, and user interface specialists, help design the respective areas and create the product together.

While developing the product, the architecture will change a bit. It may be because of changing requirements, some of the requirements requested may not be feasible to meet because of technical complexity, building as per the original architecture may require a lot of effort, or new technologies are available which was found after the architecture was designed. This is common. Unlike house construction, while it has to be right one time, software architectures evolve over a period of time as the project goes along. However, an absolute total change will be very costly. To avoid this, it is better to brainstorm the architecture along with the domain leads so that all the viewpoints are processed while designing the architecture.

Topics to be kept in mind while designing the architecture of a product are listed in the following table:

Serial number	Topics	Description
1	Objective	What problems it is trying to solve?
2	Overall architecture	Describe the overall architecture of the project.
3	References to the requirements	What requirements is the architecture addressing. What it is not addressing.
4	Architecture diagram	A diagram or multiple diagrams to show the overall architecture.
5	Explanation of different components of the architecture	Different components of the architecture and its description.
6	Interaction between the different components	Interaction between the different components of the architectural components.
7	Ability to extend the architecture	Extendibility of the architecture for future. It should be easy to extend if required to meet changing requirements or future requirements.
8	Ability to maintain the architecture	Maintainability of the architecture. Meaning it is easy to maintain the architecture.
9	Rules or policies while designing the subcomponents	Any rules or policies governing the architecture for designing the components of the architecture. It can also be for extending, maintaining.
10	Sequence diagrams	Sequence diagram across multiple components.
11	Scalability	Ability to scale the application to handle many requests, large amount of input data, large amount of output data, how to process the data, how to design the data base tables, what type of bus to use to interact with the hardware.
12	Performance	Adhering the architecture to the performance parameters of the overall system as has been requested by the product manager.
13	High availability	How the product can be made highly available, meaning the robustness of the product.
14	Disaster recovery	Resiliency against failures.
15	Testing requirements	Testability of the architecture also needs to be understood from the beginning. Test architecture and manager need to understand the requirement and plan for the test environment, setup for testing the product.

Serial number	Topics	Description
16	Principles of reusability across the team	Often teams do not interact and prepare the same components independently. Architect should specify the reusable sub-modules and make sure that they are reusable across the teams and components.
17	Debuggability	Debugging problems should be relatively easy.
18	Supportability	Support teams should have enough logs and messages to help customers. Call centers should have specified recipes based on the error messages seen in the screen.
19	Limitations of the architecture	What are the limitations of the architecture, what it is not addressing, why it is not important to cover in this document and where it will be covered if required.
20	Any omissions or special mentions	Any requirements not captured in the requirement.

Table 6.1: Architecture document topics

An architect normally defines the architecture of the product. They are typically someone who has experience developing software for 15+ years and has experience with different types of architectures. Without a strong architect, the product developed will most likely not be good. So, identifying good architects and having them on the team is crucial to project success.

As we saw in the previous chapter, requirements change as the project progresses, and hence, the architecture may also change. It is very important to update the architecture document every few months. If updated, it will help the project teams refer to this document. The team can follow these methodologies for keeping the architecture updated and to get the project:

- The **Rational Unified Process (RUP)**
- The **Architecture Development Method (ADM)**
- The spiral model

The objectives are to get the project done in a planned and systematic way and also to manage the changes happening in the project as the implementation is going on.

Not everything about architecture may be known in the beginning. Some points may require investigation before the architecture can be updated. So, the investigation can go in parallel, and once it is over, the architecture document can be updated.

Design phase

Next is the design phase after the architecture phase. In the design phase, each of the major features is designed for implementation.

Firstly, in the design phase, the team must be organized correctly. There are two ways to make the design; that is, the team can be divided in two ways to create the design document. They are as follows:

- Common layers can be done by one team; business logic can be done by another team.

  o One team can complete the middleware and lower layers, while another team can complete the application layer. The representation is as follows:

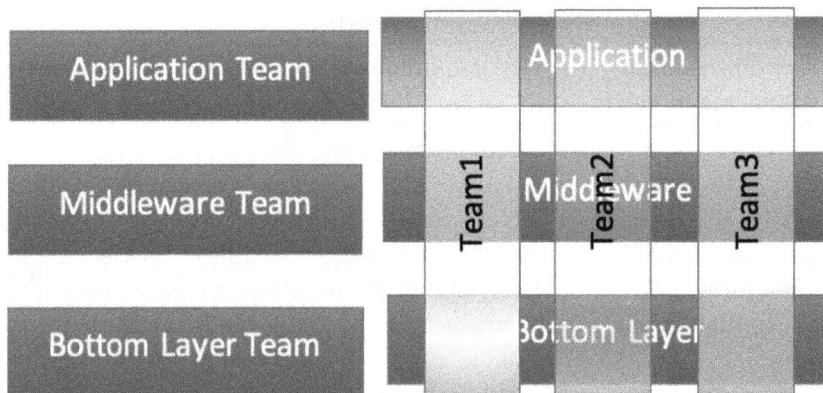

Figure 6.1: Team organization

  o For example, in an embedded software project, an entire team can be involved in developing the device driver layer, which is the bottom-most layer. Another team can be involved in developing the middleware, such as the graphics library and messaging system. Another team can be involved in developing the application layer.

- The second option is that the entire vertical can be developed by one team developing a particular feature. The team will be responsible for the application layer, middle layer, and bottom layer.

  o It depends on the team's expertise, and depending on that, the teams can be divided to work on the modules. It is hard for a team to have expertise in both applications and device driver development in an embedded software development project. So, it is better to create a team for device driver development, another for the middleware, and another for the application layer. Depending on this division, the design documentation can be done by the respective teams.

There are many advantages of a team doing a single layer:

- Consistency in the design
- Consistency in the Interfaces to different layers
- Expertise in a single-layer, quicker implementation
- Governance, as prescribed by the architect, will most likely be maintained well

However, there are disadvantages as well. The disadvantages are as follows:

- The common layers may have dependencies on many modules. So, the queue for the team may become very long. The other teams will be forever dependent on the common layers team.
- The common layers team may not be synchronized in development with the other layers. So, there will be planning issues during implementation.
- The more siloed the teams are, the more communication and integration issues can happen.

Designs should consider the module's functionality, UML diagrams for object interactions, sequence diagrams, flow charts, module interactions with other modules, performance, module scaling, resiliency, and security.

In short, it should cover all the aspects discussed in the module's architecture documentation and follow the governance model documented in the architecture documentation.

Test design

After the architecture, the team must start with the test design doc. This will give an idea about the hardware and software resources required, and the way to test the design document typically includes the following constituents:

- **Test plan overview**: This section provides a high-level summary of the test design document, explaining its purpose, scope, and objectives. It may also include information about the intended audience and stakeholders involved in the testing process.
- **Test objectives**: This section outlines the specific objectives or goals of the testing effort in more detail. Objectives may include validating functional requirements, ensuring system stability, improving usability, or enhancing performance. The objectives should align with the overall project goals and provide a clear direction for the testing activities.
- **Test strategy**: The test strategy section describes the overall approach and techniques that will be used for testing. It may include information about the test levels (e.g., unit testing, integration testing, system testing), test types (e.g., functional testing, performance testing, security testing), and any specific methodologies or frameworks to be followed (e.g., Agile, Waterfall). The strategy may also address

factors such as the allocation of resources, test environment management, and the use of automation tools.

- **Test environment**: This section provides detailed information about the test environment required for executing the tests. It includes specifications for the hardware, software, and network configurations needed. Additionally, it may cover details about the installation and setup of the test environment, including any dependencies or prerequisites. The section may also discuss the availability of test data and any considerations for managing test data sets.

- **Test scope and coverage**: Here, the scope of testing is defined in more depth. It may include a breakdown of the features, modules, or components that will be tested. The section may also outline the coverage criteria, specifying which requirements, use cases, or scenarios will be covered by the tests. It may include information about prioritizing test coverage based on risk analysis or business priorities.

- **Test cases**: This section provides a comprehensive description of individual test cases. It includes the test scenario, which outlines the specific conditions and inputs to be tested. The test steps describe the sequence of actions, including any expected results. The section may also include information about preconditions or test data required for executing the test case. Additionally, it may discuss techniques for test data generation, such as using boundary value analysis or equivalence partitioning.

- **Test execution schedule**: This part outlines the planned schedule for executing the test cases. It may include a timeline or calendar view indicating the test execution sequence. The schedule may also consider any dependencies or constraints, such as the availability of resources or the need for specific test environments. It may provide estimates of the effort or resources required for each testing phase.

- **Test deliverables**: This section lists the expected deliverables from the testing effort. It may include test reports summarizing the test results, defect reports documenting identified issues, and any additional documentation or artifacts produced during testing. The section may also mention specific templates or formats for generating the deliverables.

- **Test risks and mitigation**: This section identifies potential risks or challenges associated with testing and provides strategies or mitigation plans to address them. It may include risks related to resource availability, time constraints, technical dependencies, or environmental factors. The section may also discuss contingency plans or alternative approaches to mitigate the identified risks.

- **Test sign-off criteria**: This part defines the criteria that must be met for the testing phase to be complete and successful. It may include criteria related to test coverage, defect density, performance benchmarks, or stakeholder acceptance. The section may outline the process for obtaining sign-off or approval from relevant stakeholders, indicating the necessary documentation or evidence required.

- **Test dependencies**: This section identifies any dependencies or interdependencies between different test cases or test activities. It helps in managing the sequencing and coordination of tests. It may include information about the order in which tests should be executed, any prerequisites for executing specific tests, or any shared resources that must be coordinated.

- **Test tools and infrastructure**: If specific testing tools or infrastructure are used, this section details the tools, their configurations, and any integrations or dependencies. It may include information about test management tools, test automation frameworks, or performance testing tools. The section may also discuss any necessary training or expertise required for using the tools effectively.

Remember, the contents and level of detail in a test design document can vary depending on the project and organization. It is essential to tailor the document to suit the specific needs and requirements of the testing effort.

Scaling vs. toy application

A scaled application and a toy application represent two different levels of complexity and purpose in software development. The details of each are as follows:

- **Scaled application**: A scaled application refers to a software system designed to handle a significant amount of data, users, or transactions. These applications are typically built for large-scale operations, such as enterprise-level systems or high-traffic websites. Scaled applications require careful consideration of performance, scalability, reliability, security, and maintainability to meet the demands of real-world production environments.

  o Characteristics of a scaled application may include:

    ▪ **High availability**: The application is available 99.99% of the time. The application should have a replica of its own running all the time. If the primary application goes down, the replica application should be able to service the requests. Example, a shopping application is hosted in a data center in Mumbai, India and let us say there is a infrastructure outage and the application becomes unavailable. Then the replica application running in Chennai, India, can take over and service the requests.

    ▪ **Scalability**: The application architecture allows horizontal or vertical scaling to accommodate increasing demands. For example, let us say that traffic to an application increases. In horizontal scaling, many machines can be added, and the traffic can be distributed to all the machines. In vertical scaling, the processing power, CPU/memory of the machines can be increased to handle the increased traffic.

- **Distributed systems**: Scaled applications often involve multiple components or services working together to achieve desired functionality. Example, hosting application in K8s can solve some of the above problems.

- **Performance optimization**: The application is optimized for efficient resource utilization and quick response times.

- **Robustness**: The application is designed to handle failures gracefully and recover quickly.

- **Complex data management**: Scaled applications deal with large volumes of data and require advanced data management techniques.

  o E-commerce platforms, social media networks, banking systems, and **enterprise resource planning (ERP)** systems are examples of scaled applications.

- **Toy application**: A toy application is a small, simplified software application created for learning, demonstration, or prototyping purposes. It is not intended to handle real-world production scenarios and lacks the complexity and robustness required in scaled applications.

  o Characteristics of a toy application may include:

  - **Limited scope**: Toy applications focus on specific functionalities or features, often omitting advanced or edge cases.

  - **Simplified architecture**: The application may have a simplified architecture with fewer components or services.

  - **Minimal data management**: Toy applications may use simple data storage mechanisms.

  - **Limited scalability**: Toy applications are not designed to handle large-scale user bases or high traffic.

  - **Educational or experimental nature**: Toy applications are often used to learn new technologies, demonstrate concepts, or prototype ideas.

  o Examples of toy applications include small demo projects, code samples, tutorials, or proof-of-concept prototypes.

While toy applications serve their purpose in learning and experimentation, they do not realistically represent the challenges and considerations involved in developing and maintaining a scaled application. Scaled applications require careful planning, architecture design, and engineering practices to operate in real-world scenarios successfully.

24x7 running

Running software applications 24x7 refers to the continuous operation and availability of an application without any scheduled downtime. This means the application remains accessible and functional, including weekends, holidays, and non-business hours. Running an application 24x7 is often a requirement for critical systems, services, or applications that need to be available to users or customers without interruption.

The key considerations for running software applications 24x7 are as follows:

- **High availability**: The application must be designed and implemented with redundancy and fault tolerance to minimize the impact of hardware or software failures. This may involve using load balancers, clustering, or replication techniques to ensure uninterrupted service. All these techniques are to distribute the workload across multiple replicas of the same application running in different machines concurrently.

- **Scalability**: The application architecture should be scalable to handle increasing user loads or growing data volumes. This may involve horizontal scaling by adding more servers or vertical scaling by upgrading hardware resources.

- **Monitoring and alerting**: Implementing robust monitoring and alerting mechanisms is crucial to detect issues or anomalies in real-time. This allows for proactive identification and resolution of potential problems before they impact the application's availability.

- **Automated recovery**: Implementing automated recovery mechanisms can help restore the application to a working state in case of failures or issues. These mechanisms may involve automated failover, restarts, or backups. Failover means, if the primary application fails, then the standby application takes over and services user requests.

- **Continuous deployment and testing**: Adopting continuous integration and practices helps ensure that updates, patches, and new features can be deployed seamlessly without disrupting the application's availability. Thorough testing processes are essential to validate changes and prevent regressions.

- **Performance optimization**: Optimizing the application's performance is crucial to ensure smooth and efficient operation. This may involve performance profiling, caching strategies, database optimization, and code optimization techniques.

- **Security**: Implementing robust security measures is essential to protect the application and its data from potential threats. This includes secure authentication, encryption, access controls, and regular security audits.

- **Disaster recovery and backup**: Having a comprehensive disaster recovery plan and regular backups in place helps ensure the application can be quickly restored in case of catastrophic events or data loss.

Running software applications 24x7 requires careful planning, robust architecture, and proactive monitoring and maintenance. It is crucial to have a dedicated team or resources to handle any issues that may arise and ensure the continuous availability and smooth operation of the application.

Power saving, memory optimization

Power saving and memory optimization are crucial considerations in embedded software development for several reasons. The reasons are as follows:

- **Energy efficiency**: Embedded systems often operate on limited power sources, such as batteries or energy harvesting mechanisms. Power-saving techniques help extend the battery life or reduce power consumption, enabling the device to operate for longer without frequent recharging or replacement. This is particularly important in portable devices, IoT devices, or systems deployed in remote or inaccessible locations.

- **Cost reduction**: Power consumption directly impacts the cost of operating embedded systems. By optimizing power usage, organizations can reduce energy bills and operational costs associated with running and maintaining the devices. Additionally, power-efficient designs allow the use of smaller or less expensive power sources, reducing overall system costs. For example, the electricity requirements may be reduced. Let us say a circuit needs 12V/1A electric requirement, however, because of efficient design, the requirement is reduced to 5V/1Amp. So the size of the electric source as well as the physical size may be reduced because of the design.

- **Heat dissipation and thermal management**: Power efficiency is closely related to heat generation in embedded systems. Reduced power consumption leads to less heat dissipation, which simplifies thermal management and reduces the need for complex cooling mechanisms. This is particularly important in compact devices or systems with size constraints.

- **Extended battery life**: Power-saving techniques help maximize the battery life of portable or battery-powered devices. This is crucial in applications such as mobile phones, wearables, medical devices, and remote sensors, where users expect extended usage without frequent recharging. Prolonged battery life enhances user experience and reduces the need for frequent battery replacements.

- **Memory utilization**: Embedded systems often have limited memory resources. Memory optimization techniques aim to minimize memory usage, allowing more efficient utilization of available memory. This is important for devices with constrained memory, where every byte counts. Optimized memory usage can result in cost savings, improved performance, and the ability to run on devices with lower memory capacities.

- **Performance optimization**: Efficient power usage and memory utilization can also positively impact the overall performance of embedded systems. By reducing unnecessary power consumption and optimizing memory usage, system resources can be allocated more effectively, resulting in faster response times, improved responsiveness, and smoother operation. For example, in a laptop when the laptop is idle for a few minutes, the laptop goes to sleep mode. This reduces memory, CPU usage thereby improving battery performance.

- **Real-time constraints**: Many embedded systems have real-time requirements, where timely response and predictable behavior are critical. Power-saving techniques and memory optimization are vital in meeting real-time constraints by ensuring efficient resource utilization and minimizing delays or interruptions.

In summary, power saving and memory optimization are essential in embedded software development to achieve energy efficiency, extend battery life, reduce costs, manage heat dissipation, optimize memory utilization, improve performance, and meet real-time requirements. By prioritizing these aspects, developers can create embedded systems that are more reliable, cost-effective, and energy-efficient.

Post-sales, support, maintenance, and augmentation plan

Planning for a project's post-sales support, maintenance, and augmentation involves considering various factors to ensure the smooth operation and ongoing improvement of the software system. The following are some pointers to help you in the planning process:

- **Define objectives and scope**: Clearly define the objectives and scope of the post-sales support, maintenance, and augmentation phase. Determine what support and maintenance activities will be provided and establish the boundaries of the project's augmentation plan.

- **Identify support and maintenance requirements**: Identify the specific support and maintenance requirements based on the nature of the software system, customer expectations, and industry standards. Consider factors such as bug fixes, troubleshooting, user support, performance optimization, security updates, and compatibility with new platforms or technologies.

- **Establish Service Level Agreements (SLAs):** Define the expected response times, resolution times, and SLAs for different support and maintenance requests. SLAs can help set clear expectations for the project team and the customers or end-users.

- **Build a support team**: Determine the resources and skills needed for effective support and maintenance. Consider establishing a dedicated support team or assigning specific team members responsible for support and maintenance tasks. Ensure that the team has the necessary expertise and knowledge to address various issues that may arise.

- **Create incident and change management processes**: Establish incident management processes to handle reported issues, including ticketing systems, escalation procedures, and communication channels. Similarly, define change management processes to handle planned enhancements, updates, or modifications to the software system.

- **Documentation and knowledge management**: Develop comprehensive documentation that includes user guides, troubleshooting guides, FAQs, and knowledge base articles. This documentation will be a valuable resource for users and the support team. Implement a knowledge management system to capture and share knowledge gained during the support and maintenance phase.

- **Continuous improvement and augmentation**: Plan for ongoing improvement and augmentation of the software system. Define a process for collecting feedback from users and stakeholders, prioritizing feature requests or enhancements, and incorporating them into future releases or updates. Consider implementing agile methodologies or DevOps practices to facilitate continuous integration and delivery of improvements.

- **Training and skill development**: Invest in training programs to enhance the support team's skills and knowledge. Provide training on new features, technologies, troubleshooting techniques, and customer service skills. Continuous learning and skill development will enable the support team to provide better assistance and stay updated with industry trends.

- **Communication and customer engagement**: Establish effective communication channels with customers or end-users to gather feedback, address concerns, and inform them about support and maintenance activities. Regularly engage with customers through newsletters, webinars, or user forums to foster community and gather insights for future improvements.

- **Performance monitoring and analytics**: Implement monitoring and analytics tools to track the software system's performance, usage patterns, and user satisfaction. Analyze the collected data to identify areas for improvement, detect potential issues, and make data-driven decisions about future enhancements.

By following these pointers, you can effectively plan for post-sales support, maintenance, and augmentation of your software project, ensuring a positive user experience, ongoing system reliability, and continuous improvement.

Conclusion

Software architecture acts as the blueprint for applications, ensuring development follows a structured, scalable, and maintainable path. Key factors in design include scalability, maintainability, and testability, crucial for creating robust systems. Architectural patterns like layered or microservices come with unique benefits and trade-offs to consider. Clear documentation and communication are vital for stakeholder understanding and successful design. While architectures can evolve, considering various perspectives early on minimizes costly changes. Engaging domain experts and regularly reassessing architecture against new requirements ensures it remains relevant. With insights from this chapter, readers can confidently design effective software architectures. Plan for scale, continuous operation, energy efficiency, and post-sales support from the start for a successful product.

In the next chapter, how to kick off the project will be covered. Since the architecture is in place, the project manager can now take steps to break down the architecture into components and kick off the project. This kickoff is to bring all stakeholders, team members to the same understanding level.

Points to remember

- Define the purpose and scope of the architecture to align with project goals.

- Consider scalability, maintainability, performance, security, and user experience.

- Choose appropriate architectural patterns based on system needs.

- Document and communicate the architecture effectively.

- Evolve and adapt the architecture to changing requirements and technologies.

- Focus on important aspects of the software that are key apart from the functionality. Plan for scalable, robust, cost-effective solutions.

By remembering these points, managers can create effective software architectures that meet project objectives and contribute to long-term success.

Multiple choice questions

1. **What is the primary purpose of software architecture in the development process?**
   a) To write code for the application
   b) To define the structure and blueprint of the software system
   c) To manage project budgets and timelines
   d) To perform quality assurance testing

2. **Which factors should be considered when designing a robust software architecture?**
   a) Scalability, maintainability, and testability
   b) Marketing strategies and target audience
   c) User interface design and color schemes
   d) Employee skillsets and training programs

3. **What is the role of an architect in software development?**
   a) Writing code for the application
   b) Guiding the development process and designing the architecture

    c) Managing the project budget and finances

    d) Conducting user acceptance testing

4. **What is the purpose of architectural patterns in software design?**

    a) To make the code more readable and maintainable

    b) To define the specific components and their interactions

    c) To ensure compatibility with different programming languages

    d) To provide proven solutions for common design problems

5. **Why is effective communication important in software architecture?**

    a) To confuse stakeholders with technical jargon

    b) To ensure that developers have no say in the design decisions

    c) To facilitate a shared understanding among stakeholders and team members

    d) To eliminate the need for documentation

6. **How does software architecture differ from physical house architecture?**

    a) Software architecture is more expensive to design

    b) Software architecture can evolve over time

    c) Software architecture does not require planning

    d) Software architecture does not involve the use of blueprints

7. **What is the purpose of lower-level architecture in software design?**

    a) To provide a high-level overview of the system

    b) To define the specific components and their interactions

    c) To outline the project timeline and milestones

    d) To create visually appealing diagrams for presentations

8. **How does software architecture evolve during the development process?**

    a) It remains static and unchanged

    b) It adapts to changing requirements and emerging technologies

    c) It becomes more rigid and inflexible

    d) It is completely discarded and rebuilt from scratch

9. **What is the role of domain experts in software architecture design?**

    a) To write code for the entire application

    b) To create visually appealing user interfaces

    c) To provide expertise in specific areas, such as server management or database design

    d) To manage the project budget and timeline

10. **What is the importance of documentation in software architecture?**

    a) It helps confuse stakeholders with technical jargon

    b) It ensures that the architecture is never questioned

    c) It provides a clear understanding of the design decisions and rationale

    d) It is optional and not necessary for successful development

Answers

1. b
2. a
3. b
4. d
5. c
6. b
7. b
8. b
9. c
10. c

Exercises

1. What topics should be covered in the architecture specifications of a software product?

2. Explain how teams can be organized to manage the design of a particular product feature.

3. What are the topics that need to be covered as a part of the test design?

4. What are the most important non-functional requirements of a software application for running it 24x7?

5. What are the most important non-functional requirements of an embedded application?

6. After the software has been released, how is the software supported? Explain with an example.

Join our book's Discord space

Join the book's Discord Workspace for Latest updates, Offers, Tech happenings around the world, New Release and Sessions with the Authors:

https://discord.bpbonline.com

CHAPTER 7
Project Kickoffs

Introduction

This chapter covers different aspects of kick off. What are the different kickoff meetings the manager needs to organize, what is the importance of doing kick-offs, and how does a project kickoff? Managers need to set realistic targets for the team and should help the team reach those targets in a finite amount of time. Also, it is not just about the team; the entire ecosystem around the project should be aware of what is being delivered as a part of the project and the timelines for the project. Based on that, the adjoining marketing, sales, etc., activities can be planned. Kick-off is at the beginning of the project. A similar communication has to be maintained at every stage of the project so that the stakeholders are aware of the project's status and progress.

Structure

In this chapter, we will discuss the following topics:

- Types of kickoff
- Kickoff the overall project
- Project kickoff under the manager
- Feature or Epic kickoffs
- Manager's role in the kickoff

Objectives

By the end of this chapter, you will have a comprehensive understanding of the various types of kickoff meetings essential for project success. You will learn how to effectively initiate the overall project, as well as specific versions and features within it. The chapter will guide you on how to organize these kickoff sessions, detailing the critical elements that need to be included and the pivotal role of the project manager. Additionally, you will gain insights on maintaining clear and consistent communication with all stakeholders and the broader community, ensuring everyone is aligned with the project's objectives and timelines.

Types of kickoff

Project kickoff can be divided into multiple categories. These are as follows:

- **Overall project kickoff:** When the project is started, the overall project kickoff is organized. This will lay down the overall vision of the project and what is the objective of the product which will be developed. The product manager holds the vision for the product, and the engineering team helps to implement the vision portrayed by the product manager. For example, the product manager requests to develop a custom iot application to gather battery health in electric vehicles. The battery will send information to a SaaS application and the SaaS application will analyze the data. This requirement is passed to the engineering team thru the kick off. All the project stakeholders like the project teams, product marketing, support, program manager, product manager are at this kickoff.

- **Kickoff for a particular version of the project:** A project can then be divided into multiple milestones. For example, it can be divided into version 1, version 2, version 3, etc. These versions can have individual kickoff sessions. For example in the above example, in the 1st version, the product manager may first target to gather the data and display in simple reports in the UI in a SaaS application. In the 2nd version, the product manager may want the data to be displayed in different graphs and dashboards. In the 3rd version, the product manager may want to detect the batteries that are behaving anomalously. The kickoff sessions again are attended by all the stakeholders of the project. The focus of the kickoff meeting is only on the specific versions of the project.

- **Epic kickoff meeting**: In a particular version, some Epics are planned. Normally the Epics are larger than what has been prescribed by agile. These need to have Epic kickoff meetings. These need to be conducted by the engineering team and need to be attended by the product manager and all the dev and QA leads. If the leads attend, then they will be aware of the dependencies that this feature will bring in for the product. Epic is a small feature that is to be implemented in the product. In the previous example, implementing a data streaming feature from the IoT device to the SaaS application can be an Epic. A particular report generation mechanism can be an Epic.

- **Feature kickoff:** Feature kickoff is done when a particular small feature is being implemented. It may be part of an Epic. If the design is complicated, then a kickoff meeting can be organized to discuss the feature. If it is simple, an email communication or an update in Jira will help to make others understand the feature.

The following is a flow chart that visually represents the hierarchy and structure of different kickoff meetings within the project lifecycle:

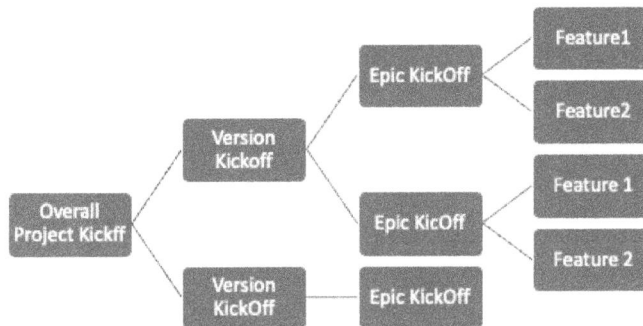

Figure 7.1: Hierarchy of kickoff meetings

Continuing with the example of the IoT application as has been discussed above, let us say for the overall vision of the product, there can be a kick off. For example, for the custom IoT application to gather battery health in electric vehicles, there can be a kick off meeting. As discussed above, the application can have multiple release versions. In the 1st version the product manager may first target to gather the data and display in simple reports in the UI in a SaaS application. For this phase there can be a kick off session which goes little deeper into the exact requirements. After that, for the streaming Epic as discussed above, there can be another kickoff. Likewise, there can be multiple Epics, and each Epic can have a kickoff before the design is started.

Kickoff the overall project

There are two types of project kickoffs that need to be done. The first thing to do is organize a project kickoff for the entire product. This is to let people know how deep project implementation will take place. This is to give an idea about the entire architecture of the project, what the unknowns are for the project, what the risks are for the overall project, and what the dependencies on the other teams for the project are. The project manager needs to present the project management part of the presentation, and the architect can present the architecture part of the presentation.

When the project kickoff happens, it is better to organize a meeting with the entire team and present the requirements, timelines, and specific non-requirements to the team. The points discussed in the following list must be presented to the entire cross-functional team so that everyone knows what they are doing.

Starting a software project involves several key steps. A general outline of the process is as follows:

1. **Define the project scope**: Clearly define the project's goals, objectives, and requirements. This has to be defined by the product manager or the business analyst. This is the first step for the project. The product manager should have interviewed the customers and gathered a set of core requirements for the project. Identify the problem you are trying to solve and determine the expected outcomes. This is for the entire cross-section of the team. The product team should know what is being delivered. The requirements of the product should be met within the timeline with good quality. That is the goal of the presentation. However, that is not all. This has to be repeated every quarter because changes to requirements will keep on happening for many reasons. Hence, it is important to keep communicating with the overall team about all the change requests and their impact on the project.

2. **Feasibility study results and what needs to be done:** Present the feasibility studies that have been done and what needs to be done. What are the risks associated with the results of the feasibility study, and how can the risks be mitigated? By the time this is presented, all feasibility studies may not have been completed. So, there is a significant risk associated with the project at this stage.

3. **Create a project plan and present the project's high-level approximate milestones:** Develop a comprehensive plan outlining the project's timeline, deliverables, milestones, resources, and responsibilities. This plan serves as a roadmap for the entire project. The overall team may not be willing to understand the detailed plan. However, present the high-level milestone plan. A Gantt chart, which can be prepared with Microsoft Project helps prepare a detailed plan. However, that might not be understandable to everyone. Keeping a running plan, as shown in the following table, helps the entire team understand the milestone plans and dates:

Milestones	Features	Date of delivery
Milestone 1	Feature 1	<Put the delivery date>
	Feature 2. Sub Feature 1	
Milestone 2	Feature 3	<Put the delivery date>
	Feature 2. Sub Feature 2	

Table 7.1: Running plan

Teams need regular communication about where we are with respect to milestones. So, this is not just a one-off; it is a regular process. In case the Microsoft Project license is unavailable, Microsoft Excel can be used to create the same. However, to do so in a detailed manner in Microsoft Excel is difficult; only a high-level plan can be prepared with it.

4. **Design the system architecture**: Create a high-level system architecture that outlines the overall structure, components, and interactions of the software system. Internal designs may not be available, but a high-level architecture should be available and should be made available to the entire team. Factors like scalability, security, and performance are the key things that the product needs to address. However, at this stage, everything may not be clear, but the architecture should be geared to address scale, security, and performance from the very beginning. The cross-team should also review and see if the architecture meets these requirements. Majority of software team can develop toy applications, which are small proof-of-concept applications. However, developing an enterprise-grade application that is stable, scalable, secure, and performs requires a great deal of understanding of software development. From the very beginning, design and architecture should focus on the above aspects.

5. **Test and quality assurance**: As consumers, we prefer not to buy poor-quality products. The same is true for enterprise customers. They prefer good-quality software that meets their requirements. A solid plan from the test and quality perspective needs to be presented to the team. Testing will require cross dependencies to be present to test fully.

6. **High-level dependencies across the cross-functional teams:** The cross-team should have expectations set regarding what is expected of them. Dependency discussions should start from the very beginning of the software implementation. During the design/architecture stage, discussions should start about the dependencies and SLAs should be defined for the dependencies coming later in the project. Dependency management should continue throughout the lifecycle of the project. Later on, it should not come as a surprise, and they should have it in their plan.

7. **Deployment and release**: Prepare the plan for software deployment, meaning how it will be deployed, so that the overall team has an idea of how the software will be made available. How frequent will the upgrade cycles be, and how can maintenance be done? Once the software is deployed, how will it be monitored, and how will it address any issues or bugs that arise? How ongoing maintenance and support needed will be provided? Customers generally submit issues, which are addressed by a dedicated customer support team. If these cannot be addressed by the customer support team, it is escalated to the next level team which is intermediate between support and engineering. If it cannot be addressed by this intermediate team, then it is escalated to engineering. These issues should be tracked through Jira tickets or through the ticketing system used in the organization.

Remember that the specific steps and their order may vary depending on the project's nature, size, and development methodology (for example, waterfall, agile, etc.). Adapt the process to suit your project's requirements and constraints. The above is for the cross-functional team and for the executives who want to be kept up to date with what is happening in the project.

Project kickoff under the manager

Ultimately, the manager is dependent on the team that is going to work on the project. So, appraising the team about the project, expected outcomes, and plans is paramount. At the very beginning of the project, there may be some whispering going on within the team about the project. Some of the individuals may have heard about the project, and some may not. This becomes a lunchtime discussion, and people are generally inquisitive about the new project and what the role of the individual will be in the project. So once the project is formally approved, the manager should apprise the team of the abovementioned product goals.

The team should be set with specific goals so that the team can achieve them. If a goal is set and the team is supported, the team will most likely achieve the goal. The kickoff for the team should set the following:

- **Setting goals for the software team:**
  - **Delivery**: The team should deliver what is expected and as per the requirements.
  - **Quality**: Software should be of good quality.
  - **Timeliness of delivery**: Delivery should be on time.
  - **Security**: The product should be secure so the customer can fully rely on the software.
  - **Usability**: The usability of the product should be good.
  - **Reliability**: Software should be reliable. Poor design, testing, and coding lead to unreliable software.

- **Setting the team up for success:**
  - The team should be made successful, and the manager's responsibility is to make each individual successful so that the overall team is successful. Managers should unblock the difficult issues and provide the required infrastructure to make the team successful. A message should be delivered to the team stating that the manager will support the team.
  - The team should be organized in a way that makes it successful. Many college graduates cannot be expected to deliver a complex project. Most often, that is the case. However, there are some exceptions too. Here, we are talking about the majority of cases. There should be a senior engineer who should always be guiding and mentoring the new engineers or the young engineers with a proper ramp-up. The team also should be organized in such a way that there are experienced engineers who are guiding the junior engineers. An agile team

of six engineers should have a scrum master, a relatively senior developer with 14+ years of experience, and one mid-level developer engineer with ten years of experience. The following table shows the team composition:

Scrum team members	Number of engineers	Experience level in years	Skills
Scrum lead	1	14+	Developer
Mid-level engineer	2	10	Developer, QA
Junior engineers	3	1-5	Developer, QA

Table 7.2: Team composition

It becomes difficult to run projects without this kind of experience level in the team. The team should have a good mix of experience and skills. Additionally, the team should gel well. Generally, without experienced software developers and appropriate skills, it is difficult to deliver the project. The team organization should be presented to the team so that the team has an overall view of the composition. Some engineers may express reservations about the team composition. So, it is better to correct the team composition at the onset. This can change when the project is ongoing. If it changes, then the manager should present it to the team at that time.

- **Showing metrics that they should keep track of:**
  o Unit test coverage should be more than 85%.
  o QA should not leak more than five major defects in a feature.
  o No unreviewed code should be checked in.

- **Processes and tools followed for development:**
  o It should explain the process followed for development.
  o How are the tools to be used, and what is the process for using the tools?
    ▪ Code repository
    ▪ Bug repository
    ▪ Document repository

Keep it short and simple. Do not present a 30-page PPT, which the team may not be willing to sit through and listen to. Keep it within ten slides with less content so that the team can comprehend the message. Keep it short and simple and drive the important messages to the team so that the team is geared up for the project.

Feature or Epic kickoffs

Once the above are done, the teams are set. Distribute the features to the team. Distribute at least six months of projects to the team so that the team has enough visibility, with a caveat that things can change. The team does not like requirements given in installments, meaning 1-2 weeks of work or, worse, a day's work. These features can be mapped to Epics in Jira:

Teams	Requirements to be met	Start date	End date
Team1	Feature 1 (Epic1)	<Date>	<Date>
Team2	Feature 2 (Epic2)	<Date>	<Date>
Team3	Feature 3 (Epic3)	<Date>	<Date>

Table 7.3: Team organization by Feature

A large feature can be broken down into smaller features. This small feature can be mapped to an Epic. The Epic should be broken down into multiple user stories, which can have sub-tasks. The same is represented as a figure:

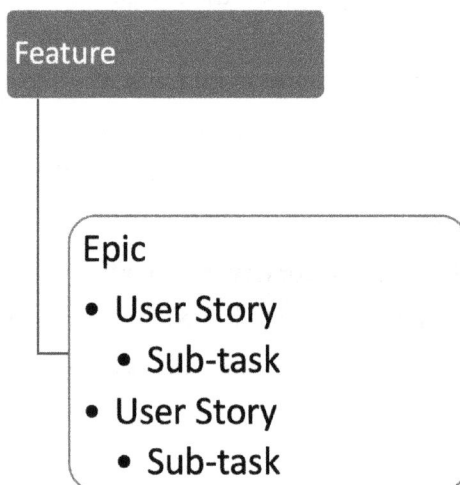

Figure 7.2: Mapping feature to Epic, User Story, and Subtask

The requirements that each team should fulfil are as follows:

- Assign them requirements that they must work on.
- That team has to organize a kickoff.
- The kickoff should set the requirements for what they are working.
- It should set the goals of the team clearly.

The scrum lead has to organize this kick-off before the start of any project. The scrum lead, along with the team, should present the following:

- What is the feature about?
- What will be implemented?
- A high-level software design.
- A high-level or rough timeline for implementing the same.

Again, it can be a short PowerPoint or a Confluence page on which it can be presented. If it is a PowerPoint presentation, it should be less than ten slides so the team can maintain interest in it.

When the design kickoff occurs, the team performing the design and implementation needs to present what they have understood, what they are implementing, and when they expect it to be completed. This keeps the implementation aligned with the project's requirements. The following can be covered in the design kickoff:

- What are the requirements the team is implementing?
- What Business Problem is the team implementing?
- Is it aligned to the requirements of the overall project?
- What is the high-level design of the implementation?
- What is the team size that is implementing?
- Are there different phases of implementation? If yes, then what are the different phases?
- What language will be used for the implementation?
- Any low lights or high lights for the implementation?
- Approximate timeline for the implementation.

Each Epic that is taken up for implementation should have a presentation like this. This way, the entire team, who is involved with the development of the Epic, will be aligned with the requirements. Preparing and presenting this will take time, so an appropriate time should be provided to the team.

Manager's role in the kickoff

The roles of the manager in the kickoff meeting are as follows:

- Review the plan.
- Identify the shortcomings in the plan.
- Review the design.
- Understand the dependency complexities. Plan with the dependent team for the dependencies.

- Understand the hardware dependencies and plan for these.

- Understand that the scrum teams can achieve very little in a few months. So, we should guard against the lofty ambitions of the scrum team.

- Understand the feasibility of the timeline.

- Plan for technical training, which might help them to achieve the goals of the project.

- Plan for allied activities like certifications and security testing.

- Focus of the manager should be to get the project done despite hurdles.

- Look at how the non-functional requirements will be met.

- Understand how this project will impact the overall non-functional requirements.

- Is the team ticking OFF all checklist items for this project?

Guiding the team early will help them plug loopholes much earlier in the project, increasing the success rate.

Keeping stakeholders in the loop

It is very important to keep all the stakeholder teams, like the cross-sectional team, the management team, and the internal team in the loop at each stage of the project. Communication is one of the key aspects, and it should be maintained throughout the project lifecycle.

Software development is a slow process, so the management team should be patient. Now the question can be how slow it is? And how long should management be patient? A bug fix may take a few days. A feature development may take a few weeks or a few months of time. Anything that can be done in a few days' time does not create any doubts. But when the project is expected to run for a few months, then the management team will have a lot of questions regarding the duration of the project. The manager must understand and communicate to the management chain about the justification for the duration, expectations, and the project's progress. At the same time, the manager should keep the team's morale high.

As per the agile principle, if the features are delivered and success ceremonies are performed, the team will feel motivated and willing to do more.

Conclusion

The kickoff for a project involves organizing meetings and presentations to inform the team about the project's goals, requirements, risks, and dependencies. It sets clear expectations, establishes project plans and milestones, and defines the system architecture. The manager plays a crucial role in appraising the team, setting goals, and ensuring the team's success.

Individual project kickoffs involve distributing features, organizing meetings, and presenting requirements, design, and implementation timelines. Effective communication with stakeholders, including cross-sectional teams, management, and internal teams, is essential throughout the project. Celebrating successful feature deliveries and conducting success ceremonies can boost team motivation and maintain morale. By following these kickoff practices and maintaining open communication, project teams can enhance their chances of success and deliver high-quality software that meets project goals.

In the next chapter, the design and execution phase will be covered. The most important aspect of the project is design and execution. This is where the product gets built.

Points to remember

- There are three levels of kickoffs:
  - For the cross-section team
  - For the internal team
  - For the Epics
- Set clear expectations at each level.
- Managers should catch defects early through the presentations, should guide the team to success.
- Maintain a wide level of communication with everyone.
- Do not forget to celebrate small successes in the team. An Epic completion will require a successful celebration.

Multiple choice questions

1. **What is the purpose of a project kickoff?**
   a) To organize team-building activities
   b) To inform the team about project goals, risks, and dependencies
   c) To celebrate the completion of a project
   d) To assign tasks to team members

2. **What is one of the key responsibilities of a project manager during the kickoff?**
   a) Presenting the system architecture
   b) Setting goals for the software team
   c) Staying away from the kickoff meeting
   d) Conducting success ceremonies

3. **What should be presented during an individual project kickoff?**

    a) Implementation results

    b) High-level design

    c) The entire project management plan

    d) Detailed implementation timeline

4. **How can communication with stakeholders be maintained throughout the project?**

    a) By organizing team-building activities

    b) By conducting success ceremonies

    c) By keeping the management team informed about the progress

    d) By assigning tasks to team members

5. **What is the importance of celebrating successful feature deliveries?**

    a) To boost team motivation and maintain morale

    b) To assign new tasks to team members

    c) To inform stakeholders about the progress

    d) To identify risks and dependencies

6. **Which of the following is a key aspect of the development process mentioned in the chapter?**

    a) Usability testing

    b) Financial analysis

    c) Market research

    d) Competitive analysis

7. **What is the purpose of setting clear expectations during the kickoff?**

    a) To assign tasks to team members

    b) To define the system architecture

    c) To inform stakeholders about the project's goals

    d) To establish project plans and milestones

8. **How can the manager ensure the team's success during the kickoff?**

    a) By organizing team-building activities

    b) By providing support and unblocking issues

    c) By conducting feasibility studies

    d) By reviewing the system architecture

9. **How can effective communication be maintained with stakeholders throughout the project?**

   a) By conducting success ceremonies

   b) By setting goals for the software team

   c) By organizing regular meetings and providing progress updates

   d) By assigning tasks to team members

Answers

1. b
2. b
3. b
4. c
5. a
6. a
7. c
8. b
9. c

Exercises

1. Create a kickoff for the cross-functional team for your project.

2. Create a kickoff for the team under the manager for your current project.

3. Organize your current project team so that they will be able to complete the Epics without any problem.

4. Pick an Epic from your current project and prepare a kickoff for the Epic.

5. Create a Confluence page for communicating the plan and status of the project.

Join our book's Discord space

Join the book's Discord Workspace for Latest updates, Offers, Tech happenings around the world, New Release and Sessions with the Authors:

https://discord.bpbonline.com

CHAPTER 8
Designing Execution

Introduction

Effective team organization is a fundamental aspect of successful execution. How a project team is structured and organized can significantly impact the project's outcomes, including its efficiency, quality, and overall success. This chapter looks at the importance of thoughtful team organization and explores various team structures, such as vertical and horizontal teams, that can be employed to optimize project execution. Additionally, it examines key considerations such as team size, composition, collaboration between development and QA teams, and the role of centralized testing teams. By understanding and implementing effective team organization strategies, project managers and team leaders can enhance collaboration and resource utilization and ultimately achieve their project goals.

Structure

In this chapter, we will discuss the following topics:

- Execution model
- Vertical vs horizontal teams
- Typical size of the team
- Common integration testing team
- Designing project execution model

- Analyze and alter execution design
- Executing turnkey projects for customers

Objectives

By the end of this chapter, the reader will have explored the importance of effective team organization in project execution and provided insights into various team structures, such as vertical and horizontal teams. It discusses the considerations for team size, composition, collaboration between development and QA, and the role of centralized testing teams. Additionally, the chapter emphasizes the need for continuous analysis and adaptation in the execution model to ensure successful project outcomes. By examining real-world examples and best practices, this chapter seeks to equip project managers and team leaders with the knowledge and strategies necessary to design well-balanced teams, foster collaboration, and optimize resource utilization throughout the project lifecycle.

Execution model

The execution team has to be designed to perform efficiently, and the project can be delivered with ease. If not done correctly, it can lead to time overrun, poor quality, fights within the team, and attrition. So, great care must be taken when designing the team's structure. This includes what kind of experience level each team member will have, how many developers will be in each scrum team, and how many QA engineers will be in each scrum team. Additionally, what kind of specialties does the development team need to possess among the developers? For example, how many server engineers will be required for a web server application, and how many UI engineers will be required? How many device driver development engineers will be required for embedded system development, and how many application developers will be required?

Without a proper execution model, the team will not be balanced, which may lead to poor execution.

Vertical vs. horizontal teams

A particular **project** will typically have a few layers for implementation. The architecture defines these few layers, which typically consist of a bottom layer, a middle layer, and an application layer, as shown in the following figure:

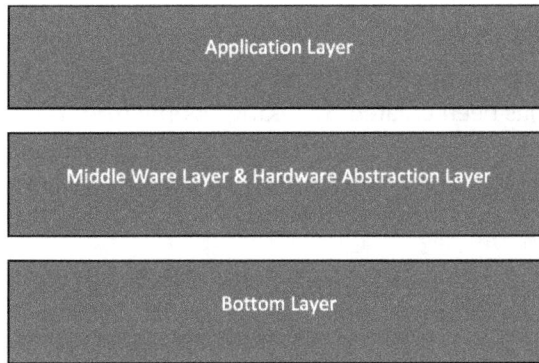

Figure 8.1: The layered approach to software development

Horizontal teams

In a horizontal team, each layer can be managed by an individual team. For example, one team can manage the bottom layer, one team can manage the middleware layer, and another team can manage the application layer.

For example, in an embedded software development project, the bottom layer can be the device driver development layer, the middleware layer can be the hardware abstraction layer, and the third one, which is the application layer, can implement the application software.

In short, the bottom layer implements the code that interacts with the hardware. The hardware abstraction layer implements code that makes the upper layers agnostic of the hardware present below. The hardware abstraction layer can also build middleware; for example, a graphics library can be built in the middleware. For example, a device driver helps to draw a particular pixel in an LCD screen in an embedded system. The middleware creates a graphics library that helps draw basic objects like a square, a line, etc., on the LCD screen. The application layer uses this graphics library to give meaning to the UI on the screen. For example, the application software can join a few lines to draw an object on the screen.

Similarly, the bottom layer in an enterprise software application can be the database layer. The middle layer can be some common libraries that help access the database. The application layer implements the business logic.

In this model, each team operates its Scrum team and develops the layers. There is a contract between the teams, and each will have certain interfaces developed in the layers. Any breach of this contract can lead to difficulty integrating the layers. Each of these teams will have developers as well as quality assurance engineers. These teams ensure that the layers are built completely and delivered with good quality.

Vertical teams

Vertical teams have a cross-section of all these layers in one team. As shown in the following figure, a vertical team has been created by taking people from the different departments:

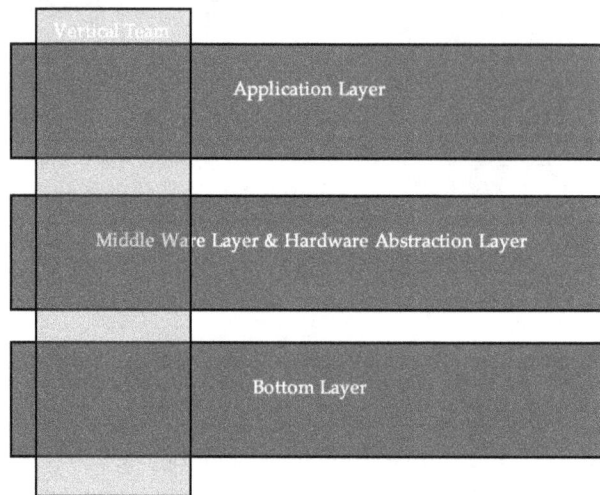

Figure 8.2: Vertical teams

A vertical team has team members from across the cross-section of the different layers. This vertical team must also interact with the parallel vertical team when common code is touched in the different layers. Any miscommunication can lead to integration issues and poor quality.

For example, in the above example, in order to draw an object on the LCD screen, the team responsible will work on all the layers in the tech stack. This will require full stack knowledge of the engineers in all the layers which might be difficult to have. Some engineers who are good in application or middleware development may not be knowledgeable in developing device drivers.

Typical size of the team

The typical size of the team, as instructed by the scrum methodology, should be around six. So, multiple teams of six members can help deliver a large project. This six-member team should have a scrum lead and one member each from different cross sections of the software stack.

In a vertical team, for example, one embedded software development project, a scrum team can have one member for the device driver development team, one member from the middleware team, and two members in the application software development team. The team can have two QA members who will help verify the software written by the team. So, in all, there are six members in the team, which develops a complete vertical of the software stack.

Like that, there can be multiple 6-member teams, as shown in the following figure:

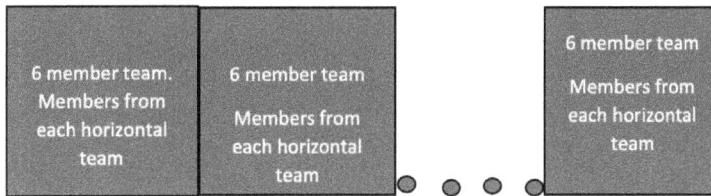

Figure 8.3: Size of teams

There can be multiple teams that can be created in this manner, to build the entire software. However, this was rather easy. It is not mandatory to have a team of six engineers. Depending on the project, it can also be a three-member team.

Division within dev

What happens if all team members do not have enough work in that specific layer? What if the engineers do not have the skills to work in multiple layers? There is a chance that some of the engineers may be idle and cannot be utilized to work on the project. In this case, it is a loss of manpower.

In this case, the layer-wise team works out well. There can be a smaller team for device driver development, which will have enough work throughout the project. Depending on the proportion of work, the middleware team can be the next biggest team. Again, depending on the proportion of work, the application team can have the requisite number of engineers. For example, there can be a 6-member device driver team since it cannot be divided any further. However, above that, it can have multiple other middleware and application teams:

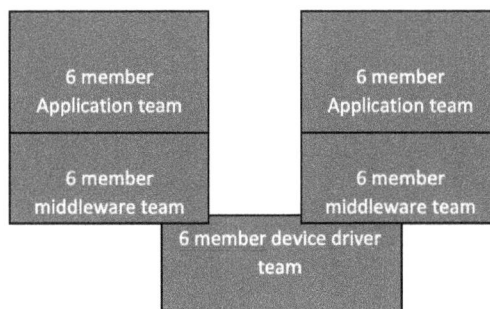

Figure 8.4: Team structure according to work needs

Dev-QA organization in a team

Also, agile is very popular these days; however, perfect agile is hard to follow. For example, device drivers cannot be completed in a 2-week sprint. A small feature also may not be available in the device driver for the quality assurance engineer to test in this 2 weeks sprint. So, what will the QA engineer do during that time? There may be a need for a QA engineer in another team; for example, the middleware team may already have developed something and may be looking for QA engineers to test it. So, there is a scope for optimization here. In this case, Kiwi may be a separate scrum team that can help to perform the QA across multiple scum teams, or the QA engineer may overlap multiple teams to optimize their efforts. Examples of an overlapping QA team are shown in the following figures. *Figure 8.5* shows the common QA team across horizontal teams, and *Figure 8.6* shows the common QA team across vertical teams:

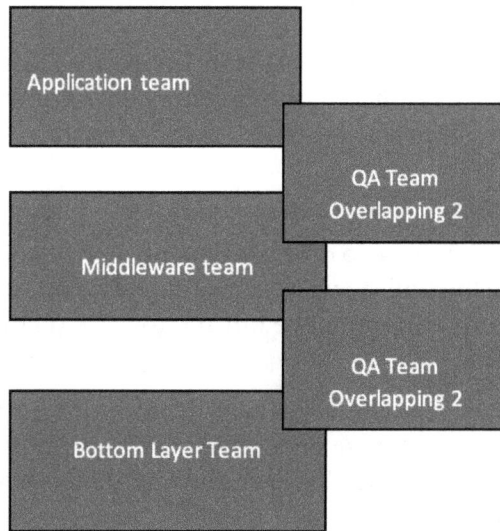

Figure 8.5: Common QA teams for horizontal teams

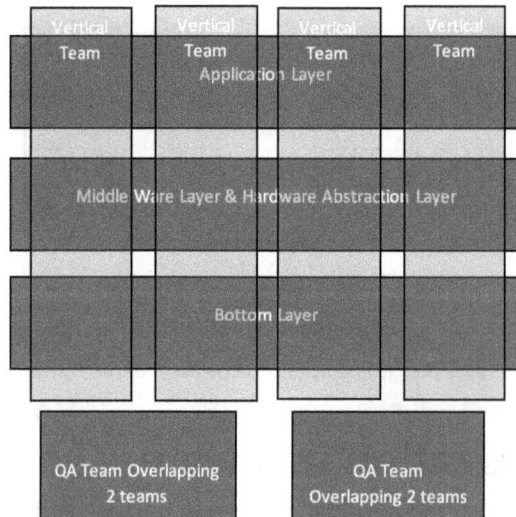

Figure 8.6: Common QA teams for vertical teams

The project manager must understand all these nuances and then design the execution team accordingly so that the engineers' efforts are effectively utilized. Managers often tend to follow the perfect Agile to make the Agile way of development successful. However, the focus should be on making the project a success by tweaking the teams according to the project's needs.

Common integration testing team

As can be seen above, each QA is associated with either a vertical team or a horizontal team. No team is testing the overall system. To test the overall system, there is to be a team that does the integration testing or system testing of the entire system. This is to ensure that the overall system is working fine. Each module working fine did not mean that the overall system was working fine. So, there has to be another team that checks the overall system.

This can be named the continuous integration team or system testing team. The integration and system test QA team can be one that does the overall integration testing of the system as a whole. An example is shown in the following figures:

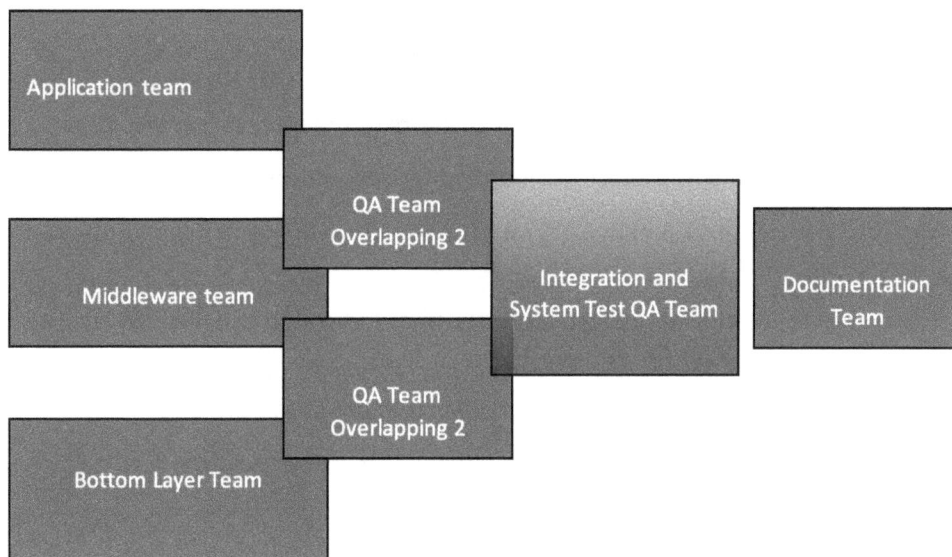

Figure 8.7: Common integration, documentation team for horizontally layered teams

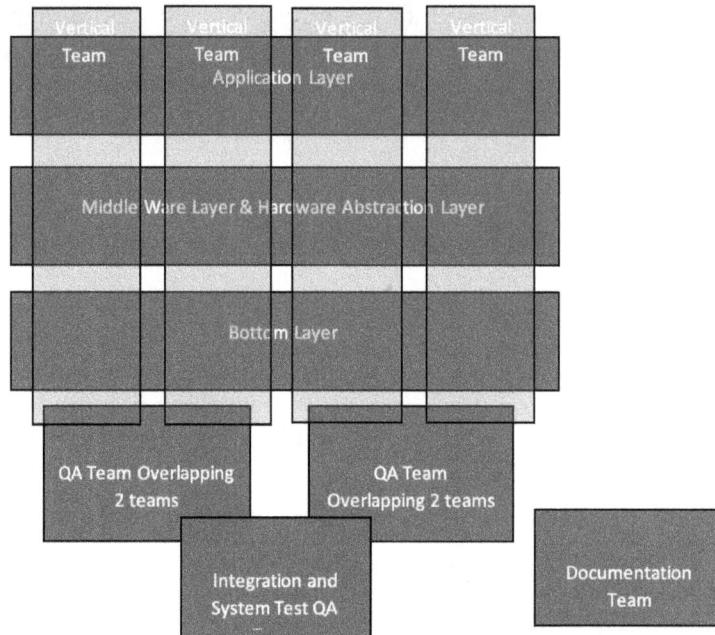

Figure 8.8: Common integration, documentation teams for vertical teams

The following can be the key performance indicators of the integration test team:

1. Measure the number of defects found during integration testing.

2. Measure the extent to which integration tests cover the system's requirements and functionalities.

3. Time taken to execute all integration tests. Should be able to cover a wider set of test cases in a short period of time.

4. Measure the percentage of integration tests that are automated.

5. Measure the severity of defects found during integration testing.

6. Measure the customer found bugs post release to determine the integration testing process effectiveness.

There can also be a scale and performance test team. The performance testing team has specialized skills to test the performance and scale of the product. These teams also have specialized tools and setups to test the performance and scale of the system. For any application sold to the customers, performance and scale are two of the most critical non-functional requirements that need to be met. An application that is not performing and scaling is a toy application that cannot be sold to customers. The performance and scale team can be a part of the project team, or they can be a part of the bigger organization that provides this kind of testing as a service:

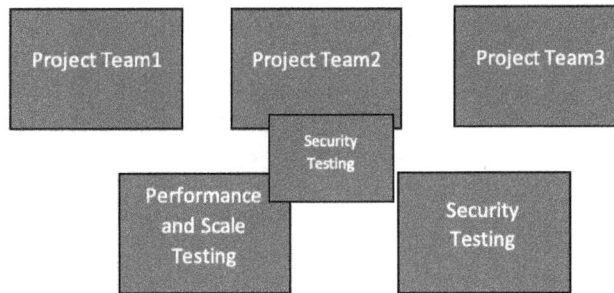

Figure 8.9: *Centralized performance, scale, and security testing teams*

Another example is security testing. Security testing requires specialized skills not available in the developer community. It also requires a specialized setup and specialized skills to test. A common security team across the organization will help test many projects in a sequence.

The project manager's role should be to interact with these teams and then include in their road map the need to test the project being executed under the manager. This should be put in the respective teams' schedules. In the absence of centralized teams, the manager has to plan for testing by the manager's own team. So, this will require considerable time to set up the environment and train the engineers who will test it.

Documentation is another such aspect that can be done by the centralized team.

The following are a couple of teams that can be centralized in the organization:

- Usability team
- Security testing team
- Performance and a skilled team
- Documentation team

However, this requires excellent coordination with the centralized team. They have their schedules, and any delay in the project schedule can jeopardize their schedule. These teams might be unable to accommodate the project's schedule changes. That can lead to delays in project execution. So, the management team must decide whether to fund an internal team for these activities or whether a centralized team has to be used. Both have their pros and cons, so the management team needs to decide based on the pros and cons of the situation.

Designing project execution model

Considering overall aspects, the manager has to decide on the project execution model. Now, one model does not suit everyone. Whatever model suits the execution needs to be created and then communicated to the team. External project teams are not bothered about the project execution model. This is internal to the team.

Once created, the team needs to be announced to the team members. Some team members may not be okay working with another team member. So, either the team members need to be counseled, or the team needs to be organized so that there is minimal overlap between the team members who are not gelling with each other. Before communicating with the entire team, discuss with the scrum leads. At any stage, reviewing with the leads can help plug the gaps.

Additionally, it can be a hybrid model. For example, at the beginning of the project, the team can be a layered one, and once the layers are built, vertical teams can be created. So initially, the entire team can split into two teams, building the bottom layer and the middleware layer. Once the layers are built, the entire team can build the application layer. During that time, the bottom layer and the middleware layer will require some work. So, the number of engineers in the bottom layer in the middle may be minimal, and the application layer can have more engineers.

For example, let us take a development team size of 12. This team can be split into two teams initially. Of the 12 members, nine are in development, and three are in QA. Initially, the team is split into two. One team will have four developers, and another will have five developers. Also, one QA engineer on each team can do functional testing. The remaining engineers can concentrate on performance testing and integration testing. This can be at the beginning of a fresh project when the entire stack has to be built from the ground up. For example, in a team of 12 members, the team composition can be something like this:

Teams	Area of work	Number of developers	Number of QA engineers	Number of QA engineers
Team A	Bottom layer	4	1	
Team B	Middleware	5	1	
System test and integration	Both the layers	0	0	1

Table 8.1: Layered team organization of 12 engineers

Once the stack has been built, the team can be reorganized. Most of the engineers can be moved to the application layer, with minimum investment in the middleware and bottom ware layers. Then, the team can be organized as shown in the following table:

Teams	Area of work	Number of developers for Application layer	Number of developers for middleware, bottom layer	Number of QA engineers	Number of QA engineers
Team A	Entire Stack	3	1	1	

Team B	Entire Stack	3	2	1	
System test and integration	Both the layers	0	0	0	1

Table 8.2: Team organization post initial stack development

There are many engineers available, let us say 18 engineers. Then, the team can be divided into layers, and then they can start working as well. Now, in the absence of the middleware and the bottom layers, how will the application layer continue to develop? So, the recommended approach is to develop a simulator that stimulates the middleware and the bottom layers and then continue developing the application layer. Developing a simulator helps continue the application-level development with the eventual integration with the middle layer of the application and the bottom layer. A similar thing can also be done for the middleware. So, the middleware team can rely on a simulator for the bottom layer and continue development.

Development tools need to be determined, and proper tools and licenses should be procured ahead of time so that all the tools are ready for development.

Some of the basic tools are as follows:

- Development tools, like Microsoft Visual Studio and Eclipse.
- Jira for bug tracking, user story creating, and tracking.
- Confluence for documentation.
- Bitbucket or GitHub for a code repository.

Any other project-specific tools also need to be established. The process of using these tools needs to be defined and documented, and the team needs to be trained on it.

Check this checklist to understand if the design has been set correctly:

1. Dev engineers has been divided based on the need of the project.
2. Each dev engineer has assigned roles and responsibilities clearly defined.
3. Dev engineers do not have an overlap with each other, there is enough room for each dev engineer to play their role.
4. QA engineers have been given specific roles to play. They have defined responsibilities.
5. Integration test team has been created and roles and responsibilities has been defined.
6. All tools are in place.
7. Orders have been placed for the tools which are not in place.

8. For all the available tools setup has been done and all engineers has role based access to the tools.

Analyze and alter execution design

Once the execution team is designed, that is not the end of the execution design. At every point, it needs to be analyzed what changes need to be made for smooth execution. It is difficult to say what changes may be required, so the manager has to analyze the changes and then make changes accordingly. For example, if the execution of a particular team is becoming slow because of a lack of QA engineers, then the manager needs to request to add more QA engineers to the team. However, getting an additional resource may not be feasible because of cost constraints, so the manager has to think about a solution. So, for some time, the performance and system test engineer can help in functional QA because, from the very beginning of the project, when the stack is unavailable, this engineer may not be able to do much system test engineering. However, if the engineer is moved, the setup for these specialized tests may be impacted. So, the manager needs to plan to create the infrastructure later.

Again, too much chopping and changing is not advised. This may mean that something is wrong with the team's organization. Changing every three to four months is a good cadence.

The team also needs to be informed about the change and its reason. Any change will initially be resisted; however, it will become a norm, and with proper communication, this will not be a surprise for the team.

Executing turnkey projects for customers

When executing turnkey projects, the team executing the projects may be remote. For example, when a services company is executing a project in a remote location like India, and the customer is in the USA, it is important to have an onsite engineer in the customer location in the USA.

The role of the person locally placed in the customer location will be:

- **To clarify the requirements:** Though initially, the requirements are signed OFF, while implementing, there will be a lot of doubts, which were kind of unknowns in the beginning. The onsite engineer on the customer site will be able to clarify the doubts of the customer.

- **To help with installation**: Once the product has been built and delivered to the customer, there are often challenges in installation. This onsite engineer will be able to help with the installation by coordinating with the remote team.

- **To help in testing along with the customer:** The engineer should be able to sit with the customer and test the product. Should capture the customer raised issues and submit those as bugs. Sometimes, if the bugs are not understandable, the onsite engineer should be able to explain to the remote team what the bug is all about.

- **Help in documenting the features:** The engineer should work with the customer to document the features. Sometimes, the features have to be documented in a local language, which the remote team may not understand. The onsite engineer should be able to take the help of the customer to translate the document into the local language.

- **Business development**: The onsite engineer can also help in business development. The engineer can develop a network with the other teams and help in getting more business for the remote workers.

- **To help in understanding the usability issues**: The remote team may have developed something that the customer is unable to use easily. This means the customer is having some usability issues. The onsite engineer should understand the issues and report them back to the team.

As seen above the onsite engineer has quite some responsibilities to execute while being in the customer location. The engineer needs to have multiple skills, and choosing a candidate who is adaptable and has the right attitude will help in executing the project smoothly. Getting feedback from the customer on a regular basis and incorporating those in the product will help to get a better experience. If the project size is big, meaning if the project is 30 people, being executed remotely, it is better to have two engineers onsite. Otherwise, the workload on the one engineer will be very high.

Conclusion

Effective team organization is crucial for the successful execution of a project, as it directly impacts factors such as efficiency, quality, and team dynamics. The choice between vertical and horizontal team structures depends on the project's specific requirements, and each has its advantages and considerations. Team size and composition should be carefully determined, considering the necessary skill sets and ensuring a balanced distribution of workload. Collaboration between development and QA teams is essential for ensuring quality throughout the project, and strategies such as shared QA teams or overlapping team members can optimize resources. Centralized testing teams, such as those for performance, security, and integration testing, play a critical role in validating the overall system and meeting non-functional requirements. Continuous analysis and adaptation of the execution model are necessary to address challenges, optimize team performance, and align with evolving project needs. By understanding these principles and applying best practices, project managers and team leaders can design and manage teams effectively, fostering a productive and successful project execution. Remote teams should have an on-site engineer to facilitate communication with the customer.

Now the execution model has been established, the next phase will be to track the execution of the project. Tracking execution and taking corrective actions are key to delivering the project on time with good quality.

Points to remember

- **Designing the team structure**: Carefully consider the experience levels, skill sets, and specialties required for each team member. Based on the project's specific needs, determine the optimal team structure, whether vertical or horizontal.

- **Continuous analysis and adaptation**: Regularly analyze the team's performance and adapt the execution model. Be prepared to adjust team size, composition, or roles to optimize resource utilization and address challenges that arise during the project.

- **Integration and quality assurance**: Establish clear interfaces and contracts between teams to ensure smooth integration between different layers or components. Consider the role of centralized testing teams to conduct system-level testing and ensure overall quality.

- **Team communication**: Communicate changes to the team and consult the scrum leads before making changes.

Multiple choice questions

1. **What is the purpose of team organization in project execution?**
   a) To assign roles and responsibilities to team members outside the project team
   b) To optimize resource utilization and enhance efficiency
   c) To communicate with external teams
   d) None of the above

2. **Which team structure involves separate teams managing different layers of a project, such as the bottom layer, middleware layer, and application layer?**
   a) Vertical teams
   b) Horizontal teams
   c) Cross-functional teams
   d) Agile teams

3. **What factors should be considered when determining team size and composition?**
   a) Required skill sets for the project
   b) Workload distribution and balance
   c) Collaboration and coordination are needed
   d) All of the above

4. **How can collaboration between development and QA teams be optimized?**
   a) Overlapping team members between the development and QA teams
   b) Shared QA teams that work across multiple development teams
   c) Regular communication and coordination meetings
   d) All of the above

5. **What is the role of centralized verification teams in project execution?**
   a) Conducting system-level integration testing
   b) Ensuring overall quality and adherence to non-functional requirements
   c) Providing specialized skills and tools for performance testing
   d) All of the above

6. **Why is continuous analysis and adaptation important in the execution model?**
   a) To address challenges and optimize team performance
   b) To align with evolving project needs
   c) To make necessary adjustments in team structure or roles
   d) All of the above

7. **What is the role of the onsite engineer?**
   a) To facilitate communication with the customer and the off-site team
   b) To help install the product in the customer environment
   c) To understand the issues faced by the customer
   d) All of the above

Answers

1. b
2. b
3. d
4. b
5. d
7. d

Exercises

1. Consider a software development project for building an e-commerce platform. Design a team structure, specifying the roles and responsibilities of each team

member. Determine the number of developers and QA engineers needed for each layer, such as the database layer, middleware layer, and application layer.

2. Compare and contrast the advantages and disadvantages of vertical teams and horizontal teams in the context of project execution. Provide scenarios where each team structure would be most suitable and explain why your choices are made.

3. Discuss the potential challenges when integrating multiple layers or components developed by different teams. Identify strategies and best practices to mitigate these challenges and ensure smooth integration. Provide real-world examples or case studies to illustrate your points.

4. List down the issues related to team organization in your current project. Determine how organizing the team can help overcome the issues related to the team.

Join our book's Discord space

Join the book's Discord Workspace for Latest updates, Offers, Tech happenings around the world, New Release and Sessions with the Authors:

https://discord.bpbonline.com

CHAPTER 9
Tracking Execution

Introduction

When the project is in progress, regular tracking is required to understand how much has been completed and how much is pending. Based on the tracking, the manager can understand whether or not the project will meet the milestone. Initially, everything will look fine for the first one or two months; however, things will start to get off track. This is typically the case in many projects. Only in some projects does execution move perfectly. Those are very few.

Structure

In this chapter, we will discuss the following topics:

- Tracking execution through tools
- Using QA test cases as an indicator
- Tracking execution through total bugs filed
- Tracking execution through bugs
- Product maturity score
- Domino effect of tasks
- Communicate status to stakeholders

- Pure agile vs. making project successful
- Tracking project progress

Objectives

During the execution, knowing the project's status will become hard. It may seem that Jira or outstanding stories will give a true picture of the situation. However, that will not be the case. The Jira stories will emerge with more understanding, which needs to be broken down. New stories will come. Bugs from the existing stories will take time to fix. In short, all hell will break loose during this time. All plans made will fall apart; presentations at this stage will not have any meaning. This chapter will suggest two reliable ways to track the execution of the project.

Tracking execution through tools

Execution is hard to track. Gantt charts in Microsoft Projects are practically hard to use; managers are not so diligent in updating the Gantt charts in Microsoft Projects. There are continuous new tasks, some things are getting moved out, some tasks are split with other engineers, and tasks often will take more time to complete. Overall, it becomes very difficult to track. Additionally, granular tasks are very difficult to track in Microsoft Projects. It is good for periodic assessments of the project, maybe quarterly; however, weekly or bi-weekly tracking is a big issue with Microsoft Projects.

Hence, people started using Jira. Understanding the overall schedule of the project gets hard in Jira as well. Jira is good for creating Epics, user stories, bugs, and subtasks. Assigning the work to the engineers to keep them on track is good. From the velocity of the team chart, which can be derived from Jira, it may also look possible to track the project and then estimate the completion date. However, there is a catch here. The future Epics and stories may not have been groomed. The existing stories, while implemented, may bring about new tasks. These tasks will increase the project's timeline when added to the current tasks.

Also, these tools are good as long as the engineers and managers constantly update them, which is not always the case. Engineers and managers do not update the tools frequently, so the data may not be correct. Sometimes, under pressure, engineers and managers may mark the tasks as complete, though they may actually be work in progress. The data in the tools may be quite skewed. It may not give the actual status of the work.

The reasons why actual project progress may not be clear from Jira are listed as follows:

- New tasks always get added
- It depends on engineers updating the data correctly
- Epics may be complete for the current scope, but overall, some may remain. These remaining stories may skew the tool's tracking

If you are using XCEL sheets or Confluence pages to track the projects, it will be equally difficult to track them correctly. It will be even more difficult and incorrect than the above two. If the team diligently updates all the tasks in Jira, then it is good. The tool can be safely relied upon. However, most often, teams do not update correctly on their own. It is the managers responsibility to ensure that Jira is updated at least at the end of the sprint and before the new sprint begins.

Using QA test cases as an indicator

Then, how to track the project. One way to correctly get the status is to do early QA along with development. How can QA do the test if the product is not ready? If interfaces are becoming ready, ask QA to test them. If QA qualifies the builds, you can be sure the project progresses.

The indicators from the QA team are as follows:

- Total number of test cases executed for that feature getting developed
- Total number of test cases passed for that feature
- Total number of bugs filed for that feature
- Total number of outstanding bugs

Once the tracking is quantified by the number of test cases or by the number of bugs filed for that feature, tracking becomes easier. However, how can it be tracked until then? Well, until then, we must rely on the updates made in the Jira, provided that the Jiras are updated frequently.

There are a couple of ways to track from the Jiras, as follows:

- Total number of user stories completed
- Total number of user stories remaining
- Total number of user story points completed
- Total number of user story points remaining

Tracking execution through total bugs filed

In a project, the test case execution to total bugs filed should be continuously plotted in a graph. The manager should ensure that the metrics are gathered regularly and the graph is plotted on a regular basis to understand the progress. Best practice is to automate the generation of these graphs so that no manual intervention is needed. For an ideal project, the graph will look like this, as is shown in the following figure below:

Total Number of Bugs

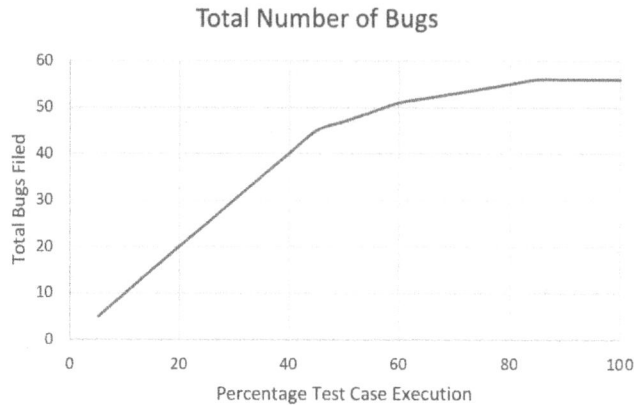

Figure 9.1: *Test cases executed vs. total bugs filed*

As the test case proceeds, the total number of bugs filed keeps increasing. We can understand by the slope of the graph that the project is in progress and whether it is near completion. If the slope of the graph reaches the horizontal flat line, which is 0 degrees, then the project has matured. QA has tested enough, and repeated testing is not yielding any more bugs. Again, this is an indication that the project is nearing completion. However, there could be 1 or 2 bugs that are very important for the product and are still not fixed. Those may be supercritical for the product. For example, the response time of a particular feature. Though the graph may show the project is completed, 1 or 2 issues may take a long time to fix. Hence, it is better to look at the contents of the Jiras to understand the complexity of the work remaining before concluding.

Tracking execution through bugs

If the number of open bugs is tracked in a project that is based on the agile way of executing, the number of open bugs in the test cases will be as follows:

Out Standing Number of Open Bugs

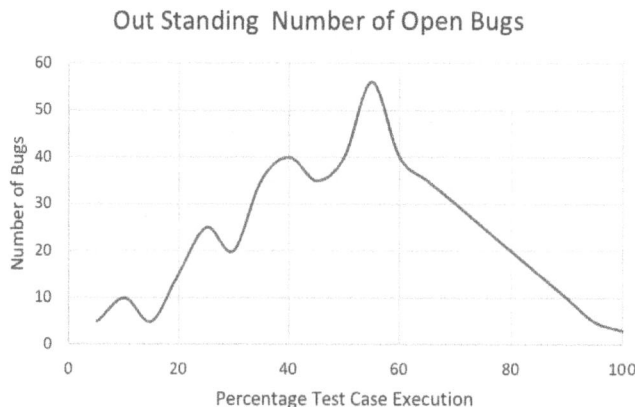

Figure 9.2: *Outstanding open bugs to understand progress*

As and when a feature is released, there is a spike in the number of open bugs. Then, the development team fixes those bugs, and the peak comes down. Again, a new set of features are developed and verified. Again, the open bugs peak and then come down. It continues till all the features are developed and released. Once the final feature is developed and released, the number of open bugs should continue to come down. It should come down to near zero. Practically, it cannot be zero. The tail can also be long if the bugs are difficult to fix.

If the graph does not gradually come down after the highest peak is reached, then there is some problem with the project's design. If one bug fix gives rise to another bug, then there is some problem with the software design.

Product maturity score

Another simple way to understand product readiness is the product maturity score. All the different metrics can be combined to create the product maturity score, a single metric showing product maturity. It can be compared to a stock market index, where the index shows the health of the market. The product maturity score can be derived from the number of user stories open, the number of bugs, the percentage of test completion, etc.

For example, a simple but effective product maturity score can be derived from the following:

Product maturity score = Total number of user stories or user story points pending for completion + Number of non-low priority bugs open + Number of test cases pending to be executed

If the total is more than five, the product may be considered unsuitable for release. However, it may depend on the organization; some organizations can take a call that if the product maturity score is less than 10, then the product may be fit for release.

Domino effect of tasks

Additionally, if there is a milestone plan that has been defined by the team, check with respect to the milestone where the team is. This has to be checked either verbally or with the help of QA. Most likely, the team will achieve the 1st milestone, with some tasks being moved to the second milestone. This leads to an impact known as the domino effect of tasks.

Let us say a project is divided into multiple milestones. M1, M2, M3, M4,M5. The total number of user story points planned for M1, M2, M3, M4, and M5 is 15, 15, 15, 16, and 14, respectively. All the milestones are planned for each sprint. Each sprint is of a two-week duration. Let us say that in M1, the user story points completed are 12. The number of story points moved to M2 is 3 in that case, since in M1, only 12 story points out of the planned 15 story points have been completed.

You will see that in M2, an equal or greater number of story points will not get completed, and those will move to M3. Example of a typical sprint in terms of story points is shown as follows:

Milestone	Planned Story Points	Unknowns added in the middle of the Milestone	Total story points	Completed Story Points	Moved to next Sprint	Total Moved to Next sprint
M1	15	0	15	13	3	3
M2	15	1	16	12	4	7
M3	15	2	17	11	6	13
M4	16	3	19	10	9	22
M5	14	2	16	12	4	26
Total	75	8	83	58	26	

Table 9.1: Domino effect

So, the project has to be extended by two milestones, M6 and M7, which will be to close the remaining 26 story points.

Milestone	Planned Story Points	Unknowns added in the middle of the Milestone	Total story points	Completed Story Points	Moved to next Sprint	Total Moved to Next sprint
M6	13	0	13	13	0	
M7	13	1	14	12	2	2

Table 9.2: Project timeline extension because of the domino effect

These two low-priority user stories may not be done in the project at all. This is what a typical milestone plan looks like during execution. Unless features are omitted from development, it will not be easy to complete within M5.

Now, how will the features be omitted? Omission can happen in 2 ways:

- If the features are prioritized, the lower-priority features can be dropped from the implementation.
- If the sub-feature within a feature is prioritized, then the lower-priority sub-features can be dropped from implementation.

Knowing that the domino effect of the first few milestones will delay the subsequent milestones, it is better to plan fewer user stories in the subsequent milestones.

Plan for progressively smaller stories in the subsequent milestones, as shown in the following table. Delivering in the current duration of the project is not possible. Proceeding without any scientific approach will stress the team, and the team will get exhausted and leave the project. This can have several detrimental effects on the team.

Milestone	Planned story points
M1	15
M2	13
M3	11
M4	9
M5	8
M6	7
M7	6
Total	69

Table 9.3: Plan for lesser stories in the later sprints

Now, convincing people of this plan will be tough when it is presented to everyone higher up in the management chain. However, one good thing is that no one micromanages to this level. Planning stories in Jira and user stories is the scrum team's responsibility. A little bit of guidance from the manager can go a long way toward achieving this goal.

Communicating status to stakeholders

Communication is one of the keys during project tracking. Communicate the correct status to other teams and management. Do not hide anything under the carpet. It is extremely important to highlight issues and communicate immediately as it happens rather than communicate in the end. If the right status is not bubbled up, then these issues will bubble up in the project later, and people will not have time to react. The longer the reaction time, the better the ability to react to the situation.

Internal stakeholders

Effective communication with internal stakeholders, including team members and management, is vital for project success. Regular and transparent communication ensures everyone remains aligned and focused on the same objectives. Here is how to approach it:

- **Regular updates**: Hold weekly or bi-weekly meetings to discuss the project's progress, potential roadblocks, and upcoming tasks. This keeps everyone in the loop and provides a platform for addressing any concerns promptly.

- **Dashboards and reports**: Utilize project management tools like Jira to create dashboards that display the current status of tasks, sprint progress, and overall project health. These visual aids can be shared with the team and management to provide a clear picture of the project's state.

- **Transparent communication**: Be honest about any issues or delays faced during the project. It is better to address problems early on, as soon as it happens, rather than allow them to escalate. Encourage an open-door policy where team members can voice their concerns or suggestions.

- **Feedback loops**: Implement regular feedback sessions, such as sprint retrospectives, to gather insights from the team on what's working and what is not. This helps in making necessary adjustments and improvements in the workflow.

External stakeholders

When communicating with external stakeholders, such as clients, investors, or other departments, clarity and professionalism are key. Here are some strategies:

- **Structured reports**: Provide structured and concise status reports at agreed intervals. These reports should highlight major milestones achieved, upcoming tasks, potential risks, and how they are being mitigated. Avoid technical jargon and focus on the overall progress and outcomes.

- **Client meetings**: Schedule regular meetings with clients to discuss progress and gather their feedback. These meetings can be monthly or at key project milestones. Ensure that the discussions are focused and that any client concerns are addressed promptly.

- **Visual presentations**: Use visual aids like Gantt charts, progress maps, and timelines in your presentations to make the status updates more engaging and understandable for stakeholders who may not be familiar with the technical details of the project.

- **Consistency**: Maintain consistency in your communication format and frequency. This builds trust and ensures that stakeholders know when and how they will receive updates.

- **Highlight achievements and challenges**: While it's important to communicate successes, it's equally important to discuss any challenges and how you plan to overcome them. This demonstrates transparency and proactive problem-solving.

By establishing clear communication channels and maintaining a transparent flow of information, you can ensure that both internal and external stakeholders are well-informed and engaged throughout the project lifecycle.

Communication channels can be through:

- Emails
- Bi-weekly project review meetings
- Program review meeting notes
- Program chat groups

Overcommunicating any issues is always better than undercommunicating the same.

Pure agile vs. making project successful

In many companies that have started to practice agile, managers want to make agile projects successful. Sometimes, making agile successful takes more priority than making the project successful. Remember, everything else is secondary; the project's success is primary. Agile, Scrum, and Jiras are tools that help make your project successful. These processes may be successfully used in the project; however, the project may not be successful. It is important to keep the priorities right. For example, if the stories of M1 cannot be completed in the sprint as planned, do not coerce the team to complete everything in the sprint. They may stretch and complete M1, but the same thing will repeat in M2. They ultimately will get exhausted and leave the project.

A sprint retrospective is a good way to analyze a particular sprint, understand where the project is, take feedback from the execution, and alter the execution accordingly. This is without the manager's involvement, and the team should reflect and understand the pros and cons of the sprint and modify its execution accordingly.

A sprint retrospective is a review conducted after a sprint and is generally conducted by the scrum team after the sprint is over. A sprint retrospective aims to determine what went well and where the scrum team had problems and identify areas where the team can improve.

If the timelines are planned as per the estimates without any buffer, then the project is going to slip unless features are removed during the implementation stage. Now, that means that some buffer has to be kept in the project. How much buffer must be kept? Is it 5%, 10%, 20%, etc.? The initial stage of the project is an indicator as to how much buffer has to be kept.

Buffer can also be derived from previous projects. If the team continues from previous projects, the buffer can be derived from the history of the previous project. For example, how much the estimate and time it took to complete the project will give an estimate of the buffer to be chosen. In the absence of any background information, it is generally hard to justify the buffer chosen. If a 20% buffer is chosen, then the question will be, why 20%?

Not every sprint will complete whatever has been planned for completion. Practically, this is not always possible in a two-week sprint. It is fine; the incomplete items can be completed in the next sprint. This is the Kanban working style rather than a pure agile way of working. Most of the time, the team will end up following the **Kanban** method of execution. In Kanban, stories are planned for the sprint, and depending on the bandwidth availability, new stories are pulled from the backlog for implementation if work is completed.

Retrospectives help the team self-correct instead of the manager telling them what needs to be improved. The team can process the retrospectives and incorporate them into the next sprint. This way, the team will gradually improve.

Focus on project completion rather than on making the process a success. Project completion, to a large extent, depends on the technical skills of the team; the process is just a helper in achieving completion.

Technical success is more important than anything else. The team should gradually improve technically year on year. New technical challenges should be given to the team so that they can conquer these new challenges.

Software development is a very slow process. Nothing happens very fast. It takes a lot of time for software to be developed, and any new development will take a lot of time to complete. Nothing can be done in the order of a week unless the development is microscopically small.

If not all the principles of agile, take some of the best practices from agile. Remember, the focus is on making the project a success rather than agile success.

Tracking project progress

Project managers experience stress when the project is actually in execution. The key to countering stress is to have better visibility into the project and communicate the issues and their impact on the project timeline. Maintaining transparency and discussing solutions is the key. All projects will experience the same kind of issues; some may have more, and some may have less. Assessing this early with enough time will help mitigate the risks and, subsequently, stress on the managers.

When a project is successful, there will be many claimants. Everybody will claim that the project succeeded because of that person. Of course, there will be a couple of good players in the team, and the project will succeed because of them. However, ultimately, it is teamwork that is the reason for success. No one individual is bigger than the team.

However, when a project fails, the project managers are normally blamed. At that time, no one claimed responsibility, compared to when the project succeeded.

The definition of failure is as follows:

- The project is technically incomplete; there are too many bugs, and fixing one bug opens another bug somewhere else.

- The timeline has passed.

- Cost became very high, putting many engineers to complete the project.

- Integrating with the other components is just not succeeding.

However, generally, it is the manager's responsibility to make the project successful. The manager has all the keys to making the project successful. The manager should see all the metrics, zoom out, analyze the metrics, and see what changes need to be made to make the project successful. The sooner the changes, the better for the project's success.

Conclusion

Effective tracking of project execution is crucial for project success, but it can be challenging due to the dynamic nature of tasks, the emergence of new requirements, and potential delays in bug fixing. Traditional tools like Microsoft Projects may not always be suitable for granular and frequent tracking, while Jira provides better visibility but still requires diligent updates and may not capture the full scope of work. Leveraging QA testing as an indicator of project progress can provide valuable insights, such as the number of test cases executed, passed, and bugs filed, helping to quantify and track project execution. Analyzing the relationship between test case execution and total bugs filed can offer a visual representation of project progress, with a flat or declining trend indicating project maturity. Considering the number of open bugs in an agile project can provide insights into the state of development and identify potential design issues if the number of open bugs remains high after significant milestones. Utilizing a product maturity score, derived from multiple project metrics, offers a holistic view of project readiness and can serve as a guide for determining release readiness. Effective communication, transparency, and timely updates to the team and stakeholders are essential for tracking project progress, mitigating risks, and ensuring successful project completion.

By implementing reliable tracking methods, leveraging QA testing, and maintaining open communication, project managers can navigate the challenges of project execution, make informed decisions, and increase the likelihood of project success. Dependencies and change management are another aspect that needs to be taken care of carefully. It will be discussed in the next chapter.

Points to remember

- **Establish clear project goals and metrics**: Define specific goals and **key performance indicators** (**KPIs**) upfront. These metrics will be benchmarks for tracking progress and evaluating the project's success.

- **Monitor and update project status regularly**: Continuously track and update the project's status by gathering progress updates from team members, analyzing task completion, and assessing any deviations from the project plan. This helps identify potential issues early on and allows for timely corrective actions.

- **Utilize effective project tracking tools**: Choose appropriate project tracking tools, such as project management software, task boards, or spreadsheets, to facilitate efficient monitoring and reporting of project tasks, milestones, and deadlines. Ensure that the tools are accessible to all team members and regularly updated.

- **Communicate and collaborate with stakeholders**: Maintain open and transparent communication, including team members, clients, and management. Regularly share project updates, milestones achieved, and any potential challenges or risks. Collaboration and stakeholder feedback can help align expectations and ensure everyone is on the same page.

- **Continuously evaluate and adjust the project plan**: Regularly assess the project plan and make necessary adjustments based on changing requirements, resource availability, or unforeseen obstacles. Flexibility and adaptability are crucial for keeping the project on track and ensuring successful execution.

Multiple choice questions

1. **Which of the following is NOT a common challenge in tracking project execution?**

   a) Emergence of new requirements

   b) Difficulty in updating Gantt charts in Microsoft Projects

   c) Lack of diligent updates in Jira

   d) Over-reliance on QA testing

2. **What can be a reliable indicator of project progress during execution?**

   a) Number of open bugs

   b) Number of test cases executed

   c) Updates in project tracking tools

   d) Both a) and b)

3. **Why is effective communication important during project tracking?**

   a) To hide issues and challenges from stakeholders

   b) To maintain transparency and foster trust

   c) To micromanage team members

   d) To prioritize process success over project success

4. **Which tool is often used for granular and frequent tracking of project tasks in Agile projects?**

   a) Microsoft Projects

   b) Jira

   c) Spreadsheets

   d) Gantt charts

5. **What does the slope of the graph representing the relationship between test case execution and total bugs filed indicate?**

   a) Project completion

   b) Project maturity

c) Complexity of the work remaining

d) Response time of a feature

6. **How can the domino effect of tasks impact project milestones?**

a) It leads to faster completion of milestones

b) It results in the removal of low-priority features

c) It causes delays in subsequent milestones

d) It improves software design

7. **What should be the primary focus when tracking project execution?**

a) Making the process a success

b) Achieving technical success

c) Micromanaging team members

d) Prioritizing project completion

Answers

1. d
2. d
3. b
4. b
5. b
6. c
7. d

Exercises

1. Consider a project that is being tracked using Jira. Identify three potential challenges or limitations project managers may face when relying on Jira to track project execution. Discuss how these challenges can impact project tracking and suggest possible strategies to overcome

2. Imagine you are a project manager responsible for tracking the execution of a software development project. Develop a project tracking plan that includes key goals, objectives, and KPIs to monitor project progress. Outline the specific metrics you would use to track the project and explain why they are relevant to its success.

3. Review the graph representing the relationship between test case execution and total bugs filed in a project. Analyze the graph and identify the key insights it

provides about project progress and maturity. Discuss how you would interpret the graph and your actions based on its findings.

4. Create a fictional project scenario where the domino effect of tasks occurs. Describe the milestones and the number of story points planned for each milestone. Calculate and illustrate how the incomplete tasks in one milestone impact subsequent milestones. Discuss the implications of the domino effect on project timelines and suggest strategies to mitigate its impact.

5. As a project manager, draft a communication plan to track progress and updates. Identify key stakeholders and determine the frequency, channels, and communication content. Consider the importance of transparency, timely updates, and addressing potential challenges. Discuss how effective communication can contribute to successful project tracking and stakeholder engagement.

Join our book's Discord space

Join the book's Discord Workspace for Latest updates, Offers, Tech happenings around the world, New Release and Sessions with the Authors:

https://discord.bpbonline.com

CHAPTER 10

Dependency and Change Management

Introduction

In software development, large projects often consist of interconnected components and modules that rely on each other to achieve their goals. These interdependencies form the backbone of complex systems, ensuring smooth collaboration and seamless functionality. However, managing these dependencies and accommodating change requests throughout the project lifecycle can be a challenging endeavor.

Structure

In this chapter, we will discuss the following topics:

- Cross-team dependency management
- Handling change requests

Objectives

This chapter looks at the vital aspects of dependency management and change requests, shedding light on the significance of tracking dependencies, exploring various types of dependencies, discussing effective tracking methods, and addressing the impact of change requests on project execution. By understanding and implementing robust strategies for dependency management and change request handling, software development teams can navigate intricate project landscapes more efficiently and deliver high-quality products that meet stakeholder expectations.

Cross-team dependency management

Large projects depend on each other. It is important to create a dependency matrix and track the dependencies regularly. The dependencies can be like a mesh; they can be serial dependencies.

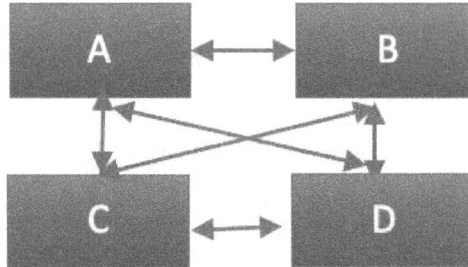

Figure 10.1 Mesh dependency

An example of a mesh dependency is shown in *Figure 10.1*, where project A is dependent on B, and B is dependent on A. This is indicated by the two-way arrows. A mesh dependency can become really messy if not tracked properly. This may derail the project from completion and impact the quality of the product.

A mesh dependency example occurs in smartphone OS development. The OS team and hardware team rely on each other's progress. For example, the hardware team creates a pressure-sensitive touchscreen, which the OS team must support. Meanwhile, the hardware team needs OS feedback to optimize this sensor. Clear communication and careful tracking are crucial to managing these dependencies, avoiding delays, and ensuring a smooth user experience.

The OS development can be divided into multiple teams. Each software team will develop its own piece. However, they will be dependent on the software developed by other teams, and also will be dependent on the hardware being developed by the hardware teams. There will always be a complex set of dependencies between multiple teams.

A serial dependency is when project C is dependent on B, and project B is dependent on A in a serial way. For example, A delivers something, B consumes that, and delivers something, and then C consumes and delivers the final product. A representation is as follows:

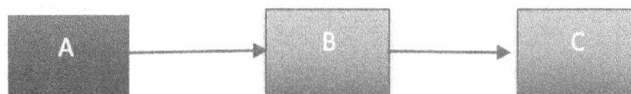

Figure 10.2: Serial dependency

A serial dependency example is seen in developing a video streaming service. Project A develops video encoding software, which Project B uses to build the **content delivery network** (**CDN**). Project C then creates the user interface using outputs from both projects.

For instance, project A's encoding software must be developed to ensure videos are ready for various devices. Project B can then optimize the CDN with these encoded videos. After both tasks, project C builds the user interface for seamless video browsing and streaming. This step-by-step reliance exemplifies serial dependency.

Tracking dependencies and tools to use

Dependencies need to be tracked from the beginning of the project. There can be many types of dependencies:

- **Requirement dependencies**: These dependencies are from the requirements perspective. One project may have multiple components. So, one requirement can be spread across multiple modules. For example, a requirement for a video player, the requirement may be stated like this: there should be a play/pause button to play and pause the video. Now this requirement can be on the hardware as well as the software. So, this is a requirement that is dependent on the software as well as the hardware.

  Requirement dependencies are tracked via the software requirements documents, then to the design documents, and then to the code. It is a hard one to track. But at least from the requirements which has been presented by the product manager, a mapping of the same has to be done from the software requirement documents to the design documents. In safety-critical software, for example, in aerospace software, the requirements have to be mapped to the code level. Numbering each and every requirement and referencing them in the documents and in the code is a good way to maintain traceability of requirements.

- **Coding dependencies:**

  o **Interface dependencies**: How the user interface looks. What are the dependencies of this module on the other modules?

  o **API dependencies**: These can be external APIs or internal APIs. Internal APIs are the ones that are consumed internally by the modules. External APIs are the ones which are the ones which are consumed by external applications.

  o **Data model dependencies**: How the data is stored and how messages are transferred across multiple modules. The schemas of all the data storage and data transferred.

  o **Hardware dependencies**: Dependencies on the hardware of the software.

  o **Software layer-wise dependencies:** Software can be layered, for example, a driver layer, middleware layer, or application layer. Each layer can have two-way dependencies.

o **Code dependencies**: Some of the code can be e and can be reused across multiple modules.

o **QA dependencies**: Testing of different modules will be dependent on each other. Overall integration testing also will be dependent on other modules.

o **Build generation dependencies**: Builds will take the latest version of the checked-in code and of the modules and do a consolidated build.

o **Deployment dependencies**: deployment of one module or modules is dependent on the other module or modules. Deployment sequence needs to be followed before some of the software can be deployed.

The requirements can be tracked via Jira, XCEL, or on a confluence page. The author prefers the XCEL or Confluence page to track the dependencies. Jira becomes a little too difficult to track the complete set of dependencies.

Each Jira can have individual dependencies on another Jira. This can be a good way to track individual dependencies. However, as the project goes on, maintaining dependencies this way becomes difficult. The following is a diagram showing how dependencies are created in Jira:

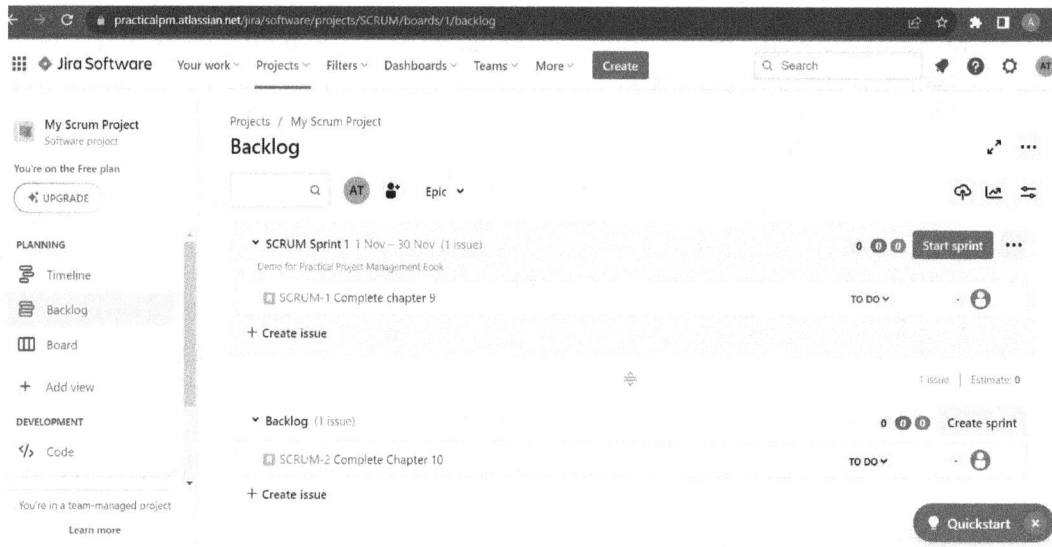

Figure 10.3 Jiras for completion of Chapter 9 and Chapter 10

Let us say that Chapter 10 is dependent on Chapter 9. This means we can start Chapter 10 only after the completion of Chapter 9. Then, a dependency can be created between the two stories, as shown in the following figure:

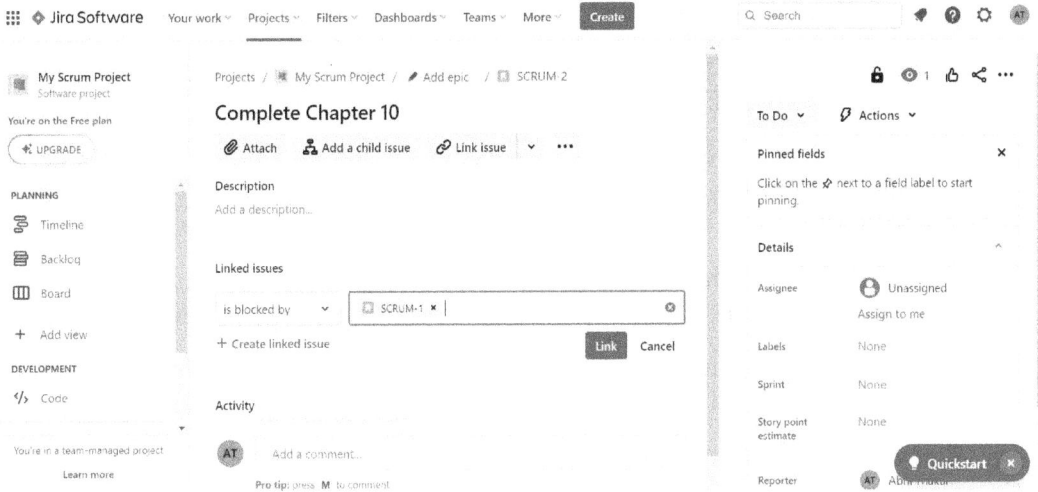

Figure 10.4: Dependency creation between Jiras

GitHub also provides a good way to manage projects. Code, documentation, issues, project management, and security upgrades through GitHub actions can be accessed from GitHub. The author has not used GitHub for issues; hence cannot comment much on it; however, since it is a Microsoft-backed product, it should be good. The author has only used GitHub as a code repository.

Dependencies will most likely not come on time. It is not always the ideal situation. This will cause a ripple effect in the schedule. The ripple effect happens because of a delay in one of the projects and causes delays in the subsequent sprints; the same type of ripple effect happens across all the projects. In this case, the delays get multiplied since they will be across the teams. It is hard to quantify how much it is. If the teams are diligent and track the stories by creating dependencies like this, it is great for the project. Mostly, the project will proceed very smoothly. However, sustaining this on a long-term basis becomes difficult, especially with changes coming in.

A combination of Jira and XCEL or Confluence is by far the best tool to track the mesh and serial dependencies. Most of the time managers use XCEL or Confluence and it is by far the best tool to track these.

A sample table for tracking dependencies can be something as shown in the following figure:

Serial Number	Dependency Topic	Description of Dependency	Dependency From Team	Dependency To Team	Dependency delivery date	Current Status	Owner	Jira Number
1								
2								
3								

Figure 10.5: Dependency tracking table in XCEL or Confluence

The following are the meanings of the columns used in the table above.

- **Topic of dependency**: A few words to describe the dependency of the topic. For example, REST API Dependency.

- **Description of dependency**: A description of the dependency in one or two sentences. For example, a REST API to get the streaming video data in a content delivery network.

- **Dependency from team**: It says the dependency came from which team? For example, in this case, it can be the UI team from which the dependency came.

- **Dependency on team**: It says the dependency is given to which team. For example, it can be the backend team to which the dependency has been given.

- **Dependency delivery date**: The date the dependency will be delivered.

- **Current status**: What is the current status? It is on track, delayed, delivered, paused, or closed.

- **Owner**: Who is owning the dependency for delivery? The name of the person.

- **Jira Number**: What is the Jira number associated with the dependency? If there are multiple Jiras, then provide all the Jira numbers. This allows for easy reference and tracking within the project management system.

Handling change requests

Changes will come all the time because of changing customer requirements or something urgent. It is important to pause the current work and address these changes. Changes come in two ways:

- **Big changes**: These come through the **change control board** (**CCB**). They are much more formalized and communicate well across the teams. They have proper discussions so everyone becomes aware and makes an informed decision. A CCB consists of people across the team, and also a representative from senior management. They determine whether this requirement is important for the project or not. They see the value of the requirement in terms of return on investment and then determine whether it should be done by deprioritizing other requirements.

- **Small changes**: These happen within the teams and can impact other teams. Sometimes, these are not communicated well, and hence, teams are caught unaware of the changes. If the development team submits a Jira across the teams, it gets addressed; however, if the development team misses and thinks it is implicitly assumed that other teams will take care of it by default, it will become a problem. Communication within and between teams is crucial to address this. If not, we can end up in a situation where the teams are completely misaligned.

Planning for mitigating dependencies

Another way to catch this misalignment is to plan for integration sprints early. Instead of having integration sprints later in the cycle, have them after a few sprints. That way, the dependencies are caught much ahead of time instead of much later in the cycle.

Even after many meetings, discussions, unit testing, and code reviews, the testing cycle ultimately stabilizes a product.

In a technically immature team, after the code is delivered, there will be a lot of bugs, and it will take a lot of time to stabilize the product. Sometimes, it cannot be stabilized at all if the design is faulty. One fix may lead to another bug. In that case, take corrective actions after seeing the results of the integration sprints. The entire design probably has to be thought through before proceeding with the integration sprints.

A technically mature team will be much more stable. As shown above, the team will proceed according to the bug maturity graphs. The product maturity graphs will also show a smoother decrease. By seeing the graphs, we can understand the maturity of the teams and the maturity of the executions.

Conclusion

Effective tracking of dependencies is crucial for large software projects to ensure smooth collaboration and avoid potential complications. Utilizing tools like Jira, Excel, or Confluence can streamline the tracking process and provide a centralized view of dependencies.

Various types of dependencies, including requirements, coding, interface, API, data model, hardware, software layer, code, QA, build generation, and deployment dependencies, should be identified and managed. Delayed dependencies can have a ripple effect on project schedules and impact multiple teams, emphasizing the importance of proactive communication and collaboration.

Whether big or small, change requests require clear communication, documentation, and integration sprints to address potential misalignment and ensure effective adaptation.

Integration sprints conducted early in the project can help catch and address dependencies and changes before they become more challenging to manage. Developing teams can deliver more stable and mature products by prioritizing product stabilization through continuous testing, bug fixing, and course correction.

By implementing robust strategies for dependency management and change request handling, software development teams can enhance project efficiency, minimize risks, and deliver high-quality products that meet stakeholder expectations.

The next chapter will focus on issue tracking. When the project comes to issue tracking, it becomes relatively easier compared to the other execution aspects of the project. Why it becomes easier will be discussed in the next chapter.

Points to remember

- **Track dependencies from the beginning**: Start tracking dependencies early in the project to ensure a clear understanding of the interdependencies between components and modules.

- **Utilize appropriate tools**: Choose suitable tools like Jira, Excel, Confluence, or GitHub to effectively track and manage dependencies, ensuring transparency and collaboration within the team.

- **Identify and manage various types of dependencies**: Consider different types of dependencies such as requirements, coding, interface, API, data model, hardware, software layer, code, QA, build generation, and deployment dependencies, and establish processes to manage them effectively.

- **Communicate and collaborate proactively**: Foster open communication and collaboration within and between teams to address delayed dependencies, change requests, and potential misalignments, minimizing the impact on project schedules and quality.

- **Plan for integration sprints and product stabilization**: Incorporate integration sprints early in the project to catch and address dependencies and changes promptly. Prioritize product stabilization through continuous testing, bug fixing, and course correction to ensure a more stable and mature product.

Multiple choice questions

1. **Which tool(s) can be used to track dependencies and manage projects?**
   a) Jira
   b) Excel
   c) Confluence
   d) All of the above

2. **What is the potential impact of delayed dependencies on a project?**
   a) Improved collaboration
   b) Accelerated project timelines
   c) Ripple effect on schedules and quality
   d) No impact on the project

3. **Change requests can come in two forms:**
   a) Big changes, small changes
   b) Formal changes, informal changes

    c) Internal changes, external changes

    d) all of the above

4. **What is a recommended approach to address misalignment caused by change requests?**

    a) Proactive communication and documentation

    b) Ignoring the changes and continuing with the original plan

    c) Delaying integration sprints until the changes are resolved

    d) Avoiding change requests altogether

5. **Integration sprints are beneficial for:**

    a) Identifying dependencies early in the project

    b) Addressing change requests promptly

    c) Ensuring effective collaboration among teams

    d) All of the above

6. **What is the importance of continuous testing and bug fixing in product stabilization?**

    a) It ensures the smooth execution of integration sprints

    b) It helps in identifying hardware dependencies

    c) It stabilizes the product and reduces post-delivery bugs

    d) It eliminates the need for change requests

Answers

1. d
2. c
3. d
4. a
5. d
6. c

Exercises

1. **Dependency identification**: Identify the types of dependencies present in the following scenarios:

    a. A web application depends on an external API for retrieving weather data.

    b. Module A relies on Module B to provide database access functionality.

    c. The design of a user interface component is dependent on the availability of specific graphic assets.

    d. Project X cannot begin until Project Y completes the implementation of a crucial feature.

2. **Tracking dependencies:** Using your preferred tool (e.g., Jira, Excel, Confluence), create a dependency matrix for a hypothetical software project. Please include at least five different types of dependencies and track their status throughout the project lifecycle.

3. **Change request assessment:** Consider a change request that has been submitted by a stakeholder. Evaluate the impact of the change request on the project by considering the following factors:

    a. Dependencies with other modules or components

    b. Project schedule and timeline

    c. Resource allocation and availability

    d. Overall project goals and objectives

4. **Communication and collaboration:** Formulate a communication plan for a project team to address dependencies and change requests effectively. Outline the key stakeholders, communication channels, and frequency of updates required to ensure smooth collaboration and alignment.

5. **Integration sprint planning:** Plan an integration sprint for a project that is in progress. Identify the key dependencies that need to be addressed during the sprint and outline the tasks, resources, and timelines required to integrate the different components or modules successfully.

Join our book's Discord space

Join the book's Discord Workspace for Latest updates, Offers, Tech happenings around the world, New Release and Sessions with the Authors:

https://discord.bpbonline.com

CHAPTER 11
Issue Tracking

Introduction

Bugs are the backbone of a software company. It is a joke that engineers write code with bugs so that their jobs are safe. Probably the easiest thing in project management for a project manager is to track the issues coming from the project. Most managers are aware of how to track bugs and use tools like Jira. There is some additional information regarding the best practices for filing and generating reports for Jiras.

Structure

In this chapter, we will discuss the following topics:

- Tracking internal issues
- Tracking external issues
- Prioritizing and fixing issues
- Triaging bugs

Objectives

The objective of this chapter is to provide a comprehensive understanding of bug tracking in software development, including best practices, tools, and metrics. By the end of this chapter, readers will be able to effectively track and manage internal and external issues, file comprehensive bug reports, prioritize and fix issues based on their impact, and utilize appropriate debugging tools to ensure the delivery of high-quality software products.

Tracking internal issues

When it comes to the issue-tracking stage, the project becomes easy to track. Normally, Jira is used to track issues that are logged for the project. Jira can be used to generate reports on a per-project basis to know how many issues are generated and how many are fixed. Instead of Jira, it can be any other tool, too. The author has personally used many different tools, but now, the dominant one is Jira.

Often, it happens in many companies, wherein, to keep the metrics low for the project, the issues are discussed verbally and then taken up for fixing. Also, sometimes issues are discussed in email, and no bug tracking is done. Sometimes, people also use Microsoft Teams and sometimes even WhatsApp to discuss issues without filing a bug report. This should absolutely be avoided. A bug report must be filed for every issue, no matter how small. Whatever the metrics, they are used to help the project. So, the right metrics have to be obtained. If no bug report is filed, the right metrics will not be obtained.

How to file a bug report

When filing a bug report, it is crucial to provide comprehensive and accurate information. Here are the mandatory parameters that need to be filled, along with detailed explanations for each:

- **Summary of the issue**: Provide a concise and clear summary of the bug to give a quick understanding of the problem. This helps in identifying the issue at a glance.

- **Description of the issue**: Give a detailed description of the bug, explaining what is happening versus what is expected. Include any relevant background information that can help in understanding the context of the issue.

- **Name of the reporter**: Mention the name of the person reporting the bug. This is important for follow-up questions or clarifications that might be needed.

- **The version number of the product in which the issue is seen**: Specify the version of the software where the bug was found. This helps in identifying whether the issue is related to a specific release or if it persists across multiple versions.

- **Steps to reproduce**: Clearly outline the steps needed to reproduce the bug. This section is critical as it allows developers to see the problem first-hand and understand how it occurs.

- **Recordings like video recordings or jpegs, which can be attached to the report**: Attach any visual evidence such as screenshots or videos that demonstrate the bug. Visual aids can provide additional clarity and help in diagnosing the issue faster.

- **Configuration in which the issue can be seen:** Describe the environment where the bug occurs, including hardware, operating system, browser, or any other relevant configurations. This information can be key to replicating and fixing the bug.

- **What is the severity of the issue**: Indicate how severe the bug is. Classify it as critical, major, minor, or enhancement, depending on its impact on the functionality of the software.

- **Is it a blocker:** Specify if the bug is a blocker, meaning it prevents further progress in the development or usage of the software. Blocker bugs need to be addressed immediately.

- **Has it been hit by customers**: Mention if the bug has been reported by customers or if it has only been identified internally. Customer-reported bugs might need to be prioritized differently. Mention the name of the customer in the bug report.

- **Will this issue be seen in any dependent components**: Note if the bug affects other components or modules of the software. Understanding the bug's impact on dependent components can help in assessing the overall risk and required fixes.

There can be many more parameters that can be created, also according to the needs of the project. For example, which patch release is required this week? Depending on the needs of the project, the project manager can decide what other fields to be filled by the reporter of the issue. If there are too many fields, it becomes taxing for the submitter to file a report. So, a perfect balance has to be struck, which can help both the project and the start submitter.

Till this stage, you can understand that only 50% of the work has been completed; the remaining 50% gets completed when testing starts and bugs are filed. Even after a thorough design, coding, review, and unit testing are done, major solidification happens during the bug-fixing stages. Understanding the issue technically helps the manager much more than just beginning to assign the bugs. If technically understood, many optimizations can be made during the execution of the project. For example, suppose some bugs are coming from a particular area, and a common area of the code is causing that. In that case, those bugs can be grouped together and assigned to a particular individual or individual. This way, things can be optimized. Also, it helps in prioritization. In a project, there will always be time constraints, so prioritization helps a lot in optimizing the effort. Of course, this must be done in consultation with the product manager or business analyst. It is always essential for a manager to be technically competent in the area where the project is being done.

A well-structured bug filing template can be created to ensure that all relevant information is captured when a bug is reported. This standardization helps in the clear communication of issues, facilitating a smoother resolution process. Some of the known fields can be prefilled in the template.

A sample bug report will look as shown in the following table. The report is about an issue where a consumer is unable to add more than ten items to a shopping cart from the catalogue. This is a very serious issue because it can adversely impact sales and needs to be fixed immediately.

Summary of the issue	Not able to add beyond 10 items in shopping cart
Description	User is unable to add beyond 10 items from the catalog to the shopping cart.
Name of the Reporter	Abhi
Version Number	2.20230615
Steps to Reproduce	1.Login as a consumer 2.Add 10 items from the catalog to the shopping cart. 3.Try adding the 11th item. 4. It fails to the add the 11th item to the cart. No error is thrown. 5. The user is able to checkout the 10 items and complete the shopping. 5. Happens both if tried from the browser or from the mobile App.
Configuration in which the issue is seen	1. Consumer login 2. Both in the browser and mobile App
Severity	Critical
Blocker	Yes
Hit by Customers	Yes
Reported by	QA Name

Table 11.1: A sample bug report

Bug metrics

When it comes to the bug-tracking stage, life becomes easy for the project manager. Even if the manager is unable to understand the project technically, he can still assign and distribute the bugs to the team members. Once the assignment is done, it becomes easier to generate metrics for the project. Also, this is a stage for solidifying the quality of the product.

The following metrics can be generated by Jira. These are the top few that can help in managing the project:

Report name	Description
Outstanding bug list	List of outstanding issues sorted by priority.

Report name	Description
Bugs which have been fixed or closed	Bugs which have been fixed or closed because the issue is obsolete, not-reproducible or it has been decided that it will not be fixed, since there is a workaround.
Bugs to be fixed by an individual	Bugs to be fixed by everyone. This helps to load balance the bugs.
Bugs fixed by an individual	Bugs which have been fixed by an individual. This can also be used during appraisals. However, the quality of the bug fixes, complexity needs to be understood too along with the number of bug fixes.
Bugs to be verified by a QA engineer	List of all bugs to be verified by the QA engineers.
Bugs verified by QA engineer	List of all bugs already verified by the QA engineers.
Fix rejects	How many times each bug fix has been rejected by the QA engineer. This is a good metrics to understand the skills of an engineer. A good engineer's bug fix will get rejected less by the QA engineer.
Velocity of bug fixes	How many bugs are being fixed in how many days? How many bugs are being fixed by individuals? Care must be taken about the complexity and the amount of work required to fix the bugs.
Incoming bug rate	The rate at which bugs are being filed by the QA engineer.
Number of test cases that have been executed	How many test cases has been executed, corresponding to the bugs which has been filed. This will give a metrics with respect to the test case executed. Then it will be easy to arrive at the number of bugs which can be filed for the remaining test cases.
Severity of the bugs	How many a critical, how many high severities and how many medium and low severity bugs have been filed.
Which bugs will get released in which release cycle.	Bugs reports can have a release target tag associated with it. So, it is easier to target the bugs to a particular release.
Priority of bugs	This will determine which one should be taken up for fixing first and which one should be taken up next.
Bugs per module	This will help in identifying which module is generating more bugs. That way, the focus can be shifted to that particular module.
Which bugs are filed by the customer which bugs are filled internally.	If it is a released product, then some of the bugs can be filed by customers also. Customer bugs should be prioritized for fixing first.

Report name	Description
How many bugs have been removed from the release.	Depending on the priority of the bugs, some of the bugs may be removed from the current release and moved to future release.
Bugs dependent on other teams	Some of the bugs will be dependent on other bugs. Some bugs will be filed on the other teams.
Bugs which have documentation impact	Some of the known obvious issues can be made online so that customers know that these issues exists and there are limitations. Sometimes workarounds are also suggested. Example, if you see the bugs filed on Jira, the tool itself or confluence, you can see that many issues are made online so that customers can see the documentation. Help manuals. technical specifications also can be updated because of the bug fixes. In that case, the bug report needs to be tagged with a documentation impact tag.

Table 11.2: Different kinds of reports about bugs

Depending on the project under execution, there may be a need to generate many kinds of reports. It needs to be seen what is required to know, and based on that, custom reports can be created. Reports give a good bird's eye view of the project from different aspects. A manager should have the acumen to generate reports. More innovation can be done by creating dashboards, charts, graphs, etc. It really depends on the need and the extent of visibility required into the project.

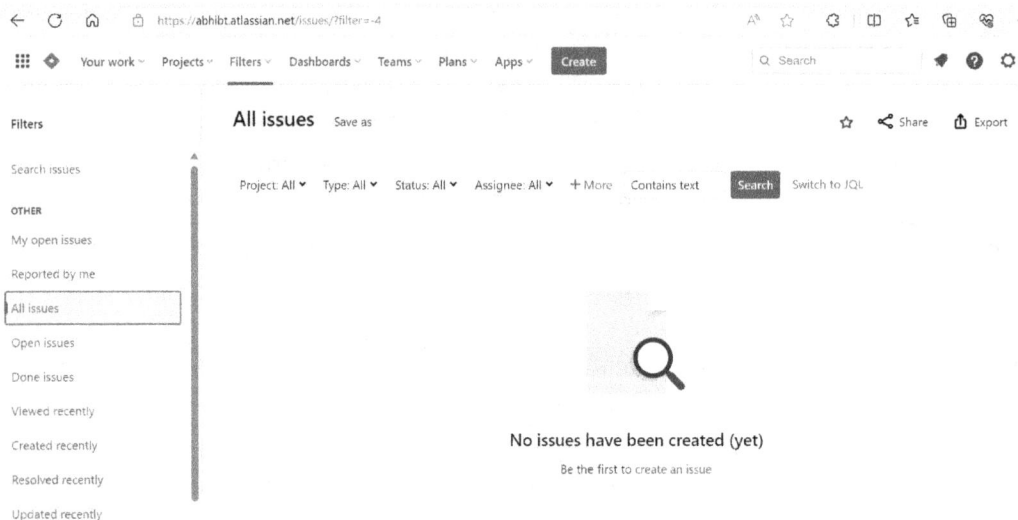

Figure 11.1: Reports in Jira

In Jira, you can create queries using the screen shown in *Figure 11.1*. There are some inbuilt queries that are provided, and managers can also create custom queries in the tool.

The project manager should create a report of the most impacting, high-severity customer issues and should keep all stakeholders informed about the status of these issues. This again can be done via email or via a program report.

Training new engineers through bugs

Assigning bug fixes to new engineers is an effective way to provide them with hands-on experience and deepen their understanding of the codebase and development processes. By tackling bugs, new team members familiarize themselves with existing features, learn the intricacies of the system, and understand the common issues that may arise. This method also helps them become adept with debugging tools and techniques, which are essential skills for any developer.

Moreover, working on bug fixes encourages new engineers to engage with different parts of the code, promoting a comprehensive understanding of the project as a whole. It allows them to see how various components interact and depend on each other, which is crucial for future feature development.

For junior engineers, this period of bug fixing can last between 4 to 6 months, providing them with ample time to gain confidence and proficiency in their tasks. Senior engineers, with at least ten years of experience, may need a shorter period, typically 2 to 3 months, to get accustomed to the codebase before moving on to more complex feature development.

Bug fixing also introduces new engineers to the QA process, as they need to ensure that their fixes do not introduce new issues. This phase serves as a valuable training ground, laying a solid foundation for their future contributions to the project. The new engineers should be provided with the design documentation and any other relevant documents for the code for which bugs have to be fixed.

Traceability in bug fixes

Traceability is an essential component in the bug-fixing process, ensuring that every change made to the codebase is documented and can be traced back to its origin. This practice helps maintain the integrity of the project and allows for seamless tracking of modifications.

One of the critical aspects of traceability is linking bug reports to the associated code changes. When a bug is fixed, it is crucial to document the check-ins made in the code repository. This linkage prevents uncontrolled check-ins and potential destabilization of the product. Metrics should be established to track how many bug fixes have corresponding code check-ins. Conducting regular audits ensures that all code changes are appropriately documented and that no unauthorized changes have been introduced.

Maintaining a comprehensive bug history

A comprehensive history of bug reports and fixes is vital for understanding the evolution of the project. Each bug report should include details such as the issue description, its severity, the steps to reproduce it, and the resolution. Additionally, it should reference the specific code changes made to address the issue. This historical data is invaluable for future debugging efforts and provides insights into recurring problems.

Using version control systems

Implementing a robust **version control system** (**VCS**) is fundamental for achieving traceability. A VCS records every change made to the codebase, allowing developers to track the progress of bug fixes and revert to previous versions if necessary. It also enables collaboration among team members by providing a central repository for code changes.

Regular reviews and audits

Regular reviews and audits of the bug-fixing process are essential to maintain traceability. These reviews should verify that all bug fixes are properly documented and linked to code changes. Audits help identify any gaps in the documentation and ensure that all team members adhere to the established procedures.

Incorporating traceability in the bug-fixing process not only improves project management but also enhances the overall quality of the software. By maintaining clear and accurate records, teams can efficiently track and resolve issues, leading to a more stable and reliable product.

QA's role in bugs

QA plays a pivotal role in the identification, documentation, and verification of bugs within a software project. Their responsibilities ensure that the software meets the highest standards of quality before it is released to the end users.

While filing the bug reports, the following needs to be taken into consideration:

- QA should know what the content of the delivery is, what is in it, and what is not.

- QA should insist on a delivery report from development to ensure clear expectations.

- Having a handshake meeting with developers before starting the testing is better.

- QA engineers should check the list of filed issues before filing a new bug report to ensure that duplicate issues are not filed.

- If possible, create a template for the description for filing the issues.

Here are some key aspects of QA's role in managing bugs:

- **Bug identification and reporting**: QA engineers are tasked with rigorously testing the software to identify any defects or issues. When a bug is discovered, it is essential that QA provides a comprehensive report that includes:

  o A clear and detailed description of the issue

  o The steps to reproduce the bug

  o The severity and impact of the bug on the software's functionality

  o Any relevant screenshots or logs that can aid in understanding the problem

  QA should ensure that all new bugs are cross-referenced with existing reports to prevent duplication. Using a standardized template for bug reports can streamline this process and ensure consistency.

- **Coordination with development teams**: Effective communication between QA and development teams is crucial for efficient bug resolution. QA should have a thorough understanding of the content and scope of each release, facilitated by delivery reports from the development team. Regular handshake meetings before testing begins can clarify expectations and set the stage for a smooth QA process. Larger teams beyond the immediate development team can be kept in the loop via emailing reports and, in some cases, having sync up meetings.

- **Verification of bug fixes**: Once a bug has been addressed by the development team, it is QA's responsibility to verify the fix. This involves re-testing the issue to ensure that it has been resolved without introducing new problems. This stage is also a valuable opportunity for new QA engineers to become familiar with the project.

- **Utilizing bug-tracking tools**: Modern bug-tracking tools offer a high degree of customization, allowing workflows, tags, and fields to be tailored to the specific needs of the project. While it is advisable to start with default settings, the system can be progressively customized to improve efficiency and accuracy in bug management.

- **Ensuring traceability:** QA must ensure that every bug report is linked to the corresponding code changes in the VCS. This traceability is vital for maintaining the integrity of the project and allows for seamless tracking of modifications.

- **Ongoing reviews and audits**: Regular reviews and audits of the bug-fixing process are essential to maintain traceability and quality. These reviews should verify that all bug fixes are properly documented and linked to code changes, identifying any gaps in documentation and ensuring adherence to established procedures.

By diligently fulfilling these roles, QA significantly contributes to the stability and reliability of the software, ultimately leading to higher customer satisfaction and a more robust product.

These days, bug-tracking tools are highly customizable. The workflows, tags, and fields can also be customized depending on the project's needs. It is advisable to get started with the default fields first and then customize the workflows, fields, and tags.

For example, in Jira, the fields are highly customizable. A custom field can be added in Jira. However, managing custom fields can become a challenge as the project progresses, because people may start asking for more custom fields.

Tracking external issues

In a software company, managing and addressing externally reported bugs is a crucial aspect of maintaining product quality and customer satisfaction. External issues are typically filed by individuals who are not part of the immediate development team, including team members from other departments, customers, and support engineers. Effectively handling these bugs requires specific practices and methodologies to ensure that they are prioritized, communicated, and resolved efficiently.

External issues are the ones that are filed by people who are not part of the immediate team. The primary sources of these issues include:

- Team members from other teams
- Customers
- Support engineers

The organization should provide tools so that issues can be filed by external people. The tools should allow only registered product users to file issues. The tool should also have the facility for engineers to suggest workarounds if available. People external to the company should have the ability to see these workarounds. These mechanisms are available in Jira or other kinds of tools. It depends on the organization to adopt these and make it easier for customers to use the product.

There are several best practices that should be followed for dealing with externally reported bugs. These practices help ensure that the issues are managed effectively and that the customers or external stakeholders are kept informed throughout the process:

- **Prioritization**: External issues should be prioritized over internal ones because they impact customers directly. Customers are the ones who contribute to the company's revenue and, therefore, their issues should be given the highest priority. This prioritization helps in maintaining customer satisfaction and trust in the company's products and services.

- **Continuous updates**: It is essential to provide continuous updates on the status of externally reported bugs. Customers and external teams are constantly looking for updates, and regular communication helps in managing their expectations. If an immediate solution is unavailable, workarounds should be proposed, and the customers should be informed about these temporary measures.

- **Visibility and transparency**: In many organizations, the entire issue is made available online through platforms like Jira and Confluence. This transparency allows customers and external teams to comment on the issues, providing additional context or feedback. It also helps in building a collaborative environment where everyone involved can contribute to the resolution of the bugs.

- **Tracking and monitoring:** Externally reported bugs need to be tracked and monitored more closely than internal ones. This is because they have a direct impact on the customers, and timely resolution is crucial. Implementing a robust tracking system ensures that the issues are not overlooked and are resolved in a timely manner.

- **Prioritizing and fixing issues**: The process of prioritizing and fixing issues involves several steps and considerations. Customer issues are treated as the highest priority, followed by issues filed by other teams, and then the internal team members' issues. However, exceptions can be made if an internal issue has a high priority and potentially impacts customers.

- **Communication**: Proper communication should be maintained among all team members throughout the bug-fixing process. In some teams, dedicated engineers are responsible for fixing customer-reported bugs, allowing the project team to focus on development while providing consulting help to the bug-fixing team. In other cases, the entire team is responsible for fixing issues reported by other teams and customers, as well as working on projects. The project manager plays a crucial role in balancing the workload across the team to prevent burnout and ensure quick problem resolution.

- **Closing old issues**: If some of the issues are very old and no longer relevant, they should be closed to keep the bug list focused and manageable. For problems that cannot be fixed, customers should be informed and advised to continue with the suggested workarounds.

Handling externally reported bugs effectively is critical for maintaining customer satisfaction and the overall quality of the software products. By implementing best practices such as prioritization, continuous updates, transparency, and tracking, and adapting methodologies like 5S, software companies can ensure that externally reported bugs are managed efficiently. Proper communication and workload balancing within the team further contribute to a streamlined bug resolution process, ultimately enhancing the customer experience and the company's reputation.

Prioritizing and fixing issues

As mentioned in the previous section, customer issues should be treated as the highest priority. Again, within customer issues, prioritization can be made. The blocker issues should be of highest priority, then come the severity high priority issues, then the medium priority issues. Low-priority issues may or may not be fixed. The manager, along with the product owner, should take a call on whether to fix the low-priority customer issues. Then, next are the issues that the other teams have filed. Next will be the issues that the internal team members have filed. However, there can be exceptions also; for example, if an internal team member has filed an issue that is of very high priority and potentially impacts customers, then that should be prioritized on top of everything else.

Through this process, proper communication should be maintained among all the team members. In some teams, there are dedicated engineers who are responsible for fixing the bugs that customers report. So, the project team does not get bothered most of the time about these issues, other than providing consulting help to the bug-fixing team. However, in some cases, the entire team is responsible for fixing issues reported by other teams and customers, as well as working on the projects. So, it is the responsibility of the project manager to balance the work across the team so that no one is stretched and is able to solve the problem quickly.

Apply for concept of 5S, explained as follows, in handling bug fixing. If some of the issues are very old, then close those issues. If some of the problems cannot be fixed, then tell the customer that the issue cannot be fixed and that they need to continue with the workarounds that have been suggested. The attempt is to triage the bugs regularly, which is equivalent to the shine part of 5S. That way, a focused list is always maintained.

While the 5S methodology is typically associated with physical workspace organization, some of its principles can be adapted and applied to software bug tracking. Here is how you can apply the 5S approach to software bug tracking:

- **Sort (Seiri):**
    - Review and prioritize the reported bugs based on their severity and impact on the software.
    - Remove duplicate or irrelevant bug reports to avoid clutter and confusion.
    - Categorize bugs based on their nature, such as functionality, performance, or usability issues.

- **Set in Order (Seiton):**
    - Establish a standardized bug tracking system or software to store and manage bug reports.
    - Define clear and consistent fields for capturing essential information, such as bug description, steps to reproduce, expected and actual results, and assigned developer.
    - Create a logical structure for organizing and categorizing bugs, such as by module, feature, or priority.

- **Shine (Seiso):**
    - Regularly review and clean up the bug tracking system by closing resolved or outdated bugs.

- o Encourage developers to provide timely updates on bug progress and resolutions.

- o Implement automated tests and continuous integration tools to catch bugs early in the development process.

- **Standardize (Seiketsu):**

  - o Establish guidelines and procedures for reporting bugs, including a standardized bug report template.

  - o Define the bug tracking workflow, including the steps for triaging, assigning, fixing, and verifying bugs.

  - o Ensure that all team members follow the same bug tracking practices and use consistent terminology.

- **Sustain (Shitsuke):**

  - o Conduct regular bug tracking audits to ensure adherence to the established processes and standards.

  - o Provide training and support to team members on bug tracking best practices.

  - o Foster a culture of accountability and continuous improvement by encouraging feedback and incorporating lessons learned from bug tracking into future development cycles.

By applying these 5S principles to software bug tracking, you can enhance the efficiency and effectiveness of the bug tracking process, improve communication and collaboration among team members, and ultimately deliver higher quality software with fewer bugs.

Tools to debug

Most often, the engineers would like to create an overall environment to debug the issue. Creating that environment might be difficult. For example, in a cloud-based system, creating the entire environment may be difficult. However, for an embedded system, creating the entire environment may or may not be so difficult. Customer issues and other team issues require quick turnaround. So, creating an overall system will always be very difficult.

To respond quickly, the development and QA teams should have good simulators to simulate the environment. This is key for quick debugging of issues and simulation of issues. When an issue is reported, a quick simulation of the issue is needed. The RCA of the issue will follow that. Once the root cause analysis is done, the next stage will be the fixing stage. If the fix is small, then it can be done quickly; however, if the fix is big, then it is important to follow the **software development life cycle** (**SDLC**) process. Otherwise, the fix will not be proper. This simulator should also be used as much as possible during development. Using simulators speeds up the work if the entire development can be done on a stand-alone computer without requiring network connectivity.

Also, proper tools should be available for network analysis, such as Wireshark and memory analysis during runtime. So, in order to debug the issue, all the parameters related to the environment need to be observed through some tools.

It is hard to describe all the tools over here, as different kinds of environments will require different kinds of tools. So, it is important to get the data through those tools, get to the root cause of the problem, and then solve the issue. If this is not done and guesswork is performed, then the issue will come back again and again, leading to unsatisfied customers.

The following are tools that should be used to debug issues.

Custom logs

This is probably the most used and most handy tool to debug any bugs. Custom logs in applications refer to the practice of generating and recording application-specific log messages that provide valuable insights into the application's behavior, events, and errors. These logs are typically created by developers and are customized to meet the specific requirements and needs of the application.

Custom logs play a crucial role in application development and maintenance. They serve as an essential debugging and troubleshooting tool, assisting developers in swiftly identifying and diagnosing issues. By strategically placing log statements throughout the codebase, developers can track the flow of execution, monitor variable values, and detect potential errors or unexpected behaviors.

Custom logs can capture a broad spectrum of information, including user actions, system events, error messages, performance metrics, and interactions with external services. They can be used to monitor the application's performance, oversee specific features or modules, and provide an audit trail for security and compliance purposes.

Furthermore, custom logs can be enhanced with additional metadata, such as timestamps, log levels, request IDs, or user context, to offer more context and facilitate log analysis. Developers can also integrate logging frameworks or libraries that provide advanced features like log rotation, log filtering, and log aggregation to manage and analyze logs efficiently.

Analyzing custom logs can yield valuable insights into the application's behavior, performance bottlenecks, and areas for improvement. Log analysis tools and techniques, such as log parsing, log correlation, and log visualization, can help extract meaningful information from the logs and identify patterns or trends.

In summary, custom logs are a fundamental component of application development and maintenance. They enable developers to gain visibility into the application's runtime behavior, troubleshoot issues effectively, and continuously enhance the application's performance, reliability, and user experience.

Some other tools are as follows:

- **Wireshark**: Wireshark is a popular network protocol analyzer that allows you to capture and interactively browse the traffic running on a computer network. It is widely used for network troubleshooting, analysis, software development, and education.

- **tcpdump**: A command-line packet analyzer that captures and displays network traffic. It allows you to analyze packets in real-time or save them to a file for later analysis.

- **Fiddler**: A web debugging proxy tool that captures HTTP and HTTPS traffic between a client and a server. It provides detailed information about each request and response, allowing you to inspect and analyze network traffic.

- **Charles Proxy**: A cross-platform proxy tool that captures and analyzes HTTP and HTTPS traffic. It allows you to view and modify requests and responses, simulate network conditions, and debug network-related issues.

- **Microsoft Message Analyzer**: A powerful tool for capturing, displaying, and analyzing network traffic. It supports multiple protocols and provides advanced filtering and analysis capabilities.

- **tcpflow**: A command-line tool that captures and stores network traffic in separate files for each TCP connection. It allows you to analyze the captured data using other tools or manually inspect the captured files.

- **tshark**: A command-line version of Wireshark, offering similar functionality for capturing and analyzing network traffic. It can be useful for automated or script-based analysis of network packets.

- **Burp Suite**: A comprehensive web application security testing tool that includes a proxy for capturing and modifying HTTP and HTTPS traffic. It provides advanced features for intercepting and debugging web requests and responses.

- **ngrep**: A command-line network packet analyzer that allows you to match packets using regular expressions and display or capture them for analysis. It is particularly useful for searching for specific patterns or content within network traffic.

- **UART**: **Universal Asynchronous Receiver/Transmitter (UART)** is a hardware communication protocol that allows for asynchronous serial communication between devices. It is commonly used in embedded systems and microcontroller projects for debugging purposes. By connecting a UART-enabled device to a computer via a serial cable, developers can send and receive data, monitor system behavior, and troubleshoot issues in real-time. This method is particularly useful for low-level debugging, where direct access to the hardware and immediate feedback are crucial. With the aid of terminal software like PuTTY or Tera Term, developers can interact with the device's firmware, log messages, and perform diagnostic checks, making UART an invaluable tool for debugging embedded systems.

These tools can help you capture, analyze, and debug network traffic to identify and resolve customer-reported issues effectively. It's essential to choose the tool that best fits your specific requirements and expertise.

Triaging bugs

Effective bug triaging is an essential part of software development, ensuring that issues are identified, prioritized, and assigned to the appropriate team members for resolution. This process begins with the creation of a bug report by the QA team or external sources such as customer support or other teams. When QA identifies a bug, they typically have the knowledge to assign it to the relevant scrum team responsible for the feature in question. If an external team reports a bug, the issue is usually passed on to the project manager for further assessment.

In cases where the QA team cannot determine which engineer should address the bug, the manager steps in to make this decision. The manager's role is crucial in balancing the workload among team members, ensuring that no single engineer is overwhelmed while others are underutilized. By carefully evaluating the nature of the bug and the current load on each engineer, the manager can assign the bug to the most suitable team member, thus promoting efficiency and timely resolution.

Once a bug is assigned, the responsible engineer must thoroughly investigate the issue, reproduce it, and identify the root cause. Collaboration between QA and developers is vital during this stage to verify the accuracy of the reported bug and to avoid duplicates. The engineer then works on a fix, tests it, and finally, QA verifies that the bug has been resolved. Continuous updates and clear communication are essential throughout this process to keep all stakeholders informed and ensure that customer-reported issues are addressed promptly and effectively.

By implementing a structured bug triaging process, software development teams can prioritize issue resolution, enhance product quality, and maintain customer satisfaction. This systematic approach not only streamlines project management but also serves as an excellent training opportunity for new engineers, allowing them to familiarize themselves with the development process, codebase, and quality assurance practices.

Conclusion

Bug tracking is a crucial aspect of software development, serving as the backbone for identifying and resolving issues that arise during the project lifecycle. Effective bug tracking requires the use of dedicated tools like Jira, which provides a centralized platform for logging, tracking, and managing issues. Filing comprehensive bug reports is essential, including mandatory parameters such as issue summary, description, reporter's name, version number, steps to reproduce, and any relevant attachments. Bug metrics play a vital role in project management, offering insights into issue resolution progress, bug fix velocity, severity distribution, and release planning. Bug tracking serves as an excellent training opportunity for new engineers, allowing them to familiarize themselves with the development process, codebase, and quality assurance practices. QA engineers play a crucial role in bug verification, ensuring the accuracy of reported issues, avoiding duplicates, and collaborating with developers to resolve them effectively. External issues, including those reported by customers or other teams, should be prioritized and addressed promptly, with continuous updates, proposed workarounds, and clear communication to ensure customer satisfaction. By implementing robust bug-tracking practices, utilizing appropriate debugging tools, and prioritizing issue resolution, software development teams can enhance product quality, streamline project management, and deliver reliable software solutions to their end users.

By implementing robust bug-tracking practices, utilizing appropriate debugging tools, and prioritizing issue resolution, software development teams can enhance product quality, streamline project management, and deliver reliable software solutions to their end users.

In the next chapter, we will discuss documentation about the product. Documentation is a key subject for making customers understand the features of the product and how it can be used.

Points to remember

- **Comprehensive bug reports**: Ensure that bug reports include essential details such as a clear summary, detailed description, steps to reproduce, and any relevant attachments or recordings.

- **Utilize a bug tracking tool**: Employ a dedicated bug tracking tool like Jira to centralize and streamline the management of issues, enabling efficient tracking, assignment, and resolution.

- **Prioritize and fix issues**: Establish a systematic approach to prioritize and address issues based on their impact, customer importance, severity, and dependencies, ensuring timely resolution.

- **Maintain clear communication**: Foster effective communication among team members, including developers, QA engineers, and stakeholders, to ensure a shared understanding of reported issues and their resolution status.

- **Leverage bug metrics**: Utilize bug metrics and reports generated by the bug tracking tool to gain insights into issue trends, bug fix velocity, outstanding issues, and the overall quality of the software product.

- **Training opportunity**: Encourage new engineers to participate in bug-fixing activities, as it provides valuable hands-on experience with the codebase, development processes, and quality assurance practices.

- **External issue management**: Prioritize external issues reported by customers or other teams, providing regular updates, proposing workarounds, and maintaining clear communication to ensure customer satisfaction and timely resolution.

By following these key points, software development teams can establish effective bug-tracking practices, improve collaboration, and deliver high-quality software products that meet customer expectations.

Multiple choice questions

1. **Which of the following is a commonly used tool for bug tracking?**
   a) Jira
   b) Microsoft Excel
   c) Google Docs
   d) Trello

2. **What are some essential parameters to include when filing a bug report?**
   a) Summary of the issue
   b) Description of the issue
   c) Steps to reproduce
   d) All of the above.

3. **Bug metrics help in:**
   a) Understanding the incoming and outgoing rate
   b) Prioritizing bug fixes
   c) Tracking the progress of bug resolution
   d) All of the above

4. **Bug tracking can serve as a training opportunity for new engineers to:**
   a) Develop new features
   b) Gain familiarity with the codebase and development processes
   c) Improve customer support skills
   d) None of the above

5. **External issues in bug tracking refer to:**
   a) Bugs reported by customers
   b) Bugs reported during integration testing

c)   Bugs found during internal testing

d)   Bugs that are difficult to reproduce

6.   **Which of the following is an important aspect of bug tracking for effective issue resolution?**

a)   Clear communication among team members

b)   Quick fixes without proper analysis

c)   Ignoring bug reports with low severity

d)   Relying solely on automated testing

7.   **Bug tracking tools can provide metrics and reports on:**

a)   Bug fix velocity

b)   Severity of bugs

c)   Test case execution status

d)   All of the above

Answers

1.   a

2.   d

3.   d

4.   b

5.   a

6.   a

Exercises

1.   Imagine you are working on a software project. Create a sample bug report for an issue you encounter during testing. Include all the mandatory parameters discussed in the chapter.

2.   Research and explore different bug tracking tools available in the market. Compare and contrast two popular bug tracking tools of your choice, considering their features, pricing, and user reviews. Write a short summary highlighting the strengths and weaknesses of each tool.

3.   Take a sample set of bug metrics (e.g., bug fix velocity, outstanding bug list, bugs verified by QA) and create a visual representation, such as a bar chart or line graph, to showcase the trends and patterns. Interpret the metrics and discuss their implications for the project.

4. Role-play a scenario where a customer reports a critical bug that impacts their business operations. Outline the steps you would take as a project manager to prioritize and resolve the issue, considering factors like severity, customer impact, and available resources.

5. Form a small group with fellow learners and simulate a bug triage session. Each group member should bring a list of bugs they have encountered or identified in a sample software project. Collaboratively prioritize the bugs based on their severity, impact, and dependencies. Discuss the reasoning behind your prioritization decisions.

Join our book's Discord space

Join the book's Discord Workspace for Latest updates, Offers, Tech happenings around the world, New Release and Sessions with the Authors:

https://discord.bpbonline.com

CHAPTER 12
Documentation

Introduction

In product development, good documentation plays a pivotal role in ensuring a product or service's success and smooth operation. While user interfaces can provide a certain level of guidance, features and complexities often cannot be adequately explained through the UI alone. This is where documentation steps in, serving as a crucial resource to bridge the gap between the product and its users. Documentation comprehensively explains features, limitations, configurations, and troubleshooting steps, empowering customers to make the most of the product's capabilities. Moreover, documentation must be continuously updated in a constantly evolving landscape to reflect new features and updates. This responsibility falls on project managers, who must ensure effective communication with the documentation team to keep the information current. The importance of timely and accurate documentation cannot be overstated, as it directly impacts customer satisfaction and the product's overall success. In this chapter, we will explore various aspects of documentation, including its types, significance in enterprise software, internal-facing documentation, user training, monetization opportunities, troubleshooting guidance, and the role of API documentation. By understanding documentation's value and best practices, organizations can empower their customers, reduce support costs, and drive revenue growth.

Structure

In this chapter, we will discuss the following topics:

- Enterprise software product documentation
- Describe limitations
- API documentation
- Describe troubleshooting steps
- YouTube videos
- User training monetization
- Monetizing certifications

Objectives

One of the key aspects of a product or service is good documentation. A product may not be able to explain everything through the UI; Some features may be difficult to understand. Limitations and configurations are best explained via the documentation. Customers will question the feature if something is missing. Documentation needs to be continuously updated for two reasons: one being that new features are being constantly developed, and existing features are being constantly updated. The project manager needs to be aware of the documentation getting impacted, and proper communication must be done with the other teams responsible for doing the documentation. Without constant updates, the documentation will be stale and incorrect. For every feature that is impacting the documentation, a corresponding Jira has to be submitted to the documentation team so that the documentation can be updated.

The project manager's role is crucial here. They must ensure that the documentation is updated in a timely manner so that the customer gets the correct information.

Enterprise software product documentation

A user manual is an absolute must for an enterprise product. It should explain in detail how to get started with the product, how to install it, and how to use it. The better the explanation of the product, the easier it is for the customers to use and for the salespeople to sell the product. It is also important to keep the documentation up to date on a regular basis so that customers get the correct information. Most of the documentation is available online and can also be provided in a PDF format.

This is almost the same as the user manual of a TV that we buy from the store. A global brand user manual is described in many languages. Global brands of TV sets operate in different languages, and a user manual can also be in different languages.

Datasheets explain the technical specifications of the product through data. For example, they describe the temperature range at which the hardware operates. To be more specific, the data sheet describes the temperature range at which cell phone hardware operates. If you Google data sheets on the Internet, you can get plenty of them.

Enterprise documentation can be in the following forms:

- Internal facing documentation
- External facing documentation

A sample datasheet typically includes a comprehensive overview of a product's technical specifications and operational parameters. It begins with an introduction to the product, outlining its main features and intended applications. Following this, there is a detailed breakdown of the specifications, such as electrical characteristics, mechanical dimensions, and environmental conditions under which the product operates. For instance, a datasheet for a cell phone hardware component would specify the operating temperature range, input and output voltages, current ratings, and physical dimensions. Additionally, the datasheet might include performance graphs, pin configurations, and a list of compatible accessories or supplementary components.

The second part of a datasheet often delves into more nuanced technical details and usage guidelines. This section can encompass instructions for proper installation and integration of the product within a larger system, as well as any necessary calibration or maintenance procedures. It may also address safety warnings and regulatory compliance information. For example, in a datasheet for a smartphone sensor, there would be guidelines on how to mount the sensor, connect it to the motherboard, and ensure it operates within optimal conditions. The datasheet serves as an essential reference for engineers, technicians, and end-users, enabling them to fully understand and utilize the product's capabilities while ensuring reliability and safety.

Internal facing documentation

Internal facing documentation is normally prepared for the teams that are part of the organization. For example, the internal facing documentation can be prepared for support organizations, for presales activities, and for post-sales onsite support. These documents have a little bit more information compared to the online documentation or the technical specifications. Better information always helps in servicing the customer better. So, it is very important to prepare very good internal documentation so that the support organizations or the onsite support engineers can handle the customer issues.

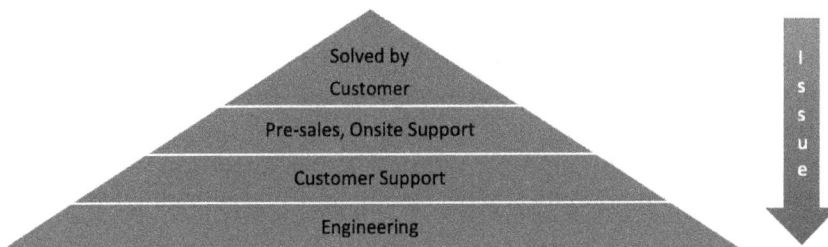

Figure 12.1: Issue fixing cost pyramid

The cost is higher if the issues are escalated to engineering. The pyramid in *Figure 12.1* shows the same. A larger base indicates more cost in the diagram. The issues move from top to bottom. If the customer can solve the issues by referencing the various documentation or by their own knowledge, the cost is less for the organization. The cost increases as it moves to engineering.

Internal documentation needs to be maintained also for the following:

- Design documentation
- Architecture documentation
- Requirement/change request documentation
- Any process documentation
- Internal troubleshooting documentation
- Test environment documentation

These are for the engineering teams. If they are not maintained, the team has to rely on tribal team knowledge to gather information when required. With attrition being a constant risk, it is good to have documentation done instead of relying on tribal team knowledge.

Internal documentation is normally kept in platforms such as SharePoint or Git to ensure accessibility and version control. These platforms facilitate collaboration among engineering teams, allowing them to update and retrieve documentation efficiently.

External facing blogs

Vlogs/blogs are good marketing tools. They can be prepared by the marketing team or by an external team. Normally, they are prepared by the marketing team for external users so that customers can learn about a particular feature.

External facing help documentation

External facing help documentation for enterprise software products plays a crucial role in ensuring a seamless user experience and maximizing the value derived from the software. This type of documentation serves as a comprehensive resource that assists users in understanding and effectively utilizing the features and functionalities of the software. It is typically created with the intention of providing clear instructions, troubleshooting guidance, and best practices to users who may have varying levels of technical expertise.

One of the key objectives of external facing help documentation is to empower users to independently navigate and utilize the software. It should provide step-by-step instructions on how to perform specific tasks, accompanied by screenshots, videos, or diagrams to enhance clarity and comprehension. By offering a structured and intuitive guide, users can quickly find the information they need, saving time and reducing frustration.

In addition to task-oriented instructions, external facing help documentation should also include conceptual and background information. This helps users gain a deeper understanding of the software's underlying principles, enabling them to make informed decisions and customize the software to suit their specific needs. Furthermore, it should provide explanations of key terminologies and concepts, ensuring users can effectively communicate and collaborate with others using the software.

Another important aspect of external facing help documentation is troubleshooting guidance. Users inevitably encounter issues or errors while using enterprise software products, and having clear instructions on how to diagnose and resolve these problems is essential. Troubleshooting sections should include common error messages, their causes, and step-by-step resolutions. Additionally, it can provide tips and tricks to optimize performance and address known limitations or compatibility issues.

To ensure the documentation remains up to date, it is important to establish a process for regular review and updates. As software evolves with new features, bug fixes, and enhancements, the documentation should reflect these changes to maintain accuracy and relevance. User feedback and support tickets can be valuable sources of information for identifying areas that need improvement or clarification.

Overall, external facing help documentation for enterprise software products serves as a vital resource for users, enabling them to maximize the value of the software, troubleshoot issues, and gain a deeper understanding of its capabilities. By providing clear instructions, conceptual explanations, and troubleshooting guidance, organizations can enhance user satisfaction, reduce support requests, and foster a positive user experience.

Tracking from feature implementation to documentation

To mark Jiras to indicate that documentation is necessary, you can follow these steps:

1. **Create a custom field:** Add a custom field in Jira specifically for documentation requirements. This field can be a checkbox or a dropdown menu with options like "Documentation Required" or "No Documentation Needed."

2. **Use labels:** Utilize Jira labels to tag issues that require documentation. You can create a label such as "Needs-Documentation" and apply it to relevant issues.

3. **Workflow transitions:** Modify your Jira workflow to include a transition that prompts for documentation. For example, when an issue moves to the "Done" status, you can add a transition screen that includes the custom field for documentation.

4. **Automation rules:** Set up automation rules in Jira to automatically flag issues that need documentation. For instance, you can create a rule that adds the "Needs-Documentation" label when an issue is moved to a specific status.

5. **Comments and checklists:** Use comments or checklists within the Jira issue to note documentation requirements. This can be a simple way to ensure that the need for documentation is communicated to the team.

Generate reports each and every week to see if any Jira require documentation. The report should query the above fields. One designated person should be there, who should take these Jiras and put them in the online help.

Describe limitations

The team can take advantage of the documentation in many ways. If a product is difficult to use, it can be shown through a video on how the product can be used. If some part of the product has limitations, it can be documented. Error codes can be documented in the documentation, and the meaning of the error code can be explained in the online documentation. The development team needs to spend significant time with the content creation team to create the documentation. It is not a trivial effort, and it is better that enough time is spent with the content creation team so that correct documentation can be created. This, in turn, will help the developers. The question may be, how? Not all engineers know each and every module, so developers who have not worked in that particular module can refer to the documentation for any help. Also, suppose the documentation is good and many issues can be resolved by on-site engineers, pre-sales engineers, or customer support engineers. In that case, a lot fewer issues will come to the engineering team for fixing. That way, the engineers will get a lot of time to work on the features. The velocity of features will increase. This, in turn, will help to sell the product more, which means more revenue.

Documenting limitations for a software product is an essential aspect of providing comprehensive and transparent documentation. Limitations refer to the known constraints, restrictions, or shortcomings of the software that users may encounter during its usage. By documenting these limitations, software providers can set realistic expectations for users and help them understand the boundaries and potential challenges they may face.

One key purpose of documenting limitations is to manage user expectations. By clearly stating the limitations upfront, users can have a realistic understanding of what the software can and cannot do. This prevents any potential frustration or disappointment that may arise from unrealistic expectations. For example, if a software product has a maximum file size limit for uploads, documenting this limitation helps users understand the constraints and plan accordingly.

Another benefit of documenting limitations is to provide guidance on workarounds or alternative approaches. While limitations may restrict certain functionalities or operations, there may be ways to achieve similar outcomes through different methods. By documenting these workarounds, users can explore alternative approaches to accomplish their goals within the limitations of the software. This empowers users to make informed decisions and optimize their usage of the software.

Documenting limitations also serves as a reference for troubleshooting and problem-solving. When users encounter issues or unexpected behavior, having documentation that outlines known limitations can help identify whether the problem is due to a limitation or an actual software defect. This saves time and effort for both users and support teams, as it helps narrow down the root cause and determine the appropriate course of action.

Furthermore, documenting limitations fosters transparency and trust between software providers and users. It demonstrates a commitment to open communication and ensures that users have complete information about the software they are using. By being transparent about limitations, software providers can build credibility and maintain a positive user experience, even when users encounter constraints.

When documenting limitations, it is important to provide clear and concise explanations. Each limitation should be described in detail, including the specific scenarios or conditions under which it applies. Additionally, it can be helpful to provide context or reasons behind the limitations, such as technical constraints, performance considerations, or compatibility issues. This helps users understand the rationale behind the limitations and appreciate the software's design choices.

In conclusion, documenting limitations for a software product is a crucial aspect of comprehensive documentation. It manages user expectations, provides guidance on workarounds, aids in troubleshooting, and fosters transparency and trust. By clearly communicating the limitations, software providers can empower users to make informed decisions, optimize their usage, and maintain a positive user experience.

API documentation

Nowadays, API documentation is key for organizations to programmatically bind their products to the rest of their ecosystem. APIs are essentially to read the data and to take actions after the data is read. Along with the API documentation, sample code also helps customers to use the product more easily. There are many examples of API documentation available on the internet. Twitter has its API documentation available online: **https://developer.twitter.com/en/docs/twitter-api**. Anyone can use it by reading the documentation here. Likewise, Facebook has online documentation available at **https://developers.facebook.com/docs/**. In the following figure, the X's API screenshot is shown:

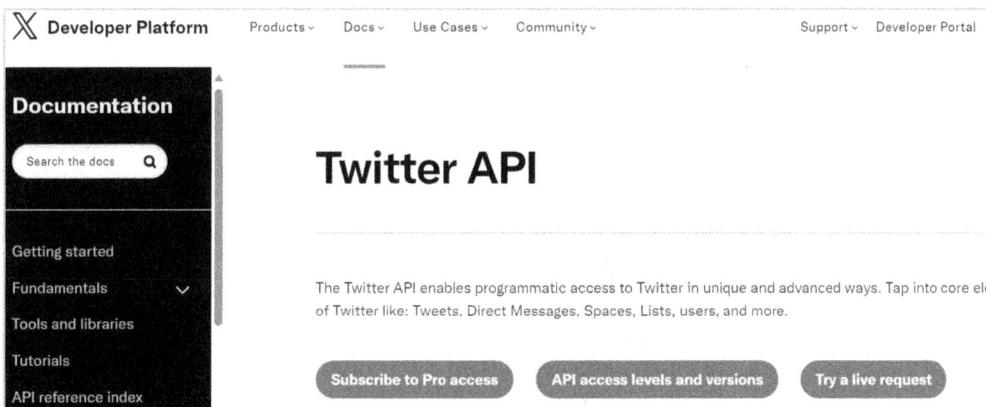

Figure 12.2: X API for developers

The objective is to make life easy for the customers to use the product. Remember, the easier it is for customers, the more the product will sell, which means more revenue for the organization. It is the collective responsibility of the development team and all the teams involved in the project to come up with good documentation. A program manager shall coordinate and ensure that the documentation is done on time and published on time so that users can use it.

It is also a continuous process because bug fixes may impact the product's features. As discussed before, bugs should have a tag for documentation impact, and the project manager should ensure that the documentation is updated and that the Jira transitions to a completed state.

Swagger is a powerful tool for API documentation that simplifies the process of designing, building, and documenting APIs. It provides a standard format known as the OpenAPI Specification, which ensures structured and consistent endpoints, methods, parameters, and responses. Swagger includes several components, such as SwaggerHub, a collaborative platform for managing APIs, and Swagger UI, an interactive interface for exploring and testing APIs.

A sample Swagger UI is shown as follows. Steps to create swagger documentation can be found in the swagger homepage **https://swagger.io/**:

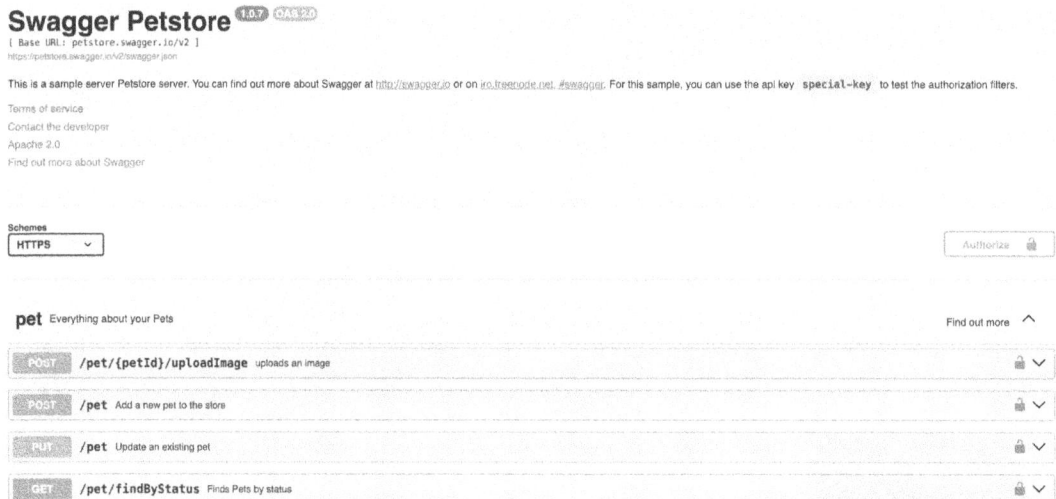

Figure 12.3: Sample Swagger UI

Describe troubleshooting steps

Online documentation is also a good place for troubleshooting issues. Organizations are always trying to reduce support costs. So, if the documentation is available online with the support guidelines, customers can resolve many of the issues independently. If clear documentation is available, for example, if any issue happens, then how can the issue be troubleshooted? If this is available, then the customers will be able to resolve many of their issues on their own. Also, if there is an error in the product and the product has an error code associated with it, then with the error code, the user will be able to go to the exact troubleshooting section.

Also, the internal support team can use the same documentation to troubleshoot issues. However, for internal teams, there can be another internal set of documentation that can have more information than the customer-facing one. This internal documentation can have more details about troubleshooting that the external customers do not need to know. Since some of the internal tools are unavailable to customers, those documents need not be made externally. These additional debugging tools help the support people to better debug the issues.

Documenting troubleshooting steps in documentation is a critical aspect of providing comprehensive support to users of a software product. Troubleshooting documentation helps users identify and resolve issues they may encounter while using the software, enabling them to overcome obstacles and achieve a smooth user experience. Here are some key points to consider when documenting troubleshooting steps:

- **Clear and concise instructions**: Troubleshooting documentation should provide step-by-step instructions that are easy to follow. Each troubleshooting step should be well-defined, with clear explanations and specific actions to be taken. This clarity helps users navigate through the troubleshooting process efficiently.

- **Diagnostic guidance:** The documentation should include diagnostic steps to help users identify the root cause of the issue. This can involve asking users to check specific settings, review error messages, or perform tests to isolate the problem. By providing diagnostic guidance, users can gather relevant information and narrow down the possible causes of the issue.

- **Common issues and resolutions**: Documenting common issues and their resolutions can be immensely helpful for users. By including a troubleshooting section that addresses frequently encountered problems, users can quickly find solutions without having to contact support. This saves time for both users and support teams and promotes self-sufficiency among users.

- **Visual aids**: Incorporating visual aids such as screenshots, diagrams, or videos can enhance the troubleshooting documentation. Visual representations can help users understand complex concepts, identify specific settings or buttons to click, and visually compare their own interface to the expected outcome. Visual aids provide additional clarity and reduce ambiguity in the troubleshooting process.

- **Troubleshooting flowcharts or decision trees**: For more complex issues, providing flowcharts or decision trees can guide users through a series of questions and actions to reach the appropriate resolution. These visual representations help users navigate through different scenarios and provide tailored troubleshooting steps based on their responses.

- **Known limitations and workarounds**: It is important to document any known limitations that may impact the troubleshooting process. If certain issues cannot be fully resolved due to constraints or limitations, it is helpful to provide alternative workarounds or suggestions to mitigate the impact. This ensures users are aware of any limitations and can manage their expectations accordingly.

- **Regular updates and feedback**: Troubleshooting documentation should be regularly reviewed and updated to reflect changes in the software, including bug fixes, updates, or new features. Encouraging users to provide feedback on the effectiveness of the troubleshooting steps can help identify areas for improvement and ensure the documentation remains accurate and relevant.

By documenting troubleshooting steps effectively, software providers can empower users to resolve issues independently, reducing the reliance on support teams and improving the overall user experience. Well-documented troubleshooting steps contribute to user satisfaction, increased productivity, and a positive perception of the software product.

YouTube videos

Video content has become a viral sensation in recent years, and organizations across various industries are capitalizing on this trend by creating and sharing training materials on their YouTube channels. For instance, software companies like Adobe and Autodesk have dedicated channels where they offer tutorials and training videos on their respective products. These videos cover a wide range of topics, from beginner-level introductions to advanced techniques, allowing users to enhance their skills and make the most of the software's features.

In addition to software companies, technology giants like Google and Microsoft also utilize YouTube as a platform for training and education. Google's YouTube channel, for example, provides a wealth of resources for developers, including coding tutorials, API guides, and best practices. Microsoft offers a similar approach to its Microsoft Developer channel, where developers can find videos on various technologies, frameworks, and tools.

Freelancers and content creators also play a significant role in the YouTube training landscape. Channels like Traversy Media, The Net Ninja, and Corey Schafer have gained substantial followings by offering in-depth tutorials on web development, programming languages, and software frameworks. These freelancers often provide comprehensive training series, covering everything from the basics to advanced concepts, catering to learners of different skill levels.

Organizations can leverage the expertise of these freelancers by collaborating with them to create training materials specific to their products. By inviting freelancers to review and present technical content, organizations can benefit from their expertise and ability to explain complex concepts in a relatable and accessible manner. This collaboration not only helps in creating high-quality training content but also enhances the visibility and credibility of the product within the community.

Maintaining positive relationships with freelancers is crucial for effective product documentation. For example, software companies may provide early access to new features or versions of their products to trusted freelancers, enabling them to create informative and timely training videos. By treating freelancers as valued partners and acknowledging their contributions, organizations can foster a mutually beneficial relationship that enhances the overall quality and reach of their training materials.

In conclusion, the popularity of YouTube as a training platform is evident through the presence of organizations and freelancers who provide valuable content to learners. From software companies offering tutorials on their products to freelancers sharing their expertise, YouTube serves as a versatile and accessible medium for training in various domains. By leveraging the power of video content and collaborating with freelancers, organizations can create comprehensive training materials that empower learners and enhance the adoption of their products.

User training monetization

Organizations also monetize this documentation via training. Training is also a good source of revenue. Trainings are created to train the users of the product. Many companies also provide certifications after the training is completed. Certifications are also a big source of revenue. Companies come out with new products, and then the users of the product undergo certifications for the new products. Of course, the products have to be popular and widely used before these types of courses can be sold to the users. Along with the in-house documentation, a lot of external 3rd party companies also create courses and then create a monetization stream for the same.

For example, Java certification is a popular course among software developers. Oracle also sells many courses, which are very popular. Many third-party companies publish books and training materials, which are available in bookstores and online. Microsoft Excel is another example. Microsoft publishes documentation about Excel, and many other organizations create training material for Excel.

These days, most people use Udemy to learn about a particular topic. A sample screenshot of Udemy is as follows:

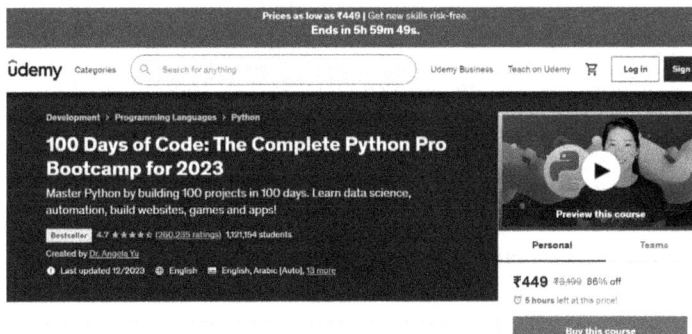

Figure 12.4: Udemy Python training page

Monetizing certifications

The monetization of certifications has become a thriving industry, with major companies such as Microsoft, Oracle, and Cisco leading the way. These companies have recognized the value of certifications and have developed comprehensive training materials, including books, to help individuals prepare for and pass their certification exams. These books serve as essential study resources, covering the necessary knowledge and skills required to succeed in the exams. The demand for these certification materials has created a substantial market, with individuals seeking to enhance their professional credentials and increase their job prospects.

However, it is important to acknowledge that developing and maintaining such extensive documentation can be a significant undertaking. The creation of certification books involves meticulous research, writing, editing, and publishing processes. These materials need to be continuously updated to align with the latest software versions, industry standards, and technological advancements. The costs associated with producing high-quality certification books can be substantial, encompassing content development, design, printing, distribution, and marketing efforts.

While larger companies have the resources, brand recognition, and customer base to support the sale of certification books, smaller companies may face challenges in this area. Smaller organizations often lack the same level of reach and influence as their larger counterparts. Consequently, they may struggle to attract a significant number of individuals interested in pursuing certifications for their products. The limited market demand for certifications from smaller companies can make it financially unviable for them to invest in developing and selling certification materials.

Moreover, the certification landscape is highly competitive, with individuals primarily focusing on certifications offered by industry giants. Certifications from renowned companies like Microsoft, Oracle, and Cisco carry significant weight and are widely recognized by employers. As a result, individuals may prioritize pursuing certifications from these established companies, further diminishing the demand for certifications from smaller organizations.

In conclusion, the monetization of certifications through the sale of books has become a lucrative industry. Major companies have capitalized on the demand for certifications by providing comprehensive study materials. However, smaller companies face challenges in this space due to limited reach, market demand, and the high costs associated with developing certification materials. The competitive nature of the certification landscape further adds to the difficulties faced by smaller organizations. Despite these challenges, certifications remain a valuable asset for individuals seeking to enhance their skills and career prospects in the ever-evolving technology industry.

Conclusion

Effective documentation is a crucial component of any product or service, providing clear guidance and information that cannot be conveyed solely through user interfaces. Timely and accurate documentation is essential for addressing customer inquiries, explaining features, and mitigating potential confusion or frustration. Project managers play a vital role in ensuring documentation is continuously updated to reflect new features and changes, maintaining its relevance and accuracy. User manuals serve as a fundamental resource, offering step-by-step instructions, troubleshooting guidance, and FAQs to enhance user experience and product adoption. Internal-facing documentation supports support teams, presales activities, and post-sales onsite support, enabling efficient issue resolution and reducing escalations to engineering. User training and certifications enhance user proficiency and provide revenue-generating opportunities for organizations. Documentation, including troubleshooting steps and error code explanations, empowers customers to resolve issues independently, reducing support costs and increasing customer satisfaction.

By recognizing the significance of documentation and employing best practices, organizations can streamline their processes, improve customer experiences, and drive the success of their products or services.

In the next chapter, we will discuss how all the components will be packaged together and delivered, and the important points to take care of to ensure a smooth delivery.

Points to remember

- **Documentation is essential**: Good documentation is a crucial aspect of any product or service, providing users with the information they need to understand, utilize, and troubleshoot effectively.

- **Keep documentation up to date**: Regularly update documentation to reflect new features, changes, and bug fixes. Outdated documentation can lead to confusion and frustration for users.

- **Clear and concise language**: Use language that is easy to understand and avoids technical jargon. Focus on providing information in a straightforward and user-friendly manner.

- **Organize information logically**: Structure documentation with clear headings, subheadings, and bullet points. This helps users navigate and find the information they need quickly and efficiently.

- **Include examples and visuals**: Use examples, code snippets, screenshots, and diagrams to illustrate concepts and provide practical guidance. Visual elements can greatly enhance understanding.

- **Collaborate with other teams**: Work closely with development, support, and other teams to ensure accurate and comprehensive documentation. Communication and coordination are key to maintaining high-quality documentation.

- **Solicit and incorporate feedback**: Encourage users and stakeholders to provide feedback on the documentation. Actively incorporate their suggestions and address any gaps or areas of improvement.

Multiple choice questions

1. **Which of the following is NOT a type of documentation?**
   a) User manual
   b) Technical specifications
   c) Internal troubleshooting documentation
   d) Sales brochure

2. **Why is it important to update documentation regularly?**
   a) To increase revenue
   b) To reduce support costs
   c) To keep the documentation team busy
   d) To confuse users

3. **Who is responsible for ensuring documentation is updated in a timely manner?**
   a) Project managers
   b) Developers
   c) Marketing team
   d) Customers

4. **What is the purpose of user training and certifications?**
   a) To generate revenue
   b) To confuse users
   c) To increase support costs
   d) To enhance user proficiency

5. **What is the role of troubleshooting documentation?**
   a) To create more confusion for users
   b) To reduce support costs

c) To increase revenue

d) To entertain users

6. **Which of the following is an example of internal-facing documentation?**

a) User manual

b) API documentation

c) Troubleshooting guide for support teams

d) Sales brochure

7. **How can visuals enhance documentation?**

a) By making it more confusing

b) By improving understanding

c) By increasing support costs

d) By reducing revenue

8. **Why is clear and concise language important in documentation?**

a) To make it more challenging for users

b) To confuse users

c) To improve user experience

d) To increase support costs

Answers

1. d
2. b
3. a
4. d
5. b
6. c
7. b
8. c

Exercises

- Imagine you are creating a user manual for a new software product. Write a step-by-step guide on how to install the software on a computer. Include any prerequisites or system requirements.

- You are tasked with updating the troubleshooting documentation for a mobile app. Choose one common issue that users may encounter and write a troubleshooting guide with clear steps to resolve the problem.

- Review the following sentence from a documentation page: "To configure the settings, access the admin panel and navigate to the 'Advanced' tab." Identify at least two improvements you would make to enhance clarity and user understanding.

- Create a short FAQ section for a customer support documentation page. Choose three common questions users may have about a specific feature of the product and provide concise answers.

- You are creating API documentation for a web service. Write a code example in the programming language of your choice to demonstrate how to make a GET request to retrieve data from the API.

Join our book's Discord space

Join the book's Discord Workspace for Latest updates, Offers, Tech happenings around the world, New Release and Sessions with the Authors:

https://discord.bpbonline.com

CHAPTER 13
Delivery

Introduction

Software delivery is the final milestone in the development cycle, marking the transition from development to providing the software to users. This chapter explores different delivery methods, including on-premises, SaaS, and remote updates. We discuss considerations and challenges faced by developers during delivery, such as scalability, monitoring, and maintenance. of thorough testing, documentation, and compliance is emphasized. Throughout this chapter, readers will have a comprehensive understanding of software delivery methods and be equipped to implement effective strategies in their projects. Let us study the world of software delivery and its intricacies!

Structure

In this chapter, the following topics will be discussed:

- Types of delivery
- Dev focus on delivery
- Scaling
- Monitoring, maintaining, and running

Objectives

This chapter aims to explore the various methods of software delivery and equip readers with the knowledge and understanding to successfully navigate the complexities of delivering software. We will look at different delivery approaches, including on-premises, SaaS, and remote updates, discussing the considerations and challenges that developers encounter during the delivery phase. Additionally, we will provide a comprehensive checklist for ensuring a smooth and successful software delivery, covering aspects such as testing, documentation, compliance, and customer communication. The chapter will emphasize the importance of scalability, monitoring, and maintenance in delivering software that can handle varying user demands and ensure a seamless user experience. Furthermore, we will address the significance of post-release support, including debugging, issue resolution, and proactive monitoring, to maintain the quality and reliability of the delivered software. By the end of this chapter, readers will have a solid understanding of software delivery methodologies and be equipped to make informed decisions and implement effective strategies in their software projects.

Types of delivery

After development and verification are completed, it is time to deliver the product. Delivery of the product can happen in different ways. These are as follows:

- On prem delivery, binary delivery through a website
- On prem delivery, putting the binary in a shared location
- SaaS delivery, running 24x7
- Delivery through embedded devices
- Code delivery

The following sections describe more about each delivery aspect, depending on the type of delivery chosen for the product.

Binary delivery through a website

Binary delivery through a website is a common method for distributing software to end customers. This approach involves creating and posting the binaries on a website, allowing customers to download them directly. For instance, let us consider the example of Java binaries, which can be downloaded from the official Java website (**https://www.java.com/en/download/**).

When providing binaries for download, it is essential to include certain components to ensure a smooth installation process. Let us explore the typical contents of a binary package:

The main file that customers need to download and install is the binary itself. In the case of Java, it may be a **Java Development Kit (JDK)** or **Java Runtime Environment (JRE)** package. Additionally, it is crucial to include a license agreement that outlines how the binary can be used. This helps establish the legal terms and conditions for the software's usage.

To ensure compatibility and help users choose the appropriate browser for a smooth download experience, it is important to specify the browsers through which customers can download the binary. Furthermore, clearly state the minimum system requirements necessary for running the software. This includes details such as operating system versions, processor specifications, memory requirements, and disk space.

Providing step-by-step instructions on how to install the binary is crucial. This should cover prerequisites, configuration options, and any additional setup steps required. Comprehensive installation instructions help users navigate the installation process with ease.

Even with comprehensive information provided, customers may still encounter difficulties during the installation process. To address this, it is crucial to offer support through online help documentation and videos. While the engineering team may find the installation process straightforward, customers may have varying levels of technical expertise.

Create detailed documentation that covers the installation process, common issues, and troubleshooting steps. This documentation should be easily accessible on the website and provide clear explanations and solutions. Additionally, consider creating video tutorials that guide customers through the installation process. Videos can be particularly helpful for visual learners and provide a more interactive experience.

Project managers play a vital role in addressing installation issues. They should allocate time and resources to assist customers with installation issues. This includes providing support channels, such as email or a dedicated forum, where customers can seek help and receive timely responses. For example, for Jira support following are the channels available on their website. There is a community to answer queries. Also, there are ways to submit bug reports and suggestions as shown in the following figure:

Jira Cloud support

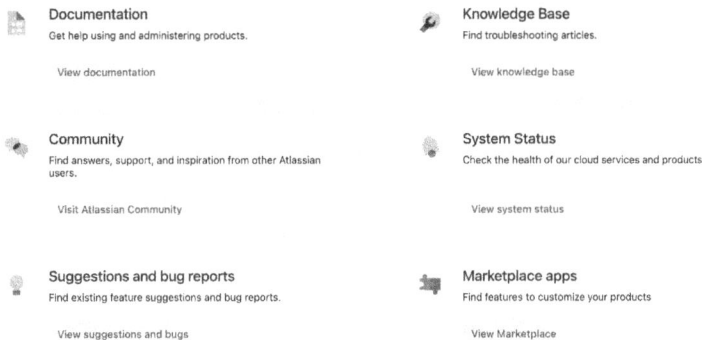

Documentation Get help using and administering products. View documentation	**Knowledge Base** Find troubleshooting articles. View knowledge base
Community Find answers, support, and inspiration from other Atlassian users. Visit Atlassian Community	**System Status** Check the health of our cloud services and products View system status
Suggestions and bug reports Find existing feature suggestions and bug reports. View suggestions and bugs	**Marketplace apps** Find features to customize your products View Marketplace

Figure 13.1: Support channels for Jira

Despite providing comprehensive documentation and support, some customers may still face challenges during installation. Common issues include compatibility problems with operating systems, hardware, or other software dependencies. Clear system requirements and troubleshooting guidance can help address these issues. Additionally, incorrect configuration settings or missing dependencies can lead to installation errors. Detailed instructions and troubleshooting steps can help customers resolve these configuration-related issues.

The following is a short template for troubleshooting:

- **Check system requirements:** Ensure that your system meets the following minimum requirements:

    o **Operating system**: Specify the supported versions (e.g., Windows 10, macOS 11, Linux Ubuntu 20.04).

    o **Processor**: Detail the required processor specifications (e.g., Intel i5 or equivalent).

    o **Memory**: Indicate the minimum RAM required (e.g., 8 GB).

    o **Disk space**: State the necessary disk space (e.g., 500 MB).

    o **Additional software:** List any additional software dependencies (e.g., .NET Framework, Java).

Some common issues and solutions are as follows:

- **Compatibility problems:**

    o **Issue**: Incompatibility with the operating system.

    o **Solution**: Verify that your OS version is supported. If not, consider upgrading or using a compatible system.

- **Missing dependencies:**

    o **Issue**: The required software or libraries are not installed.

    o **Solution**: Install any missing software dependencies as specified in the system requirements section.

- **Incorrect configuration:**

    o **Issue**: Incorrect settings or configuration during installation.

    o **Solution**: Review and follow the step-by-step installation instructions carefully, ensuring all settings are correctly configured.

The step-by-step troubleshooting guide is as follows:

1. Verify that system requirements are met.

2. Ensure all necessary dependencies are installed.

3. Follow the detailed installation instructions provided.

4. Refer to the common issues and solutions section if problems arise.

5. If the issue persists, check online help documentation or video tutorials.

6. Contact support through the provided channels for further assistance.

Support channels provide multiple support channels to help customers resolve issues:

- **Email support**: [Insert email address]

- **Dedicated forum**: [Insert forum link]

- **Online documentation**: [Insert documentation links]

- **Video tutorials**: [Insert video link]

By following this troubleshooting template, customers can resolve common installation issues efficiently. Clear instructions, comprehensive support resources, and multiple support channels can significantly enhance customer satisfaction and ensure a smooth installation experience.

To ensure a smooth binary delivery process and improve customer satisfaction, consider the following best practices:

Conduct extensive testing on different platforms and configurations to identify and resolve potential issues before releasing the binary. Provide concise and easy-to-follow installation instructions, including screenshots or diagrams when necessary. Continuously monitor and address customer feedback and issues related to the installation process. Regularly update the documentation and support resources based on user feedback and evolving requirements.

In conclusion, binary delivery through a website is a convenient and accessible method for distributing software to end customers. By including comprehensive documentation, support resources, and addressing common installation issues, software providers can ensure a smooth installation experience for their customers. Investing in clear instructions, troubleshooting guidance, and ongoing support can significantly enhance customer satisfaction and reduce installation-related challenges.

Putting the binary in a shared location

Putting binaries in a shared location is primarily used for internal deliveries within an organization. This approach is commonly employed when one team needs to deliver a dependency to another team. By choosing a shared location, such as SharePoint, OneDrive, GitHub, or a binary repository like Nexus or Maven, teams can easily access and retrieve the required binaries.

The shared location serves as a centralized repository where teams can copy the binaries for sharing. This can include both executables and libraries, depending on the specific needs of the recipient team. By utilizing a shared location, teams can avoid the complexities of external websites or services and maintain control over the delivery process.

While the method of delivery may change, the fundamental rules and considerations remain the same. All the documents described in the previous section, such as license agreements, system requirements, and installation instructions, are still applicable for internal deliveries. However, some of these documents can be streamlined or omitted when delivering to internal teams.

In some cases, instead of documenting every detail, a meeting between the delivering and recipient teams can be arranged. During the meeting, the delivering team can explain the usage and specifics of the delivered binaries, while the recipient team can ask questions and seek clarification. It is important to ensure that meeting notes are circulated across the team to ensure everyone understands how to use the binaries effectively.

This document outlines the procedure for handing off a build to the **quality assurance** (**QA**) team. It ensures that the build is properly communicated, documented, and ready for testing, facilitating a smooth transition and effective testing process.

The build information is as follows:

- **Build version:** [Enter Build Version]
- **Build date:** [Enter Build Date]
- **Build ID:** [Enter Build ID]
- **Built by:** [Enter Developer/Team Name]

Release notes provide a summary of the release, including new features, bug fixes, and known issues:

- **New features:** [List New Features]
- **Bug fixes:** [List Bug Fixes]
- **Known issues**: [List Known Issues]

Installation instructions

Outline the steps required to install the build, including any system requirements or dependencies:

- **System requirements**: [List System Requirements]
- **Pre-requisites:** [List any Pre-requisites]
- Installation steps

It is crucial to remember that what may seem obvious to the delivery team may not be as clear to the recipient team. Different teams may have varying levels of familiarity with the specific binaries or dependencies. Therefore, it is important to consider the recipient team's perspective and provide sufficient support and documentation to facilitate a smooth integration and usage of the delivered binaries.

Internal deliveries should not be treated casually. Missing timelines or delivering poor-quality code can have a significant impact on product quality and the reputation of the project manager and the team. Good internal deliveries are often the foundation of building a strong reputation for project managers. Therefore, it is essential to prioritize timely and high-quality deliveries within the organization.

In conclusion, internal deliveries through a shared location provide a convenient and controlled method for teams to share binaries and dependencies. While some documentation can be streamlined, it is important to ensure effective communication, meetings, and clear meeting notes to facilitate a smooth integration and usage of the delivered binaries.

Sync up should start when the initial requirements are discussed. It should be followed up by sync-ups in between. Finally, during integration or testing, the teams should work together to ensure that the handoff is smooth, following the delivery template as discussed above.

Prioritizing internal deliveries helps maintain product quality and contributes to the reputation of the project manager and the team.

Software as a Service delivery

Software as a Service (**SaaS**) is a software delivery model where applications are hosted and provided to customers over the Internet. In this delivery mechanism, the software is centrally managed by the service provider, who handles all aspects of maintenance, updates, and security. Customers access the software through a web browser or a dedicated client application, eliminating the need for local installation and infrastructure management.

SaaS is something that is always running, and software has to be delivered while the services are running. This is extremely challenging, and a competent team has to be there to make this happen. Examples of SaaS are Microsoft Office 365, Gmail, GSuite products. A couple of salient features of SaaS delivery are:

- The software has to be deployed or upgraded in production by the team delivering the same.

- The software has to be up 99.99% of the time. During delivery, the software should continue to run.

- Requires continuous monitoring.

- Each team can upgrade its own part of the software.

- Need to ensure that none of the other components are broken.

- If the customer has integrated their software with the SaaS software, the SaaS software needs to ensure that the customer's software is unaffected.

- There are many techniques for testing SaaS software before deploying it to production. SaaS itself is a big topic, so please refer to any book on SaaS software development.

When delivering SaaS, there are several key considerations:

- **Service Level Agreements (SLAs):** Clearly define the service level agreements with customers, outlining performance guarantees, uptime, support response times, and data backup policies. SLAs ensure transparency and set expectations for service quality.

- **Data privacy and compliance**: Adhere to relevant data privacy regulations and industry-specific compliance requirements. Implement appropriate measures to protect customer data and ensure compliance with regulations such as the **General Data Protection Regulation (GDPR)**, the **Health Insurance Portability and Accountability Act** of 1996 **(HIPAA)**, or the **Payment Card Industry Data Security Standard (PCI-DSS)**.

- **User onboarding and training**: Provide comprehensive user onboarding and training materials to help customers quickly familiarize themselves with the SaaS application. This may include documentation, tutorials, and interactive guides to ensure a smooth user experience.

- **Customer support and feedback**: Establish robust customer support channels to address user queries, issues, and feedback promptly. Regularly gather customer feedback to identify areas for improvement and prioritize feature enhancements.

- **Continuous improvement and innovation**: SaaS providers should continuously evolve their offerings to stay competitive and meet changing customer needs. This involves regularly releasing new features, improving performance, and leveraging emerging technologies to enhance the user experience.

In conclusion, the SaaS delivery mechanism offers numerous benefits, including accessibility, scalability, cost efficiency, and reduced maintenance overhead. By focusing on service level agreements, data privacy, user onboarding, customer support, and continuous improvement, SaaS providers can deliver a seamless and valuable software experience to their customers.

Delivering software remotely

In mobile phones, software is delivered remotely. This has become pretty common. For example, in Android or iPhone, software is upgraded remotely. The App developers, however, need not do anything for that unless there is something special in the App. Google Play store or Apple Appstore will take care of pushing the changes to mobile phones or other compatible devices.

However, there could be some custom applications that may require the entire ecosystem to be built. For example, in a satellite, software is upgraded remotely. The satellites are not using Android or iPhone OS. They are using their custom installation and remote upgrader system. These can be flaky and sometimes lead to problems. These are hard to debug and solve. For example, if an upgrade problem happens in a satellite, it will become very difficult to fix. There must be enough fault-tolerant mechanisms built into the installation system so that even if the installation fails, the previously installed version continues to work. The timing of the upgrade is another thing to take care of. When an important sports entertainment program is going on, it will be wrong to upgrade the software of a Set Top Box. The timing of the upgrade needs to be correctly determined. The following are important things to take care of while upgrading software remotely:

- Even if the current upgrade fails, previously installed software should continue to work

- The timing of the upgrade needs to be correctly determined

- Like in mobile phones, the choice and timing of an upgrade can be left to the end user to decide

- The customer's system, if integrated with the remote software, should continue to work

- It should have an excellent debugging mechanism so that the issue can be debugged and resolved remotely

- Should have the mechanism for testing it internally

Again, these are some of the high-level points that need to be taken into account. More can be found in the literature covering this type of software development.

Delivery through embedded devices

Automotive software, aerospace software, and small electronic devices that are not connected to wireless networks are some examples of software delivered through embedded devices. Nowadays, EV car software is delivered through wireless networks, too. However, there are a lot of vehicles, the majority of vehicles on the planet, whose software is not upgraded wirelessly. Automotive software is loaded into the car while in the factory. They run for years without any upgrades. Sometimes, they can be upgraded at the service station. However, most often, they are not. The quality of this software has to be extremely good. Bug fixes will be challenging to do while the car is on the street, so the quality of the software has to be excellent. An electronic gadget, for example, a software-controlled coffee machine, may not undergo software upgrades too often in its lifetime. So, the quality of the product has to be extremely good. It should give the right flavor of coffee every time for a certain number of years, and it should not be buggy. In short, here are some of the important points to take care of:

- The quality of the product has to be excellent.
- Upgrade of the product is next to impossible.
- Only in the next factory refresh can the software be upgraded.
- Bugs in the software has a detrimental effect on the revenue of an organization.

- Pressures on delivering before the festive season are very high. Many of these electronic devices are for consumers, and the pressure to deliver before the festive season is very high.

- Debugging can only be done in service centers. Service centers should be equipped with debugging capability.

The fewer features of the product, the smaller the code size. So, it is easier to ensure the quality of the product, provided the design is right. If the design is not right, then the quality of the product may not be good, even after repeated testing.

Dev focus on delivery

The development team needs to adhere to the following checklist, as a bare minimum, when the software is released:

Checklist	Yes/ No
Is the binary that meant to be shipped being shipped? Is the binary number matching?	
Before release, has it been downloaded and tested by internal QA engineers?	
After release, has it been downloaded and tested by internal QA engineers and friendly customers?	
Is release notes created and uploaded? Does it mention what is the content of the release?	
Has an update been sent to the customers about the release so that they know that release has happened?	
Has support team been updated about the release?	
Has documentation and known issues list been updated?	
Are the service stations updated with the tools for updating the software?	
Has export compliance check been done? Some countries have export embargo to certain countries.	
Do all third party components used in the product have proper license to be used in the product?	
Is the software deployment planned in Off Peak hours?	

Table 13.1: The checklist

Depending on the type of deployment, there could be some additional checklists. Managers should factor in time for the above activities. These are not trivial. Often, after a binary release, the binary does not work. It may be because a configuration file is missing or some other dependencies are missing. Checks and balances have to be there at each stage to ensure that the quality is maintained.

Scale is another aspect that cannot always be tested internally. When deployed in production, the software may not be able to scale according to the customer's environment. It may not function at all. Most software fails in this. In that case, it is important to define the software's limitations. It cannot be used to scale beyond a certain limit.

Scaling

Delivery of this software should scale so that customers are able to download it without any problem. Sometimes, many customers try to download the software from the website, and the software does not get downloaded.

Also, SaaS software should be able to scale to handle a variable number of requests. For example, if a SaaS software is able to handle 100 requests per minute and the number of requests grows to 1000 requests per minute, then the software should be able to scale to handle these many requests. Let us say that release becomes very popular, then many people will start accessing the software. So, at that time, the scale of the software needs to be dynamically improved so that the SaaS software handles the customer's requests.

In the case of mobile software, where hundreds and thousands of mobile phones are downloading the software, the backend needs to be scaled so that when downloading the software, it gets downloaded very quickly. If it takes a long time, then the download may not happen correctly, and repeated downloads may be required.

The manager needs to ensure that the platform for releasing this software is good enough for scaling and the performance of the release platform is tried and tested. Enough testing should be done to parallelly download the software to test that the release platform is scaling. This should be done in a hidden mode so that customers cannot see this. This may not be the work of the development manager, but the person who is responsible for the release management platform should ensure that the release platform is proper from all aspects. This, preferably, should be another team that is solely responsible for the release platform. One development manager cannot own everything. Though in smaller companies that might be the case also.

Monitoring, maintaining, and running

Once the release is made to the customers, that is not the end of the software development life cycle. Most often, just after the release and when the customer starts using the product, the customer faces some problems. It may be because of environmental differences, the way the customer is using the product or some corner cases in which the customer is using a product that has not been tested.

The manager needs to absolutely plan about these unforeseen activities few weeks in advance when the release has been planned. This most certainly will happen sometimes, and the manager needs to react quickly to the situation. A quick fix needs to be arranged and released. Also, customer and support communication needs to be made when this kind of situation happens, and a release is being planned.

This is not a desired process and should be avoided, but it happens sometimes. A quick reaction can mitigate the situation.

Also, the backend monitoring system should be there to monitor the software. Whether it is on the prime product, an embedded systems product, or a SaaS product, all these systems should provide some information to the back-end systems regularly, So that the backend systems know that this software is running properly. This proactive monitoring can help to address a lot of issues before customers notice. For example, a mobile phone can send crash information to the backend. Now, if the backend is monitored and the developers analyze the root cause of the crash quickly, this issue can be addressed before many other users actually face this. This backend system requires engineering effort, and the same development team may not be responsible for it. This can be another development team, preferably the release platform development team, which manages this kind of backend.

One effective way to achieve robust backend monitoring is by employing the ELK stack, which consists of Elasticsearch, Logstash, and Kibana. This powerful trio works in harmony to collect, analyze, and visualize log data from multiple sources.

Elasticsearch is a distributed, RESTful search and analytics engine capable of ingesting large volumes of data swiftly. It indexes logs and makes them searchable in near real-time, allowing developers to query logs quickly and pinpoint issues.

Logstash acts as a data processing pipeline that collects logs from various sources, transforms them, and sends them to Elasticsearch. It can handle multiple inputs, filter logs based on specific criteria, and structure the data to make it more useful.

Kibana, the visualization layer of the stack, provides an intuitive interface to create dashboards and visualizations. This helps teams monitor application performance, track errors, and analyze patterns over time. Using Kibana, managers and developers can gain valuable insights into the system's behavior and make informed decisions.

Implementing the ELK stack as a backend log-gathering system enhances monitoring capabilities and helps in swift issue identification and resolution. It also allows for proactive maintenance, ensuring that problems are addressed before they affect a larger user base.

Conclusion

There are many ways to deploy the product. Why should a project manager know some of these ways? Nowadays, software is interdependent. A SAP tool can have mobile software that can be used to update or view data. An automated application can be updated remotely. Aerospace software can upload data to the central server when the aircraft is at the airport. There can be many interdependent systems, and a little bit of knowledge is necessary for a software project management job. Of course, there will be individual managers for every functionality, but having an overall idea always helps manage the project.

In the next chapter, we will discuss how the product is made secure. Be it an on-prem product or a SaaS product, security is of paramount importance. Any breach in security can cause havoc to the organization. Project managers should devote ample time and resources to solving security issues.

Points to remember

- **Understanding deployment methods**: Project managers should be familiar with various deployment methods since modern software systems are often interdependent, requiring seamless integration across different platforms.

- **Importance of overall knowledge**: While individual managers handle specific functionalities, having a comprehensive understanding aids in effective project management.

- **Proactive monitoring with ELK stack:** Implementing the ELK stack (Elasticsearch, Logstash, Kibana) enhances backend monitoring, enabling swift issue identification and resolution.

- **Benefits of Kibana**: Kibana's intuitive interface allows for effective data visualization, aiding in performance monitoring, error tracking, and pattern analysis.

- **Logstash's role:** Logstash acts as a data processing pipeline, transforming and routing logs from various sources to Elasticsearch, making data more useful.

- **Elasticsearch's capabilities**: Elasticsearch efficiently indexes and searches large volumes of data, enabling near real-time log queries and issue pinpointing.

- **Proactive issue address** issues before they impact users, requiring coordinated efforts from specialized development teams.

Multiple choice questions

1. **What is the primary benefit of a robust backend monitoring system?**

   a) Decrease in server costs

   b) Increased user engagement

   c) Enhanced UI design

   d) Preemptively addressing issues before they impact users

2. **What does Elasticsearch enable through its efficient indexing and searching capabilities?**

   a) User interface enhancement

   b) Near real-time log queries and issue pinpointing

   c) Secure data transactions

   d) Automated backups

3. **What function does Logstash serve in the ELK stack?**
   a) Data processing pipeline, transforming and routing logs from various sources to Elasticsearch
   b) Frontend development
   c) User authentication
   d) Database administration

4. **Which feature of Kibana aids in performance monitoring and error tracking?**
   a) Machine learning
   b) Intuitive interface for effective data visualization
   c) Cloud storage
   d) User profiling

5. **How does implementing the ELK stack (Elasticsearch, Logstash, Kibana) benefit backend monitoring?**
   a) Reduces code complexity
   b) Enhances backend monitoring with swift issue identification and resolution
   c) Minimizes user interaction
   d) Promotes hardware efficiency

6. **Why should project managers be familiar with various deployment methods?**
   a) To improve marketing strategies
   b) Because modern software systems are often interdependent, requiring seamless integration across different platforms
   c) To enhance coding skills
   d) To reduce the server load

7. **What is the primary reason for ensuring the delivery platform of mobile software is scaled properly?**
   a) To ensure the software is downloaded quickly and correctly.
   b) To reduce the size of the software.
   c) To enable the software to be used by only a few users.
   d) To enhance the graphics of the software.

8. **What is the primary reason to have a release checklist?**
   a) To ensure that the customer is aware of the release
   b) To ensure that all steps are adhered to

    c) To ensure QA tests the product

    d) All of the above.

Answers

1. d

2. b

3. a

4. b

5. b

6. b

7. a

8. b

Exercises

- Imagine you are developing a web application and need to decide on the most suitable method of software delivery for your project. Write a brief analysis comparing and contrasting the advantages and disadvantages of binary delivery through a website versus SaaS delivery. Consider factors such as ease of deployment, maintenance, scalability, and customer experience.

- Create a checklist for software delivery that includes essential items to consider before releasing a software product. Include elements such as binary integrity, testing, release notes, export compliance, documentation, and communication with support teams. Explain the importance of each item on the checklist and how it contributes to a successful software delivery process.

- Choose one of the types of delivery discussed in the chapter (e.g., delivering software remotely, SaaS delivery) and create a step-by-step guide outlining the process for that specific type of delivery. Include key considerations, best practices, and any challenges that may arise during the delivery process. Highlight the critical steps and potential pitfalls to be aware of.

- Research and select a real-world example of software delivery through embedded devices (e.g., automotive software, IoT devices). Describe the specific challenges and considerations involved in delivering software through these devices. Discuss how quality assurance, fault tolerance, and customer support are crucial in ensuring successful software delivery for such devices.

- Design a monitoring and maintenance plan for a SaaS application. Outline the key metrics and indicators that should be monitored to ensure the software's smooth operation. Discuss how you would handle performance degradation, scalability challenges, and customer support. Consider the tools, processes, and resources required to monitor and maintain the software in a production environment effectively.

These exercises will help readers engage with software delivery's concepts and practical aspects, encouraging them to think critically and apply their knowledge to real-world scenarios.

Join our book's Discord space

Join the book's Discord Workspace for Latest updates, Offers, Tech happenings around the world, New Release and Sessions with the Authors:

https://discord.bpbonline.com

CHAPTER 14
Security of the Product

Introduction

Security nowadays is extremely important. Through the internet, people sitting in one corner of the world can hack into another system in another part of the world. This can cause chaos, monetary loss, or bankrupt companies or individuals. The chapter is for educating the managers on the steps that need to be taken to improve the security of the product.

Structure

In this chapter, the following topics will be discussed:

- Security is a specialized domain
- Security is non-compromisable
- Methods to improve security
- Monitoring security, continuous improvement

Objectives

The objective is to understand the steps to be taken to improve the product's security. The chapter will also focus on how engineers can be trained in security. Also, how to integrate the security lifecycle into the software development lifecycle. What are the steps to be taken to ensure that the security issues are addressed? The manager should also understand how much time it takes to work on the security issue. Security is a recurring issue, and it is not enough to fix it once and then forget about it. It is an ongoing cycle that needs to be executed for security analysis and fixing. To understand whether a security issue has been fixed requires specialized knowledge.

To achieve robust security, a comprehensive approach that includes regular security audits, continuous monitoring, and timely updates is essential. Collaboration with external security experts can provide valuable insights and help identify potential vulnerabilities that may be overlooked.

Security is a specialized domain

Security is a specialized domain. Special care has to be taken to improve the security of the product. What will happen if the application is not secure? Anyone can hack into the system and gain complete access. In many instances, hackers log in to the system and completely shut down the entire system. This may cost the organization millions of dollars, and sometimes, it may be irrecoverable.

At home, TVs are Wi-Fi enabled. Every gadget is getting connected to the Wi-Fi network. If someone can log into the Wi-Fi network, then they can show some unwanted content on the TV. From the Wi-Fi network, the hacker can steal a lot of data. Mobile phones are reaching every person's pocket and are also a significant source of security breaches.

People on the team should be experts in security to take care of it. It is not compensable. There are two types of security tools. One can be used during development, and the other can be used post-deployment. A brief explanation of the same has been provided below.

Security analysis, fixing, and continuous updates require plenty of time to be invested. In a project, 20% of the bandwidth of the entire team needs to be reserved for security fixes. 20% may be less in some cases, but it can be even more. These are some aspects that can derail the delivery timeline. The development and testing effort is not trivial, and without a security engineer understanding and guiding the fixes, it may take even longer. Most of the time, managers are caught unaware of the effort required, and hence, projects slip milestones.

For a software engineer, if they do not have sufficient knowledge about security. It is difficult to understand the security issues. One engineer needs to be trained in the OWASP top 10 issues to gain knowledge about how to interpret security issues. The engineer needs to know about each of the OWASP top ten contributors present on this website **https://owasp.org/www-project-top-ten/** to understand the security issues. Dedicated training sessions are required for the engineer to understand the issues. Please investigate the details of each top 10 issues and look into the contributing CWEs. If an engineer can understand the CWEs, then 80% of the security issues can be understood.

Security is non-compromisable

Security is non-compromisable because the consequences of neglecting it can be catastrophic. Failing to secure an application exposes it to potential hacks, which can lead to unauthorized access and manipulation. Often, hackers exploit vulnerabilities to shut down entire systems, causing significant financial losses that may be irrecoverable. With the increasing connectivity of devices, such as Wi-Fi-enabled TVs and mobile phones, the risk of security breaches has amplified. Hackers can infiltrate home networks to display unwanted content or steal sensitive data.

Ensuring security requires a dedicated team of experts and substantial investment in time and resources. It is essential to integrate security measures during both the development and post-deployment phases.

Neglecting security can have a far-reaching impact on the organization.

If security is compromised, several severe implications can arise:

- **Unauthorized access:** Hackers can gain complete access to the system, leading to unauthorized manipulation. Actual data can be manipulated, and manipulated data can be sent to applications, leading to wrong calculations by the applications.

- **System shutdown:** Hackers might shut down the entire system, affecting its functionality and accessibility. It may cause disruption to the users who are accessing the applications for their work.

- **Financial loss:** The organization could incur millions of dollars in losses, some of which may be irrecoverable. The share prices of the organization can drop significantly in the case of a security issue. This may impact the investors as well as the employees of the organization.

- **Data theft**: Hackers can steal sensitive data from connected devices via Wi-Fi networks. People will lose trust in organizations if data is stolen.

- **Unwanted content display**: Hackers can display inappropriate content on Wi-Fi-enabled gadgets like TVs. It may be harmful to kids who are watching TV.

- **Project delays:** Security issues can derail project timelines, requiring significant development and testing efforts. If not taken into account early, it may cause delays in the projects. Just before the release, some security issues may pop up and delay the project.

- **Continuous investment**: Security requires ongoing analysis, fixes, and updates, demanding substantial time and resources. There is an increase in the cost of the project, there is no doubt about it. However, if not invested, then the overall cost may be much higher.

Overall, neglecting security can have catastrophic consequences, making it a non-negotiable aspect of any application development and deployment process.

Methods to improve security

Firstly, let us consider secure development practices. The developers need to be trained in security. They should write code in a secure way.

The following checklist is a good example of what developers should do to ensure the security of the code:

Check your code for vulnerabilities	Examine your code against the latest OWASP Top 10 web application vulnerabilities list present at his location, https://owasp.org/www-project-top-ten/. It is also listed below:
	<ul><li>A01:2021-Broken Access Control</li><li>A02:2021-Cryptographic Failures</li><li>A03:2021-Injection</li><li>A04:2021-Insecure Design</li><li>A05:2021-Security Misconfiguration</li><li>A06:2021-Vulnerable and Outdated Components</li><li>A07:2021-Identification and Authentication Failures</li><li>A08:2021-Software and Data Integrity Failures</li><li>A09:2021-Security Logging and Monitoring Failures</li><li>A10:2021-Server-Side Request Forgery</li></ul>This list is extensive and requires a deep understanding of various security aspects. If a developer can grasp all these aspects and code accordingly, a major milestone is already achieved. Utilize static code analysis tools (SCA) such as Coverity, SonarQube, Snyk, Checkmarx, and Veracode. Stay updated by subscribing to vulnerability bulletins. The team should read the associated CWEs to understand what each of the bullet point in the above list means.
Use encryption to protect data during transmission and while stored.	Enable HTTPS using website security certificates. Employ robust encryption methods wherever possible. Use SSL whenever there is a communication across 2 computers or 2 applications. When data is stored, make sure that the data is encrypted and the keys are securely stored. Basically, you lock your house when you are leaving your house. And the key for the house is stored in a secure place so that no one gets access to the key to enter the house.

Implement strong access management through authentication and authorization	Enforce **multifactor authentication (MFA)**, such as OTP-based authentication. Consider alternatives like passwordless authentication, including fingerprint or iris scan-based systems. Regulate access authorization strictly, ensuring only authorized individuals are granted access.
Log relevant data, but do not store sensitive data in your code	Log errors, suspicious activities, and code changes. Avoid storing sensitive data or personal information within your code. For instance, passwords should never be hard-coded.
Secure web apps and software applications with digital certificates	Use digital certificates (SSL/TLS for web apps and code signing certificates for software applications) issued by a trusted **Certificate Authority (CA)**. Allocate budget to purchase certificates from a CA when needed. Add a timestamp to your signature.
Audit information	All system logins should be audited. Record all login details in an audit log.
Detect dynamic errors	Run dynamic memory allocation detection tools to ensure no memory leaks occur. If leaks and crashes do happen, it may result in internal information being printed in the crash logs, potentially visible to the end-user. Therefore, it is best to prevent leaks. Tools like Valgrind, GCeasy, Eclipse MAT, and Glowcode can help identify dynamic memory leaks.
Check for network errors	Employ tools capable of detecting network vulnerabilities, such as Invicti.

Table 14.1: Checklist to improve security

All of the above can be integrated into the continuous integration pipeline. If any of the tests fail, then the entire build should fail. It is practically impossible to fix all security bugs before a release. Then the release will not happen. Prioritize the security issues and fix the high-priority issues. Do continuous patch updates post-release.

It also becomes extremely difficult to install software that is released once and not upgraded in a customer environment. This software will be vulnerable to attacks.

Monitoring security, continuous improvement

Secure software development is a continuous cycle. It should start from the beginning of the project till the end, as shown in the following figure:

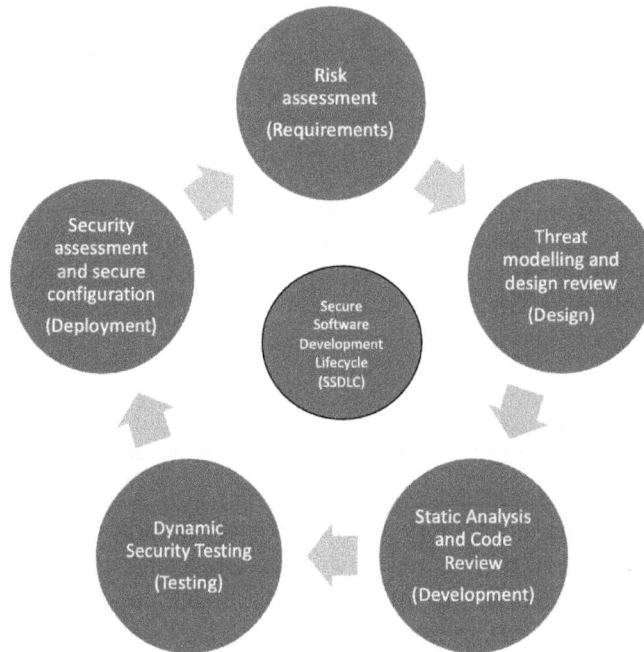

Figure 14.1: Secure software development life cycle

Instead of viewing security as a hindrance in the **software development life cycle** (**SDLC**), it should be integrated into every phase to enhance the process. Incorporating security at each development stage involves:

- Assessing risks during the requirements gathering stage
- Reviewing the design for potential vulnerabilities
- Conducting architecture analysis for risk during the design phase
- Performing both static and dynamic analysis
- Engaging in interactive application security testing during the development and testing phases

Your development team should be well-versed in secure coding practices and security frameworks. This ensures uniformity and helps establish a consistent security policy across the enterprise.

Incorporate security requirements during planning

Alongside business, performance, and functional requirements, ensure your development team gathers security needs from all stakeholders before starting the development process.

For security considerations, you will need to decide on the technologies and languages to use and the best practices for detecting and managing vulnerabilities and other harmful code. This stage also involves ensuring that frameworks are secure within the application environment and checking the compatibility of technologies and languages. Addressing these prerequisites early on is crucial, as encountering such issues later can lead to development challenges and potentially expose your software to security threats.

Often, security requirements are integrated with functional specifications. For instance, if a feature requires a user to enter their password to access their account, a corresponding security measure might be to encrypt the password input.

Mitigate through secure design principles

The design phase in software development is where the software product's and its features' blueprint is crafted to meet technical and business requirements. This blueprint guides developers in writing the source code.

Security is paramount at this stage. Thorough reviews of both the code and design are essential to mitigate defects that could lead to security risks. These issues might not be classified as bugs, so they can go unnoticed during testing if not addressed early.

Methodologies like **architecture risk analysis (ARA)** and threat modeling are crucial for identifying design flaws. ARA ensures that the design adheres to security principles, while threat modeling uncovers potential vulnerabilities that attackers might exploit.

Adhere to secure coding standards

Performing a thorough security review of your source code is essential to identify any vulnerabilities. The code quality review focuses on detecting logic errors, specification flaws, and adherence to style guides, among other defects. This process is typically done using automated tools that scan your source code based on predefined rules to identify insecure coding practices.

Secure coding guidelines are crucial security rules that should be integrated into the software development process, regardless of the technology used. Implementing these practices is vital to protect against cyberattacks. Key guidelines include validating inputs from untrusted sources, designing and implementing robust security policies, employing multiple defense strategies, following the principle of least privilege, and strictly adhering to quality assurance techniques.

Continuous testing

Even after conducting various security checks throughout the development process, the final stage of code testing is essential. Once the code modules are ready, they undergo rigorous testing, including security assessments, to identify and address vulnerabilities. You can utilize various scanning tools to perform a range of tests, such as:

- **Static analysis Static Application Security Testing (SAST)** examines your source code before it is compiled, uncovering vulnerabilities and security risks that could expose your application to potential threats. Example tools, Coverity, Lint.

- **Dynamic analysis**: Dynamic analysis, also known as **Dynamic Application Security Testing (DAST)**, involves evaluating vulnerabilities while the application is running, typically focusing on HTML and HTTP interfaces.

- **Interactive application testing**: Unlike SAST and DAST, this is a functional test that interacts with your application via an automated bot, human tester, or any other type of simulated interaction.

- **Penetration testing:** In this test, you evaluate the security of your application by stimulating an attack using tools, techniques, and processes that real-life cyber attackers use. If the skills are present, internal testers can do it, and if they are not, external testers can.

Keep up with the latest threats

With evolving technology, cyberattack practices also evolve. Therefore, it is critical to keep yourself up to date with security issues. Although there are no fixed guidelines on how to do that, you can follow simple practices to ensure that you are always up to date with the latest threats on the scene:

- Follow security experts, as they usually spend the majority of their efforts researching cybersecurity issues. It is a good idea to subscribe to their blogs, newsletters, podcasts, and other updates.

- Do your own research into the cyberattack ecosystem. Although it might not be possible for you to dedicate as much time to this as experts, you can read through every reported attack, such as the Log4j vulnerability, and pore into the details.

- Attending cybersecurity events is also a great way to learn new trends. Engaging in such events will also help you build a network of security professionals who can collaborate and share knowledge on software security.

Conclusion

The project manager needs to allocate time for security activities. The developers need to be trained in security. They need to code in a secure way so that the number of bugs is less. Appropriate tools should be used to catch the security issues during development itself. At least 20% of the time must be spent on security activities. Estimation must be done accordingly. Without allocating time, the project will not be security compliant. Remember, it may be better not to deliver rather than deliver poor quality and insecure products. Damage to the organization may be severe with an unsecured product.

In the next chapter, we will discuss QA and automation. Product security and quality depend on verification, which is the last gate before the product is released.

Points to remember

- Security is specialized; ensure experts are involved.

- Integrate security throughout the development lifecycle.

- Train engineers on security best practices, including OWASP Top 10.

- Implement secure development practices like encryption and access management.

- Continuously monitor and improve security with audits and updates.

- Integrate security checks into the development process.

- Stay informed, collaborate, and follow security trends.

These concise points serve as reminders of the essential aspects to consider when improving product security.

Multiple choice questions

1. **What is the primary reason for integrating security throughout the software development lifecycle?**
   a) To meet regulatory requirements
   b) To ensure a smooth development process
   c) To proactively address security vulnerabilities
   d) To reduce development costs

2. **Which of the following is an essential practice for improving product security?**
   a) Regular security audits and updates
   b) Ignoring security concerns during development
   c) Relying solely on external security experts
   d) Treating security as an afterthought

3. **What is the purpose of training engineers on the OWASP Top 10 issues?**

   a) To become certified security experts

   b) To gain awareness of common security vulnerabilities

   c) To bypass the need for security testing

   d) To eliminate the need for external security assessments

4. **Which of the following is an example of a secure development practice?**

   a) Implementing encryption for data in transit and at rest

   b) Ignoring access management and authentication

   c) Storing sensitive data in plain text

   d) Neglecting to update software libraries

5. **What is the benefit of integrating security checks into the continuous integration pipeline?**

   a) It speeds up the development process

   b) It eliminates the need for security testing

   c) It catches security issues early in the development cycle

   d) It reduces the need for security updates

6. **How can organizations stay informed about the latest security threats?**

   a) By ignoring security bulletins and updates

   b) By attending cybersecurity events and conferences

   c) By relying solely on internal security expertise

   d) By avoiding collaboration with external security professionals

7. **What is the recommended approach for addressing security vulnerabilities discovered during monitoring?**

   a) Ignore them if they do not impact immediate functionality

   b) Prioritize and address them in a timely manner

   c) Wait for external security experts to provide guidance

   d) Downplay their significance and focus on new feature development

8. **Why is collaboration important in the context of product security?**

   a) It helps to shift the responsibility of security to external parties

   b) It allows for the sharing of knowledge and best practices

   c) It slows down the development process

   d) It eliminates the need for security assessments

Answers

1. c
2. a
3. b
4. a
5. c
6. b
7. b

Exercises

- Identify three common types of cyber threats that organizations may face. Provide a brief description of each.

- Explain the importance of integrating security into the software development lifecycle. Provide at least two reasons.

- List and briefly describe three secure coding practices that developers should follow to enhance product security.

- Explain the 5 CWEs contributing to OWASP's top 10 security issue, "Broken Access Control."

- Explain the different tools used for static and dynamic analysis of code.

- Imagine you are creating a user manual for a new software product. Write a step-by-step guide on how to install the software on a computer. Include any prerequisites or system requirements.

- You are tasked with updating the troubleshooting documentation for a mobile app. Choose one common issue that users may encounter and write a troubleshooting guide with clear steps to resolve the problem.

- Review the following sentence from a documentation page: "To configure the settings, access the admin panel and navigate to the 'Advanced' tab." Identify at least two improvements you would make to enhance clarity and user understanding.

- Create a short FAQ section for a customer support documentation page. Choose three common questions users may have about a specific feature of the product and provide concise answers.

- You are creating API documentation for a web service. Write a code example in the programming language of your choice to demonstrate how to make a GET request to retrieve data from the API.

Join our book's Discord space

Join the book's Discord Workspace for Latest updates, Offers, Tech happenings around the world, New Release and Sessions with the Authors:

https://discord.bpbonline.com

CHAPTER 15
QA and Automation

Introduction

Verification by the **quality assurance** (**QA**) team plays a crucial role in software development. While developers dedicate a significant portion of their time to architecture, design, and development, the remaining time is spent resolving issues raised by the QA team and stabilizing the product. Manual QA, a fundamental aspect of the verification process, involves meticulous planning and execution of tests to ensure the quality and reliability of the software.

In this chapter, we will delve into the world of manual QA, exploring its significance, methodologies, and best practices. We will examine the test design process, which involves understanding the product's architecture and design to create comprehensive test plans. We will also discuss the execution of manual tests, including test case creation, execution, and defect reporting. Furthermore, we will explore the collaboration between the QA team and developers, highlighting the iterative nature of bug reporting and resolution.

By understanding the principles and techniques of manual QA, software development teams can enhance the overall quality of their products, mitigate risks, and deliver robust solutions to end-users. So, let us embark on this journey to uncover the intricacies of manual QA and empower ourselves with the knowledge to ensure software excellence.

Structure

In this chapter, the following topics will be discussed;

- Manual QA
- Testing in scale
- Performance testing
- Automation QA
- Simulators

Objectives

This chapter aims to provide a comprehensive understanding of manual software verification, specifically focusing on the role of the QA. This chapter aims to equip readers with the knowledge and skills necessary to effectively plan, design, execute, and report manual tests by exploring the methodologies, best practices, and collaboration between QA and developers. Through this understanding, readers can contribute to software products' overall quality and stability, ensuring that they meet the desired requirements and deliver an exceptional user experience.

Manual QA

Verification by QA is one of the most important gates in the development process. Developers spend 50% of their time on architecture, design, and development. The remaining 50% is spent resolving issues submitted by QA and stabilizing the product.

Test design

Test design is a critical phase in the software development lifecycle where the QA team meticulously plans and documents the testing strategy for the product's features. This stage involves understanding the product's architecture and design to create comprehensive test cases covering functional and non-functional requirements. The QA team must develop appropriate test scripts and data sources to ensure a seamless testing process once development is complete. Effective test designs identify potential issues early and facilitate clear communication between development and QA teams, ensuring that all scenarios, including edge cases, are considered. This preparation is vital to achieve a high-quality product that meets the specified requirements and user expectations.

Test design should be documented in the test design document. The test design can be for the overall product, or it can be for individual features, too. Usually, it is written for the overall product and seldom for the individual features. The document, once written at the beginning, is good to update later on; however, that is seldom the case. The document is not updated later. So, treat this as the initial document, and as the project starts flowing, focus on the other subsequent documents.

Test design document format

The test design document should have the following format:

- **Introduction:** This section provides an overview of the test design document, including its purpose, scope, and intended audience.

- **Test objectives:** Outline the primary objectives of the testing process. This includes identifying the key features and functionalities that need to be tested and the goals of the testing effort.

- **Test scope:** Define the boundaries of the testing effort. Specify what will be included in the testing and what will be excluded. This helps to manage expectations and clarify the extent of the testing.

  It should be mentioned that anything beyond what is mentioned is out of test scope. Mentioning things out of scope is not possible, since there could be hundreds of things which are out of scope.

- **Test strategy:** Describe the overall approach to testing. This includes the testing levels (e.g., unit testing, integration testing, system testing), types of testing (e.g., functional, non-functional, regression), and the testing environment.

  What will be tested via manual testing, what will be tested via automation testing, etc. How will regression testing be done?

- **Test environment:** Detail the environment in which the testing will be conducted. This includes hardware, software, network configurations, and any other relevant infrastructure. Also, specify any tools or frameworks that will be used.

  There is a separate section for performance and scale testing.

- **Test data:** Outline the data requirements for testing. Describe how test data will be generated, managed, and used during the testing process. Include any specific data sets or sources that will be utilized.

  Data can either be generated in-house, or it can be obtained from the customer, or it can be bought from the marketplace, or it can be downloaded from any website. If it has to be bought, then budget has to be allotted for the same. For example, financial data is bought and used. This has to be planned much earlier.

- **Test cases:** Provide a list of test cases, including detailed descriptions of each test. This should include the test case ID, test description, preconditions, test steps, expected results, and postconditions.

  Use a tool to document the test cases. There are many tools to document test cases, examples are Jira, Qtest, TestRail, TestMo, Qase, TestCollab. During the overall test design stage of the product, it is not possible to write all the test cases. Rather than defining where the test cases will be written, what the test case columns are, and which column to use to indicate that this test case needs to be automated.

- **Test scripts:** Include reference to any specific scripts that will be used for automated testing or to be developed. Provide details on the scripts, including their purpose, how they will be executed, and any dependencies or requirements. Here, a list of test scripts can be provided, and details of the scripts can be covered in the test script design document. At the beginning of the project, it is not possible to think about all the test cases.

- **Roles and responsibilities:** Define the roles and responsibilities of the testing team. Specify who will be responsible for various aspects of the testing process, including test design, execution, defect reporting, and test management.

  This is for the start of the project. Things may not be the same as the project progresses. Seldom do people update the document later on. The projects go in a flow after the initial baseline in set.

- **Test schedule:** Provide a detailed schedule for the testing activities. This should include timelines for test preparation, execution, and reporting. Include any milestones or key dates that are relevant to the testing process.

- **Risk management:** Identify potential risks that could impact the testing process. Describe how these risks will be mitigated. Include any contingency plans or strategies to address identified risks. Again, this is what is understandable at the beginning of the project. As the project moves, the risks change. This is not the document to update at that point in time.

- **Review and approval:** Specify the process for reviewing and approving the test design document. Include details on who will review the document, how feedback will be incorporated, and the final approval process.

  The test document must be reviewed by the architect and project managers. If there are cross-team dependencies, then the cross-team should also review them.

- **Release handover process to QA:** Define the code handover process to QA. Before handing over any release to the QA team, it is imperative to ensure that several critical steps are meticulously completed to guarantee a smooth and effective testing process.

  The following are the mandatory things to do before a release is handed over to QA:

  o **Code freeze and documentation:**

    - Ensure that the codebase has reached a stable state with no more changes planned. All code should be committed, and a code freeze should be implemented to prevent last-minute alterations.

    - Update all relevant documentation, including requirements, design documents, and user manuals. This ensures that the QA team has all the necessary information to understand the new features and changes.

- o **Sanity check:** Conduct a sanity check to ensure that the application is working as expected in the testing environment. This helps in identifying any configuration or deployment issues early.

- o **Communication and training:** Communicate the features and any special instructions to the QA team. If necessary, conduct a meeting to familiarize the QA team with new features or changes in the application.

- **Bug logging, tracking:** Define the bug logging and state the transition process of the bugs.

  - o Identify and document any bugs or issues found during testing in a bug-tracking system.

  - o Each bug should have a clear and concise description, steps to reproduce, expected results, actual results, severity, and priority.

  - o Include any necessary screenshots, logs, or other supporting evidence to facilitate understanding and resolution.

  - o Track the status of each bug through to resolution. Define the state transition process of Jiras.

  - o Ensure regular updates are provided on the progress of bug fixes and retesting. Communication between QA and development teams is crucial during this phase to ensure timely and effective resolution of issues.

  - o Define a process for duplicate filing of bugs.

- **Test report:** Generate a format of the test report post a feature is done. It should contain comprehensive information to document the testing process and results. It can be an email or a document. Setting the expectations upfront helps everyone be aligned.

  The essential components of a test report include:

  - o **Summary**: A brief overview of what was tested, including the project name, dates, and a summary of the testing objectives and scope.

  - o **Objectives**: The goals and objectives of the testing effort.

  - o **Test items**: A list of the items that were tested, including software versions and configurations.

  - o **Environment**: Details of the test environment, including hardware, software, network configurations, and any other relevant details.

  - o **Test cases**: A summary or list of the test cases executed, including their identifiers and descriptions.

  - o **Results**: The outcomes of the test cases, including which tests passed, failed, or were blocked, with appropriate metrics and statistics.

○ **Defects**: A detailed log of any defects or bugs identified during testing, including their severity, priority, status, and any steps taken to resolve them.

○ **Conclusion**: A summary of the overall testing effort, including any significant findings, risks, and recommendations for further actions or improvements.

○ **Metrics**: Quantitative measures that provide insights into the testing process, such as test coverage, defect density, and test execution progress.

○ **Attachments**: Any supporting documents, such as logs, screenshots, or additional evidence that support the findings in the report.

By including these elements, the test report ensures that all aspects of the testing process are well-documented and communicated, facilitating effective decision-making and continuous improvement.

• **Appendices:** Include any additional information or reference materials that are relevant to the test design. This might include a glossary of terms, diagrams, templates, or other supporting documentation.

The test design document is a critical component of the software development lifecycle, ensuring the testing process is well-planned, structured, and effective. By following the outlined format, QA teams can create comprehensive, clear test designs that facilitate successful testing and high-quality product delivery.

Manual QA stages of testing

The sequence of testing in a development project by the verification team is as follows:

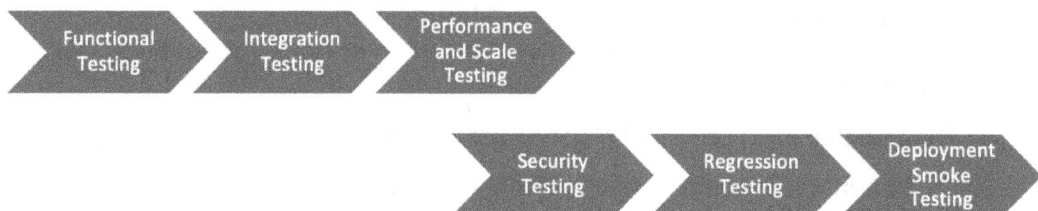

Figure 15.1: *Manual QA stages*

Functional testing

This is about testing the functionality of the product. Most people are aware of this. When the development team is working on the development code, the QA team should focus on creating a test design document and a plan for the testing of the features. For example, if a shopping cart is being developed, the QA team should focus on testing the features of the shopping cart. How the shopping cart can be created, what products have to be created in the catalog of the shopping cart, in which currency the price has to be put in the catalog, everything has to be described in the test design spec.

During this time, the QA team should develop appropriate scripts and data sources so that the data can be populated when testing starts. Test cases should be reviewed with the dev team and should be logged in a tool.

Very few teams provide reasonable-quality builds for the first round of testing, meaning all the happy paths are working, and some of the negative scenarios are not working.

- If a dev team has provided this kind of build within the estimated time or near the estimated time, then the development team's maturity can be assumed to be high.

- If QA finds issues in the happy paths in the builds provided in the initial rounds of testing, then the development team's maturity is medium. This indicates that the plans going forward will not be intact. They will miss the timelines, and the quality will be poor.

- If QA is unable to proceed with the happy path testing in the builds provided in the initial rounds of testing, then the development team's maturity is Poor. The QA manager should signal that the team is not capable of delivering the product.

During the test design stage, the QA team should do the following:

- Understanding the architecture and design
- Thinking on your feet to understand the entire product
- Writing test cases
- Keeping abreast with the changes and updating the test cases

When testing starts, QA should file a bug report for each issue. Care should be taken to ensure that each bug report contains all the necessary details so that the developers can understand the issue. These days, QA can be in one part of the world while dev can be in another part of the world. Dev needs to rely on the Bug Reporting tool to understand the issue. Occasional meetings can be held with Dev to clarify some of the problems.

Care must be taken to understand the scope of testing and reduce the submission of unnecessary bug reports.

You should find similar issues already submitted so that duplicated issues are not filed.

Should publish test reports and file bugs on a regular basis to understand where the product stands.

If 95% of the test cases pass, the product can be assumed to be mature. Anything less than that can be deemed immature and unusable by customers. In aerospace software, 99% of the Test cases should pass. Otherwise, the software is not suitable for use in aircraft. For financial software, all calculations should work correctly, 100% correct. Any bugs in the code can lead to wrong calculations and wrong data.

Some of the tools used to manage test cases and track test case execution are Xcel, New Relic, TestRail, Xray, and Qtest. Some of the tools can be integrated with Jira, which is an added advantage.

Not all issues can be fixed or need to be fixed. QA needs to understand which problems are significant and which are not. The following are the reasons why some issues may not be necessary to fix:

- There will be very little return on investment by fixing some problems.

- Fixing this issue will not give much value. However, regression effects on other modules are higher.

- The feature is excellent for customers.

QA needs to be pragmatic about which issues need to be fixed. If all issues are to be fixed and released, then the software cannot be released. QA needs to understand the impact of the bugs and stories and then suggest which need to be fixed first, which need to be fixed next, and which need not be fixed.

This triaging exercise should happen on an ongoing basis. Otherwise, a huge accumulation of issues may be difficult to handle going forward.

The list of issues that will be marked as "Won't FIX" needs to be approved by the product manager. The product manager is the final decision maker regarding what needs to be fixed and what needs not be.

Integration testing

Integration testing is when all the different dev components are added together to create the integrated product. Post the dev integration, QA does integration testing. It is to check the end-to-end functionality of the product. Integration test cases can be separately written, or some functional test cases can be marked as integration test cases. 10% to 20% of the functional test cases can be marked as integration test cases.

Integration testing can be performed incrementally by adding one module at a time to the integrated system and testing its interactions with existing modules. This approach helps in isolating defects and facilitates easier troubleshooting.

Furthermore, integration testing is essential in validating end-to-end scenarios that mimic real-world application usage. It ensures that the integrated modules deliver the desired functionality, performance, and reliability. By employing both automated and manual testing techniques, QA teams can thoroughly assess the integrated system's behavior under various conditions, paving the way for a robust and reliable software product.

Integration testing also often involves collaboration between development and QA teams to ensure the test environment accurately reflects the production setup. This collaboration is critical in setting up test data, configuring environments, and addressing any issues that may arise during testing. Ultimately, successful integration testing contributes significantly to the overall quality and stability of the software, making it an indispensable phase in the software development lifecycle.

It will be difficult for QA to identify which component is the bug when integration testing is done. After the bugs are filed in the best-guessed component, the development manager has to assign them to the correct team.

There will generally be some back and forth between the dev teams, saying that the issue is not with their module but with another team's module. The QA team should keep the momentum to identify the correct team and fix the bug as soon as possible.

Start integration tests early in the product development lifecycle. Do not wait for all functional tests to get done before starting the integration tests. Incremental integration tests should begin early on to catch defects early.

Security testing

Security testing has been covered in the previous chapter. Please refer to the chapter for more details. This is an ongoing process, and security testing needs to be conducted regularly. Knowledge about security testing needs to be built into the team. This can be done after the integration of the components. It also needs to be done when the product is deployed and made live. Because not all the issues are caught in the test bed, some testing must be done post-deployment. There are quite a few vendors who specialize in security testing, and their services can also be availed to do security testing if internal knowledge is absent.

The QA team requires specialized knowledge and continuous learning for effective security testing. Given the complexity and evolving nature of security threats, it is critical to build a foundational understanding of security principles within the team. This can include familiarizing team members with the latest security testing methodologies, tools, and best practices.

Additionally, collaboration with external vendors who specialize in security testing can provide valuable insights and support. Regularly scheduled training sessions and staying abreast of emerging threats are crucial for maintaining a robust security posture. By integrating security testing into the QA process, teams can ensure that vulnerabilities are identified and mitigated before they can be exploited, thereby protecting the integrity of the application and its data.

Security testing should be an integral part of the QA process, conducted not only during the integration phase but also post-deployment to catch any potential issues that may arise in the live environment. Regular security audits and penetration testing can help uncover hidden vulnerabilities and strengthen the overall security framework.

One easy way to become an expert in security is to understand the CWEs well as is listed in the OWASP top ten website, **https://owasp.org/www-project-top-ten/**. A QA engineer will be able to exploit the vulnerabilities if they understand the CWEs. This requires time, effort, training, and largely self-learning to become an expert in security issues.

Regression testing

Regression testing is used to check if, because of a fix somewhere, something else is broken. If something was working before and is not working now, that is known as regression. If automation coverage is good for the product, then it can be used to catch regression issues. If there is not sufficient automation, then manual testing can be used. However, this is costly and boring for the QA engineers. If there is no manpower available to automate, then it becomes difficult to do this. Also, the product cannot expand with new features because the QA engineers will be busy with regression testing, and it will be difficult to test new features because of a lack of bandwidth. Needs to be done when patches are released.

If done manually, the QA engineer has to sit with the development engineer and understand the impact the changes can have. The QA engineer then has to identify the test cases that need to be run. If multiple modules can be impacted, the QA engineer has to understand the overall impact from the component owners and design test cases according to that.

Normally, the overall product has frequently used scenarios marked with regression tests. For example, in a product, the customer uses 20% of the features 80% of the time. The QA team needs to understand these 20% of features and then mark the test cases for these features available for regression testing. If possible, these scenarios should be automated.

Smoke testing

A very high level of testing is needed to see if the product is working as expected. This is just a few test cases, 10 or 20 test cases, which can be executed quickly. It needs to be done after the deployment. Though automation can be used to test, it should be remembered that humans are ultimately going to use most of the software. Hence, one round of manual smoke testing is an absolute must after the deployment.

This is when smoke testing is performed:

- When a build is obtained from dev, do smoke testing to see if everything is working fine.

- When a build is deployed for QA, check through smoke testing to see if everything is working fine.

- When a production build is deployed, do a quick check to see if everything is working fine.

Testing in scale

This is another non-functional test. Most software works fine in a low-scale environment. That is, if one or two people are using the software, then it works fine most of the time. However, this kind of software is toy software. Software is ready for enterprise if more than 1000 users can simultaneously use it. Software should be developed so that it can scale to handle multiples of 1000 users.

Now, how can this be tested in-house? How can 1000 users be simulated? Apache Jmeter, Gatling, Loadrunner, Locust, and Webload are such tools that come in handy in this case.

The QA team should be able to generate a scale generated by many users to test whether the product's functionality is working fine. The QA automation team should own this testing since coding is required to simulate the environment. This should not be a manual activity and should run automatically.

The product should have limits defined. For example, it will work fine for 1000 users.

The QA team needs to be trained to understand how performance and scale testing can be done. Skills need to be developed in the team to test the scale and performance of the application. Some of the tools that are used for scale testing are Jmeter, Gatling, and LoadNinja are a couple of tools that are used for scale and performance testing.

Some of the needs for scale testing are as follows:

- The tool should be able to simulate many end-user connections. For example, for a shopping cart, the tool should be able to create many end-user connections, which simulate many users logging into the shopping website to shop. During a day of sale, there may be a spike in users logging into the website. There should be appropriate tools to simulate this so that the website can be tested for this.

- There needs to be a test bed where this kind of testing can be done. The QA team needs to prepare a separate test bed for this kind of testing. It may require DBs with large data to test the scale.

- The results need to be documented, with the timing measurements as much as possible, because these results will be referenced when the application needs to be scaled. The development team needs to look into the results. Also, the metrics need to be published for customers and deployers to understand the sizing guide of the product. For example, a Webserver, how many concurrent users it can handle in a particular machine configuration, will be used by customers to understand the machine requirements.

- Again, the scale can be simulated to a limited extent. The entire scale cannot always be simulated. The extrapolation method needs to be used to approximate and solve for the scale that is beyond testable limits. For example, if in production, an 8-core 64GB machine is used, testing can be done in a two-core 16GB machine because, in a QA environment, it might not be possible to provision a bigger machine. The results of this two-core 16GB can be extrapolated for an 8-core 64GB machine. Though this is an approximation, it is much better than guesswork.

- Some of these tools may require development support. Setting up and testing will be quicker if developers are involved. So, it may be wise to set up a team comprising developers and QA.

- It cannot be done continuously since it requires resources, both hardware and manpower. It can be done when the entire product is integrated.

Performance testing

It does non-functional testing. Performance testing is a critical aspect of software testing that ensures a system's performance, stability, and scalability under various conditions. When subjected to different load levels, it evaluates a software application's speed, responsiveness, and stability. The primary goal is identifying and eliminating performance bottlenecks to enhance the overall user experience.

The environment for performing performance testing should be set up carefully:

- It can be scaled down replica of the production environment.
- It should be isolated, and external traffic should not be impacted.
- It should be able to be set up repeatedly.
- You should be able to run automation tests repeatedly without changing the environment.
- We should be able to get logs for analysis.
- The environment should be constant for repeated tests going forward.

The main objectives of performance testing include:

- **Speed**: Assessing the application's response times under various conditions.
- **Scalability**: Determining the application's ability to handle increased workloads.
- **Stability**: Ensuring the application remains stable under prolonged usage.
- **Resource usage**: Evaluating efficient utilization of system resources.

Scale and performance testing should be automated together when the tools mentioned above are used. Performance results should be printed in a report format and should be analyzed.

Now, if the production environment is enormous in terms of resources, it is impossible to replicate the exact environment in the QA environment. This will require a lot of effort, and the cost will also be high. It is fine to do the tests in a smaller setup in the QA environment and benchmark the numbers. The number can be extrapolated for the production cluster. This can be done for the first time, and a benchmark can be set. From next time onwards, the results can be tallied against this benchmark.

Automation QA

The advantages of automation QA are as follows:

- Automates test cases
- Helps in regression testing
- Helps in continuous integration

- Difficulty in managing e2e test cases
- Difficulty in debugging e2e test cases
- Grouping test cases to run only 1 group
- Using simulators and not depending on actual systems for running tests
- Reliability, repeatability of testing

Automation helps in automatically testing the product. Some of the well-known products that are used to automate testing are Selenium, TestNG, Postman, and many more. There are many tools that can be used. There should be an appropriate selection criterion for selecting the tool. Selection criteria can be based on:

- Firstly, what is the need? What needs to be tested? Is it an end-to-end test tool, unit testing, or just some scripts that need to be run?

- What is the type of product for which testing is required? Is it a standalone software, embedded software, or is it a SaaS kind of application?

- The tool that is being selected, does anyone have experience with it?

- If there is no experience, is training available for that tool?

- How long will it take to learn and use it?

- Is it a paid or free tool?

- What is the complexity of the setup and maintenance requirements of the tool?

- Is it a prevalent tool in the market? You can check the search trend for the tool on Google Trends.

The team should feel confident about the tool, not only the manager, because the team is ultimately going to use it. If a tool is chosen based on the manager's preferences, then the team may be unwilling to use the tool. A balance must be attained between the manager and the team's choice. This is probably true for anything that needs to be done in the project.

Automation needs to have a captive system for testing. If possible, test it on the same machine instead of depending on the network. If dependent on another external production system, then there are chances that the external production system is unstable, and hence, the entire system is unstable. For example, if software has to be tested for end-to-end functionality in custom-made hardware, the hardware may be unstable. Now if the automation tests are run in the hardware, there may be failures. It will take time to understand whether the issue was with the software or with the hardware. It might be better to eliminate the hardware dependency and run the software only, possibly in a simulator on a standalone machine. A standalone machine running Windows or Linux is much more stable compared to custom hardware. The software part can be very well tested if run in a simulator. Of course, some of the software cannot be tested; for example, the device drivers for embedded hardware cannot be tested in a simulator. Those must be tested on the actual hardware. However, the application layer and middleware can be tested in the simulator.

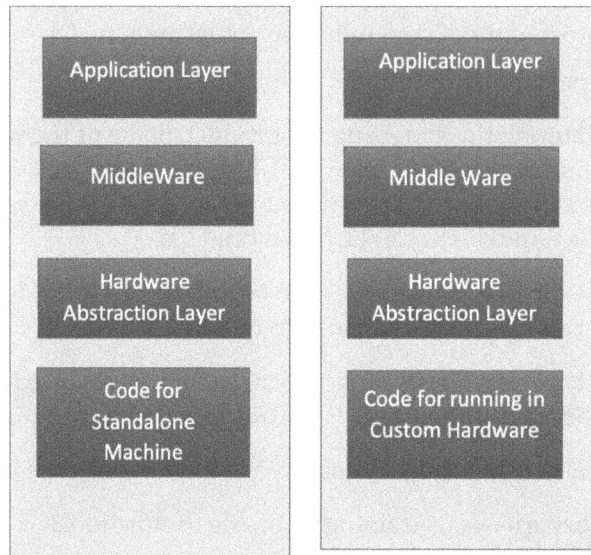

Figure 15.2: Abstracting layer switching between a standalone machine and custom hardware

This is a tremendous value addition to the development process. Many embedded projects take a longer time to execute because of a lack of a suitable environment to develop and test on a standalone machine. Work will proceed much faster if this is adopted. The majority of the testing can also be done on a standalone Linux or Windows machine. There can be a hardware abstraction layer below the middleware that can be modified to run the code either in a standalone environment or in the hardware environment.

Another common example is the Android phone simulator. Android phone simulator runs in a PC environment. An application can be written entirely and tested in the simulator. Once done, it can be downloaded to the actual hardware and tested.

Many languages can be used for testing. Python and Java are popular languages used in test automation.

Which test cases to automate are also major decision factors? There can be 100s of manual test cases. The QA team needs to identify the test cases in which the test cases if automated, will give the best return on investment. Normally, it is not possible to automate 100% of the test cases. However, if 50% of the test cases are automated, it will save QA effort.

Run in batches because if you run a single batch, then the number of test cases becomes very high. Very difficult to debug and find out the exact issue. So, the automation test cases can be batched. For example, 1-20 test cases can be in batch 1, and 21-40 can be in batch 2. The running of batch 2 should not be dependent on batch 1. This way, it will be easy to get to the root cause of a test case failure. Most often, rather than hitting actual issues, the test failure is because of the automation test environment. The systems may have occasional instability, causing the test to fail. Logs generated from the test runs can be fed to a log server, for example, Syslog or Splunk, so that the logs can be analyzed further.

Automation testing should be reliably repeatable. If continuous maintenance is required, then it will defeat the purpose of automation.

The size of the automation QA team should be 1 for every 6 developers, which means the proportion of developers to automation QA should be 6:1. With increasing maturity, it can be even lower than this; for example, the developer-to-automation engineering strength can be 9:1.

Simulators

Simulators play a crucial role in quickening the development of software projects. If a developer is able to develop most of the software on a laptop without depending on external hardware or software, then the development will be much faster, and the quality of the software will also be much better. There are many simulation software programs available. So, choose the one that is suitable for the project.

The automation team has a huge role in augmenting the simulators with new features and maintaining and troubleshooting whenever there is an issue with the simulator. They should be the primary owners of the simulator.

If the simulators are unavailable, the automation team should develop a home-grown simulator. The home-grown simulator can be developed in any high-level language, such as C/C++, Java, Python, or GoLang.

The following should be the features of the simulator:

- It should run in the laptop so that the developer does not have any network dependencies.

- It should be stable. It should not reboot often.

- It should be extendible. Meaning new features can be developed easily.

- Instead of coding, requests/responses from the simulator should be coded in config files.

- The simulator should run on the following operating systems: macOS, Windows, and Linux. Check the systems being used by the developers.

- Simulators should be bug-free.

Some of the examples of off-the-shelf simulators are Mockito, Postman simulator, and Wiremock. Besides that, plenty of API simulators are available which can be found in the internet.

Team composition

Dev to manual QA proportion should be 3:1. For every 3 developers there should be 1 QA. For dev teams with high maturity, the dev to QA proportion can be 3.5:1.

Team hierarchy can be both ways, as shown in the diagram below. If the team is small (= 12 engineers), manual QA and automation QA will be handled by a single manager. If the team is big (>=12), then there can be two managers, each managing the respective functionalities.

The reporting structure in the QA team can be as follows:

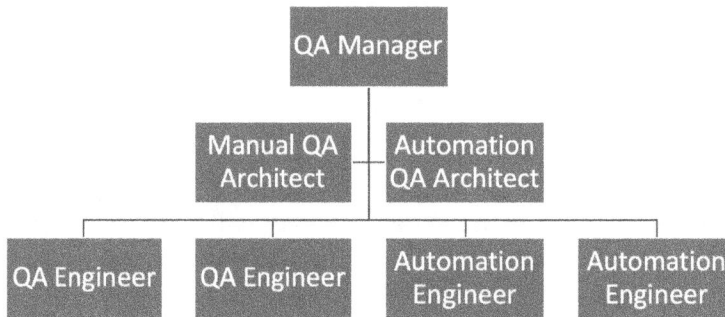

Figure 15.3: QA team organization, one manager has the entire team

There can be many other models possible. If the team is bigger, then there can be a separate **QA Manager** and a separate **Automation QA Manager**. The QA team can be managed by the **QA Manager** and the automation team by the automation manager.

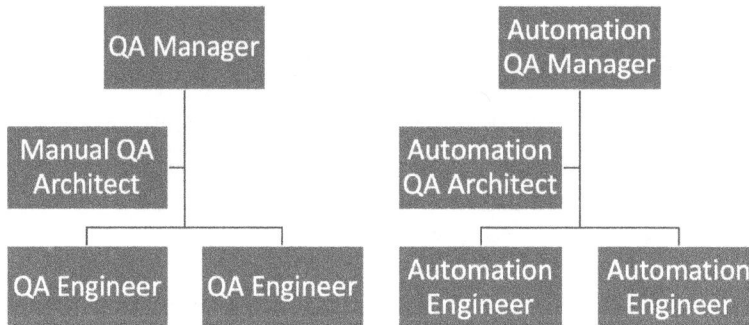

Figure 15.4: Manual and automation QA with separate managers

Scrum team models

The development scrum team can have 3 dev and 2 QA members. One QA member can concentrate on functional testing, and the other can concentrate on non-functional testing or automation testing.

Scrum team model 1

Applicable for smaller teams where the team size does not go beyond ten members including dev and QA. The following two diagrams represent the two scrum team models.

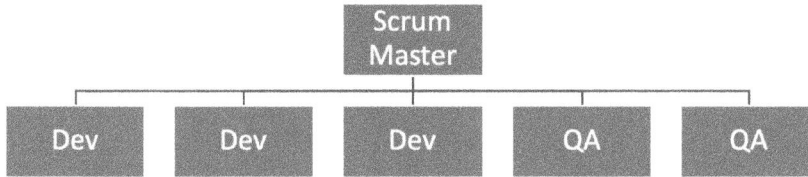

Figure 15.5: Scrum team with dev and QA team combined

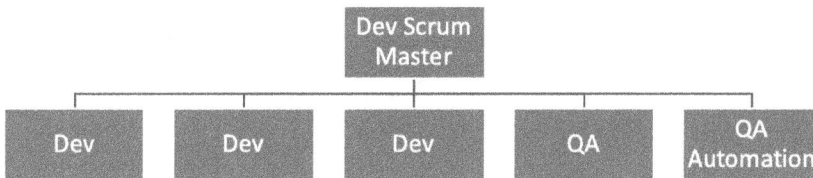

Figure 15.6: QA and automation part of scrum team

Scrum team model 2

If the project is very big, spanning more than five scrum teams, then it is better to have a common automation team, which can optimize the effort. The following can be an automation scrum team model.

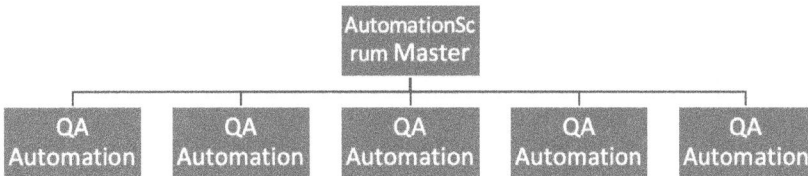

Figure 15.7: Automation as a separate team

Also, if the team is big, then there should be a separate integration QA team which should focus on the Integration testing of the overall product.

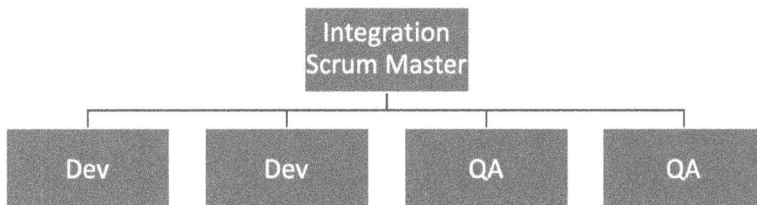

Figure 15.8: Integration scrum team

Test data, test environment

Test data will be required during testing. This means the data should be fed to the system based on which testing needs to be done. A test environment with data should be created before the testing starts. Most often, the team does not prepare the data upfront. This causes delays in testing. For example, for testing a graph that compresses data for 12 months and shows on the screen, the team needs to have different datasets spanning over 12 months to test the graph.

Many such scenarios can be there. Some of them are as follows:

- 12 months of data is required to test a feature:
    - Generate 12 months of data programmatically
    - Download the data from the internet
    - Get the data from other teams within the organization
    - Buy the data if the above three are not enough

- A test requires us to wait for 4 hours
    - Wait for 4 hours to do the test in a controlled environment
    - Instead of waiting for 4 hours, tweak the product to wait for a shorter period (15mins, let us say) and do the testing
    - Check for the possibility of advancing the clock in an isolated system and see if the test can be done

- Sampling is done at 1 hour intervals
    - Wait for sampling to happen at 1 hour intervals.
    - Another option could be to tweak the product and do the testing by having a sampling time of 5 minutes.

- The test needs to run for 30 days before certification can be done
    - If it is required for certification, then nothing can be done.
    - However, a pre-release, near-final version can be used to do the runs. That way, time will be saved. While the release activities are ongoing, the pre-release version can be used for certification testing.

Download test data from these locations from the internet.

- **https://www.kaggle.com/datasets/jacksoncrow/stock-market-dataset**
- **https://apidocs.frankiefinancial.com/docs/test-data**

The following tools can be used for test data generation:

- **https://www.lambdatest.com/learning-hub/test-data**

- https://www.datprof.com/solutions/what-is-test-data/
- https://www.mockaroo.com/
- https://tuskr.app/learn/test-data

Defining states, transitions of bugs, and stories

Bug transition states need to be well-defined so that everyone involved understands the lifecycle of a bug and what each state signifies. Here are the typical states a bug might transition through:

- **New**: When a bug or story is first reported, it is in the *New* state, which indicates that the issue has yet to be reviewed. A bug can be created by anyone, including QA engineers, dev engineers, product managers, and support engineers. A story is normally created by a product manager, scrum master, or project manager.

- **Assigned**: Once a bug is reviewed and deemed valid, it is assigned to a developer or a team member responsible for fixing it. The assignment has to be done by the project manager or scrum master.

- **In Progress**: The bug moves to the **In Progress** state when a developer starts working on it. This state reflects that the bug is being actively addressed. A developer can be a product code developer, or an automation engineer or a QA engineer. For example, QA engineer can have a story to *Create data sets for testing*. This can be marked as In Progress.

- **Resolved**: After the developer fixes the bug, it transitions to the **Resolved state**. The bug is believed to be fixed in this state, but QA has not yet verified it.

- **Verified**: Once QA has tested the fix and confirmed that the bug is indeed resolved, the bug moves to the **Verified** state. This indicates that the solution works as intended.

- **Closed**: The bug is marked as **Closed** if the fix is successful and no further action is required. This state signifies that the issue is officially resolved.

- **Reopened**: If QA finds that the issue persists or the fix causes other problems, the bug can be **Reopened**. It then transitions back to **Assigned** or **In Progress** for further work.

- **Wont Fix:** Some bugs are not worth fixing due to low impact or high risk of regression. These bugs are marked as **Wont Fix** after approval from the product manager.

- **Deferred**: Occasionally, a bug may be deferred due to time constraints or the need to prioritize other issues. These issues will be revisited at a later date.

By clearly defining these states, the team can manage and prioritize bug fixes more effectively, ensuring that critical issues are addressed promptly while focusing on overall project quality and stability. These are pretty much well-known to everyone in the software development world.

Usually, everyone is good at bug management because it is quantized. It is very clear what each person is working on. Very crisply defined.

The same cannot be said about user stories. User stories require much work and understanding before they can be broken down properly. Follow agile principles to create user stories and smaller user stories for better handling of the requirements. If the user stories are handled well, the number of bugs will be lower. The project will have a predictable finishing time.

Conclusion

In conclusion, manual software verification performed by the QA team is a vital aspect of the software development lifecycle. Through meticulous test design, execution, and defect reporting, the QA team plays a pivotal role in ensuring the quality and reliability of software products. By embracing best practices, effective collaboration, and a thorough understanding of the product's architecture, QA professionals can contribute significantly to the overall success of a project. Manual QA helps identify and resolve issues, enhances the user experience, mitigates risks, and instills confidence in the software's functionality. By mastering the principles and techniques discussed in this chapter, software development teams can strive for excellence and deliver robust, high-quality solutions to end-users. Manual QA is not just a gatekeeper; it is an integral part of the development process that empowers teams to create exceptional software products.

In the next chapter, continuous integration and delivery will be discussed. Whatever is being developed, the same needs to be continuously integrated, tested and delivered to the end customer or be made ready for the end customer.

Points to remember

- Developers spend 50% of their time on architecture, design, and development, while the remaining 50% is dedicated to resolving issues raised by the QA team and stabilizing the product.

- Test design is a critical phase in the software development lifecycle, during which the QA team meticulously plans and documents the testing strategy for the product's features.

- Manual QA involves creating comprehensive test cases based on the understanding of the product's architecture and design.

- Effective execution of manual tests involves creating test cases, executing them systematically, and documenting the results.

- Defect reporting is essential to manual QA, and accurate and comprehensive defect reports facilitate efficient issue resolution.

- Collaboration between the QA team and developers is crucial throughout the verification process. It promotes effective communication and iterative bug reporting and resolution.

- Software development teams can enhance the quality and reliability of their products by adhering to industry best practices, continuously improving testing methodologies, and staying updated with industry trends.

Multiple choice questions

1. **What is the primary role of the QA team in software development?**

   a) Writing code

   b) Resolving customer issues

   c) Ensuring software quality and reliability

   d) Managing project timelines

2. **Which phase of the software development lifecycle involves planning and documenting the testing strategy?**

   a) Design

   b) Development

   c) Testing

   d) Deployment

3. **What is the purpose of test design in manual software verification?**

   a) Creating a comprehensive test plan stating how the product will be tested

   b) Debugging code

   c) Deploying the software

   d) Managing project resources

4. **What does test execution involve in manual software verification?**

   a) Writing test plans

   b) Executing test cases and documenting results

   c) Analyzing product performance

   d) All of the above

5. **Why is effective defect reporting important in manual QA?**

    a) To assign blame to developers

    b) To communicate issues clearly and facilitate resolution

    c) To delay the project timeline

    d) To bypass the development team

6. **What is the significance of collaboration between the QA team and developers in manual software verification?**

    a) To compete for recognition

    b) To increase project costs

    c) To foster effective communication and iterative bug resolution

    d) To assign blame for issues

7. **Why is continuous improvement important in manual software verification?**

    a) To avoid testing altogether

    b) To maintain the status quo

    c) To optimize testing methodologies and stay updated with industry trends

    d) To minimize communication with stakeholders

8. **What percentage of time do developers typically spend on architecture, design, and development?**

    a) 25%

    b) 50%

    c) 75%

    d) 100%

9. **What is the ultimate goal of manual software verification?**

    a) To create bugs in the software

    b) To delay the release of the product

    c) To ensure software quality and deliver a robust solution to end-users

    d) To avoid collaboration with the development team

Answer

1. c

2. a

3. a

4. d

5. b

6. c

7. c

8. b

9. c

Exercises

- Take a software product of your choice and create a test plan for one of its key features. Include test objectives, test cases, and expected results. Consider both functional and non-functional requirements in your test design.

- Imagine you are executing a set of manual test cases for a web application. Choose one test case and document the steps you would take to execute it. Include any necessary test data and expected results. Consider different scenarios and edge cases.

- Create a defect report template that includes essential information such as bug description, steps to reproduce, actual and expected results, severity, and priority. Use this template to report a hypothetical defect in a software product.

- Collaborate with a developer or another QA team member to analyze and resolve a reported defect. Document the steps taken to investigate the issue, propose a solution, and verify the fix. Reflect on the effectiveness of the collaboration process.

- Research and explore a popular test management tool used for manual software verification. Set up a test project, create test suites, and execute test cases using the tool. Evaluate its features and usability for managing manual tests.

Join our book's Discord space

Join the book's Discord Workspace for Latest updates, Offers, Tech happenings around the world, New Release and Sessions with the Authors:

https://discord.bpbonline.com

CHAPTER 16

Continuous Integration and Delivery

Introduction

In today's fast-paced software development landscape, **continuous integration/continuous deployment (CI/CD)** has become essential for automating the software delivery process. CI/CD enables development teams to streamline building, testing, and deployment, resulting in faster feedback loops, improved collaboration, and more frequent and reliable releases. This chapter explores the fundamental concepts, best practices, and tools associated with CI/CD, covering topics such as code discipline, version control, testing strategies, infrastructure setup, and build traceability.

By integrating CI/CD practices, teams can catch bugs earlier, ensure code stability, and accelerate the delivery of new features. We will delve into the stages of the CI/CD pipeline, including CI, CD, and testing strategies. Additionally, we will discuss the infrastructure requirements, popular tools, and the benefits of integrating issue-tracking systems like JIRA with version control platforms. Whether you are a developer, DevOps engineer, or project manager, this chapter will equip you with the knowledge to optimize your software delivery process and achieve faster, more reliable releases.

Structure

In this chapter, the following topics will be discussed:

- Version control and configuration management

- Continuous integration
- Continuous deployment
- Setting up infrastructure for CI/CD
- Continuously testing
- Deploying in simulators
- Running e2e tests on embedded software
- Build traceability
- CI/CD team organization

Objectives

By the end of the chapter, the readers will have a comprehensive understanding of the critical importance of version control and configuration management in the software development process. They will be equipped with the knowledge and best practices required to implement disciplined code check-ins, ensure code traceability, and maintain high-quality standards through automated compliance checks and rigorous unit testing. Additionally, readers will learn how to effectively utilize configuration management tools to establish a robust CI and CD process, facilitating seamless code integration and project deployability. By mastering these concepts and practices, readers will be able to enhance their development processes, ensure code quality and stability, and foster efficient collaboration within their development teams.

Version control and configuration management

The code needs to be tightly version-controlled. The team needs to maintain proper discipline while checking in code. Using a good configuration tool like GitHub, Bitbucket, or CM Synergy by Telelogic does not guarantee that proper discipline will be maintained. In order to maintain proper discipline, some rules have to be followed. The rules are as follows, which need to be set automatically in the tool instead of doing manual policing. Manual policing cannot scale up if the project has too many people. It works well with a very small team, maybe a maximum of five developers:

- Only code that compiles should be checked in.
- The checked-in code should reference a bug or user story against which the check-in is being done. To track better, it is always good to have code check-ins associated with a bug or user story.
- While checking in, there should be appropriate comments.
- All the dependent code also needs to be checked in.

- All necessary compliance checks need to be completed before checking in.

- Before a release is done, the release should be tagged with a label indicating which version of the code is tagged with the label.

- A unit test is a must before check-in. Even if other tools are not run, unit tests should be a must. Unit test line coverage should be at least 80%. Otherwise, the code will be difficult to maintain as the number of lines of code grows.

The branching strategy needs to be defined using the configuration management tool so that the CI process is set. A typical branching is shown as follows:

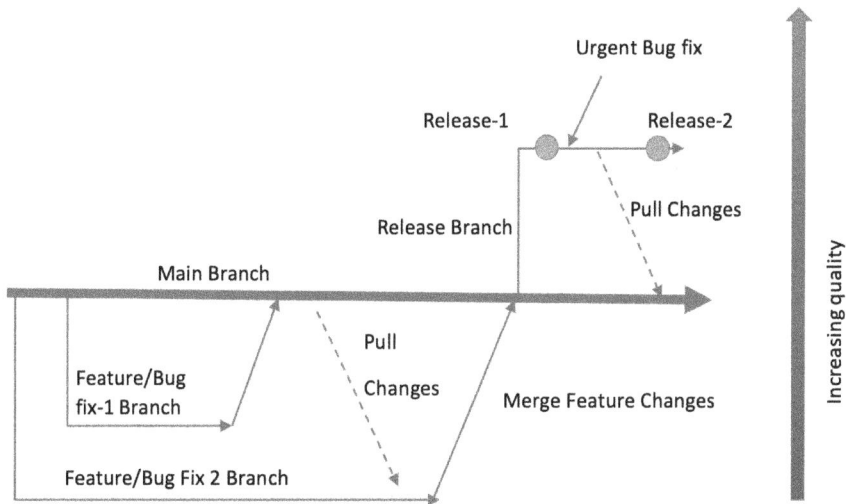

Figure 16.1: *An ideal branching diagram*

Figure 16.1 shows branching, and CI processes essential for maintaining code discipline and ensuring CI.

The strategy needs to be defined so that the CI process is set. The following are the descriptions of the branches and the rules to be followed for CI. *Figure 16.1* illustrates the branching and CI processes crucial for maintaining code discipline and ensuring seamless CI. It visually represents a hierarchical structure where the stability of branches increases from bottom to top, beginning with the most unstable branch at the bottom and culminating with the most stable branch at the top. The project should have a drawing like this to make people understand the branching diagram. Otherwise, some people will understand, and some people will not understand the branching model. The descriptions are as follows:

- **Main branch**: This is where all the main code resides and should always be green. This means the CI tools should always be able to compile this branch at any time of the day. This branch should always be stable. Any compliance checks that must be done on a nightly or weekly basis can be done in the main branch.

- **Release branch**: When a release is made, to keep track of the release and to ensure quick bug fixes on top of the release branch, a branch is created. The point at which the branch is created should be tagged. For example, in this case, a release has happened from the branch named **Release-1**. So, the branch should be tagged with the label **Release-1**. Now, what is **Release-2** used for? If a bug is reported in **Release-1** immediately after release, then the same branch is extended, and a **Release-2** is created. Now, why not from the main branch? This is because, by the time **Release-2** is done, some other changes may have come to the main branch from the other feature branches. Also, once the release has been done, the changes from the **Release-2** branch have to be pulled to the Main Branch. The team needs to appoint a branch gatekeeper who can keep track of all these and help the team in case there are issues.

- **Feature/Bugfix-1 or Feature/Bugfix-2 branch**: Branch in which the feature is being developed. Or this is the branch in which a bug is being fixed. This branch has to be linked to the bug field. JIRA has the ability to link branches. Please see the JIRA tutorial on how this can be done.

- **Pull changes**: If a branch has been merged to the main branch, then those changes have to be pulled back into the working branch of the feature. This has to be a regular feature; otherwise, some of the branches will fall behind, and during merges, there will be a lot of conflicts.

- **Merging branches**: Once the features or bug fixes are completed, the branch has to be merged into the main branch. In the other working branches, these changes need to be pulled, and the branch needs to be updated with the merged changes.

When checking in the code, maintaining a clear and informative history of changes is crucial for the success of any project. A well-structured Git commit message provides context and clarity, making it easier to understand the purpose of a change, track down bugs, and collaborate effectively with team members. This document outlines a standard template for Git commit messages to ensure consistency and readability.

A well-crafted Git commit message typically consists of the following components:

- **Subject line**: A brief summary of the change (50 characters or less)
- **Blank line:** A single blank line separating the subject line from the body
- **Body**: A detailed description of the change (wrap at 72 characters)
- **Footer**: Optional metadata such as issue tracker IDs or breaking changes

The following is one example of a properly formatted Git commit message:

- **Subject line:** Add user authentication feature
- **Body**:
  - Implement user authentication using JWT tokens.

    ○   Update the login and registration APIs to generate and validate tokens.

    ○   Add middleware to protect routes that require authentication.

- **Footer:**
  ```
  Fixes #JIRA-PROJECT-NAME-100
  ```

Using a consistent template for Git commit messages helps maintain a clear and organized project history. By following the guidelines outlined in this document, developers can ensure their commit messages provide valuable context and improve collaboration within the team.

Continuous integration

CI builds need to be triggered as soon as it is merged. This will give early feedback about the quality of the code checked in. CI can have many stages in the build process. Some of the steps are shown in the following figure:

Figure 16.2: Build pipeline process

Additionally, the figure outlines the stages of the CI/CD pipeline.

The above can be done for each of the feature branches as well as the main branch. However, it depends on the build machines' availability. If the resource is not a constraint, then it is done for each of the branches. If the resource is a constraint, then only the feature branches can go through the build cycle during the daytime. During the night, the main branch build can happen. This is an option, but not a rule. Teams need to define their own rules, balancing resource usage.

The following list shows some of the key aspects of accomplishing continuous improvement:

- There are many tools that can be used to do all the above steps. Popular tools are Gitlab, TeamCity, and Jenkins to do the above steps.

- The build code step is to build the code which has been checked in.

- The unit test is to do the line coverage and functional coverage. Line and functional coverage should be above 85% to make the product stable. It will help to build quality products. If this is low, then more time will be taken for QA tests during the testing phase. So, writing unit tests is a must. If the team thinks it is wasting time, they need to understand that the later time will be much longer.

- Integration testing is crucial in the CI/CD pipeline, as it verifies the interactions between different modules and ensures they work together as expected. This type of testing helps identify issues that unit tests might miss, such as interface mismatches or data format inconsistencies. By thoroughly conducting integration tests, teams can detect and resolve issues early, ensuring a smoother and more stable deployment process.

- The static analyzer detects issues in the static code. This means the code is not running, and the files are scanned for issues. Some of the static analyzers are sonarqube, coverity, fortify, snyk.

- Compliance checkers like Misra compliance checker, Autosar compliance checker, and OWASP dependency checker can be integrated into the pipeline. The builds can be made to fail if the compliance checks fail.

- After everything is done, the builds need to be deployed in a testing environment, which is part of continuous deployment, which will be discussed in the next section.

- While running the end to end tests, dynamic memory checking tests can be done. Also, dynamic security testing can be done while running the end-to-end tests. Tools like Valgrind for C, Appscan for dynamic security testing, Jmeter for performance analysis. A list of dynamic analysis tools can be found at this location **https://github.com/analysis-tools-dev/dynamic-analysis**.

- Each build should also generate a report of the list of JIRAs or bug reports associated with the build. It should also list the branches that have been used to generate the build. Complete traceability should be maintained between the requirements, JIRA or bug report list, build, and release. This will help to trace things back if required.

  o While unit tests are designed to test individual components or functions of the code, they focus on a specific part of the code to ensure it works as intended. Unit tests focus on small parts of the application, ensuring each function or method performs correctly in isolation.

  o Integration tests verify interactions between different modules or components. They ensure that the combined parts of the application work together as expected.

  o These tests help identify issues that unit tests might miss, such as interface mismatches or data format inconsistencies. By thoroughly conducting integration tests, teams can detect and resolve issues early, ensuring a smoother and more stable deployment process.

  o Integration tests have a broader scope as they test the interaction between multiple parts of the application.

  o Integration tests take longer to run compared to unit tests. So, before checking in, it is not always feasible to run the integration tests. So it is optional to run in the CI pipeline. However, it can be run overnight or over the weekend. In the CI pipeline, normally, the stages should finish quickly so that engineers can check the code quickly.

CI/CD accelerates the software development process by automating integration and deployment, reducing the time between writing and releasing code. It ensures that only high-quality code reaches production, minimizing the risk of bugs. This automation increases efficiency and allows developers to focus more on building features. Overall, CI/CD enhances the feedback loop with end users, leading to faster improvements and better software quality. This improves the morale and motivation of the team members, too. Whatever they are doing gets deployed in production very quickly. Also, it helps to improve the quality of the product by detecting various types of bugs much before deployment into production. All larger companies rely on CI/CD for build and deployment. For example, Netflix, LinkedIn, Google, or any other large company, everyone relies on a highly automated CI/CD pipeline. The efficient pipelines deliver builds to production a few times a day. Much of the information is available online, so it can be searched online and researched online.

Continuous deployment

CD is the practice of automatically deploying every change that passes all stages of the production pipeline to the live environment. It extends CI by deploying all code changes to testing and/or production environments after the build stage. When properly implemented, continuous deployment allows developers to focus on building software rather than manually pushing it through various stages.

The key advantage of continuous deployment is that it reduces the time between writing code and running it in production, thus accelerating the feedback loop with end users. Automated testing and validation processes ensure that only quality code reaches production, which in turn minimizes the risk of introducing bugs.

The following tools facilitate this process by providing robust frameworks for automating CI and CD:

- Microsoft Azure DevOps
- Google Cloud Build
- AWS CodeDeploy
- Jenkins
- CircleCI
- Puppet

Continuous deployment is about deploying the builds continuously into the testing environment or to the production environment.

In most mature organizations, the deployment system is such that, once built, the builds are deployed into the QA environment and to the production environment. These are true for web services, the SaaS environment, and intranet applications. However, these are not always possible for embedded environments, like mobile applications, automotive applications, and aerospace software. These softwares have to undergo multiple levels of testing and certifications before they can be deployed to the devices.

In less mature organizations, deployments are manual. All deployments and verification are manual. There can be multiple deployment scenarios:

- Directly deploying in the QA environment
- Deploy the entire release to the production environment.
- Canary deployment to a few customers:
  - Deploy a few features in production for a few customers
  - Deploy a few features in production for all customers
  - Deploy in production a few features for a few user roles for all customers
- Blue Green deployment:
  - Blue Green deployment is a strategy that reduces downtime and risk by running two identical production environments.
  - The Blue environment is the existing live system, while the Green environment is the new version of the application.
  - When the Green environment is ready and fully tested, the traffic is switched from Blue to Green, making the new version live.
  - This approach enables prompt rollback if any issues arise, as the previous version (Blue) is still available and can be resumed.

Releases are normally done manually in most of the organizations. Builds are normally packaged and released manually. This is not the ideal scenario. Ideally, it should be deployed automatically, tested automatically, and then deployed in production automatically. The maturity of the organization improves as the deployment and testing automation improve. The following table shows the maturity levels and how to measure them:

Maturity Indicator	Build, Deployment, Testing methodology
Low Maturity	Build is manual, Deployment is manual, verification is manual, compliance checks are done manually.
Medium Maturity	Build is automated, deployment is manual, verification is manual, compliance checks are manual
High Maturity	Build is automated, deployment in completely automated, verification is manual, compliance checks are completely automated.

Table 16.1: Release management maturity

Once deployed, it is not the end. It has to be downloaded and tested once more and made sure it is working fine. It is quite a common occurrence that the builds uploaded are not working because of a flaw in the deployment process.

In some of the devices, deploying via automation can be difficult because of the environment. In those cases, simulators can be created, and the software developed in simulators and tested in the simulators. For example, deployment should be done in simulators for embedded devices. It should be thoroughly tested and then deployed in the actual hardware. This strategy should be followed when deployment to actual systems may be difficult.

Setting up infrastructure for CI/CD

As listed above, there is a lot of work involved in making the CI/CD work. In order to make the CI framework, the infrastructure has to be created.

A build system has a master and agents. The master is what controls, and the agents are the ones who perform the builds, as shown in the following figure:

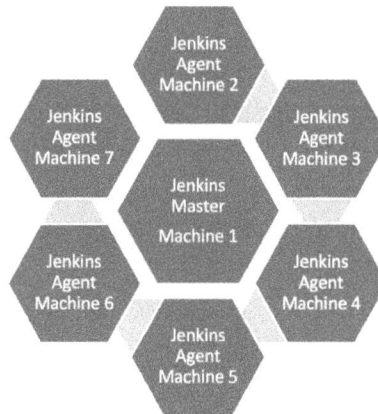

Figure 16.3: Infrastructure for CI/CD

Building the infrastructure requires hardware resources, and it has to be planned. Infrastructure has to be maintained and upgraded as and when needed.

As can be seen, the overall infrastructure requires hardware and software tools at every stage. All these require maintenance, too. Both budget and manpower need to be allotted to get this up and running and then maintained. If the software development and QA team is big, then this infrastructure takes quite a lot of effort. A team of at least 2-3 engineers needs to be allotted to get this done. To optimize effort, in larger organizations, a consolidated team is created that caters to all the development teams.

Issues related to the CI/CD infrastructure also need to be tracked. A bug-tracking tool needs to be used to track the issues related to CI/CD infrastructure. Any issue faced by the dev team needs to be filed as a bug report. These issues need to be tracked, prioritized and then fixed.

The infrastructure should always be tracked for optimization so that the cost of the systems remains minimal. It should have a system of continuously measuring the CPU/memory and should optimize the usage of the machines. If the machines are not in use, they should be put to sleep to save power costs.

Reports need to be generated and should be mailed to the project manager on a weekly basis. That way, the manager has a track of what is happening in the build infrastructure. Key indicators should be how many builds succeeded, how many builds failed, and what is the CPU/memory utilization of the machines that are doing the builds.

Continuously testing

Continuous testing is an integral part of the CI process. It involves the automated execution of tests at every stage of the software development lifecycle. The primary objective is to provide immediate feedback on the quality and functionality of the software, ensuring that any defects or issues are identified and addressed quickly.

In a CI environment, continuous testing is essential to maintain the stability and reliability of the codebase. As developers commit changes to the version control system, these changes trigger automated builds and tests. The tests can range from unit tests, which verify individual components, to integration tests, which ensure that various components work together as expected, and end-to-end tests that simulate real user scenarios.

The continuous testing process is designed to catch bugs early in the development cycle, reducing the cost and effort required to fix them. It also helps maintain a high code quality level, as any regression or new bug introduced by a recent change is quickly detected.

Moreover, continuous testing supports a culture of quality and accountability within the development team. By integrating testing into the CI pipeline, developers are encouraged to write tests for their code and ensure that it meets the required standards before it is merged into the main branch. This practice leads to more robust and maintainable software over time.

Deploying in simulators

For mobile application testing, simulators are a boon. They allow developers to test their applications in a controlled and consistent environment, replicating various device configurations and operating system versions. This ensures that the app performs well across different devices without the need for physical hardware, which can be costly and time-consuming to acquire and maintain.

Simulators provide a flexible platform for testing, enabling quick iterations and debugging. Developers can easily capture logs, take screenshots, and simulate various user interactions, which are crucial for identifying and resolving issues early in the development process. Furthermore, simulators support automated testing frameworks, allowing for extensive test coverage and repeatability, which significantly enhances the overall quality of the application.

Deploying in simulators also facilitates CI/CD pipelines, where automated tests can be executed as part of the build process. This integration ensures that any new code changes are thoroughly tested before being deployed to production, minimizing the risk of defects slipping through and impacting end-users.

Example: Android Studio is a good example of a simulator, which can be used to test mobile applications. It can help in testing many configurations, without using the hardware.

This is especially true for any embedded hardware; if the test environment is set up in a simulator and extensive testing can be done in the simulated environment before deploying in the actual hardware, the development process will be much faster.

Running e2e tests on embedded hardware

Running end-to-end tests on embedded hardware presents several challenges:

- **Variety of platforms**: Unlike mobile or desktop environments, embedded systems can operate on various non-standardized platforms.

- **Custom OS:** Many embedded devices use custom operating systems or firmware, complicating the testing setup.

- **Limited interfaces**: These devices often have restricted interfaces for interaction and data capture, hindering automation and monitoring.

Creating a robust test setup is crucial to running e2e tests on embedded hardware effectively:

- **Select the right hardware**: Ensure the test environment replicates the production hardware as closely as possible to get accurate results.

- **Test bench configuration**: Set up a test bench that can simulate user inputs (e.g., key presses, touch inputs) and capture outputs. Tools like GPIO extenders, **programmable logic controllers** (**PLCs**), and automated input devices can be employed.

- **Data capture mechanisms**: Implement mechanisms to capture outputs from the **device under test** (**DUT**). This can include signal processors, cameras for screen captures, or direct digital outputs.

In cases where the embedded hardware does not support standard automation tools, a custom test system needs to be developed:

- **Simulator integration**: Where feasible, integrate simulators to replicate certain parts of the hardware environment, reducing the dependency on physical devices. This approach speeds up testing and simplifies setup.

- **Custom scripts**: Write custom scripts to simulate user interactions and automate test sequences. These scripts can be developed using languages such as Python or using specific testing frameworks suitable for embedded systems.

- **Output verification**: Develop methods to verify outputs. For non-standard outputs, create adapters or use middleware to interpret and validate the results.

Consider a scenario where you need to test an embedded device that controls home automation:

- **Test bench**: Set up a test bench with the embedded device connected to various sensors and actuators that mimic a real home environment.

- **Automation scripts**: Write scripts to simulate user interactions, such as turning lights on and off, adjusting thermostat settings, and checking camera feeds.

- **Data collection**: Use digital capture tools to log the device's responses, ensuring they match the expected outcomes.

- **CI integration**: Integrate these tests into your CI pipeline, ensuring they run automatically with every code commit.

Build traceability

Traceability allows for the monitoring of every modification within the codebase, from initial requirements to final deployment, simplifying both debugging and compliance auditing. It is crucial that all changes are correlated with specific user stories or requirements and that each test case aligns with these stories to guarantee thorough coverage.

CI/CD pipeline reports provide an in-depth overview of the build and test stages and should include:

- **Build status**: A summary indicating whether the build succeeded or failed, accompanied by detailed logs.

- **Test results:** Detailed outcomes of all automated tests, showing passes, failures, and any errors encountered.

- **Code quality metrics**: An evaluation of code quality, including data from static code analysis tools, code coverage statistics, and potential security issues.

- **Performance metrics**: Information on the application's performance during the build process, highlighting any regressions or improvements.

- **Artifact details:** Details about the artifacts produced during the build, including version numbers and their storage locations.

Traceability ensures comprehensive oversight and accountability across all stages of development.

JIRA to Bitbucket mapping: Configure the necessary settings to link JIRA issues directly with Bitbucket branches and commits for smooth integration between JIRA and Bitbucket. This facilitates automatic updates and traceability, aligning each code modification with a specific JIRA issue. This approach creates an integrated workflow where every change is well-documented and easily traceable, promoting transparency and accountability.

Sustaining this integration helps generate comprehensive reports covering various elements such as build status, test results, and code quality metrics. This ensures the development process remains efficient and accurate. The CI/CD pipeline becomes instrumental for continuous improvement, spotlighting areas that need attention and delivering actionable insights to enhance the entire development lifecycle.

CI/CD team organization

A diverse and skilled team is essential to implement and maintain a CI/CD pipeline. The core team members and their required skills include:

- **DevOps engineers**: These professionals need expertise in automation tools, CI/CD practices, containerization (Docker, Kubernetes), and infrastructure as code (Terraform, Ansible).

- **Software developers**: Proficient in writing clean, efficient code and familiar with automated testing frameworks. They should also understand version control systems (Git) and be able to integrate their code seamlessly into the CI/CD pipeline.

- **QA engineers**: Skilled in creating, executing, and maintaining automated tests. They need to understand test automation tools (Selenium, JUnit, TestNG) and have a strong grasp of testing methodologies.

- **Security engineers**: Focused on integrating security practices into the CI/CD pipeline (DevSecOps). They should be knowledgeable about static and dynamic code analysis, vulnerability scanning tools, and security compliance standards.

- **Release managers**: Responsible for overseeing the deployment process, ensuring that releases are well-coordinated and meet quality standards. They should possess strong project management skills and a thorough understanding of the CI/CD workflow.

- **System administrators**: Experts in managing and maintaining the underlying infrastructure that supports the CI/CD pipeline. They need to be proficient in server management, network configuration, and monitoring tools.

- **Technical writers**: Essential for documenting the CI/CD processes, tools, and practices. They should have excellent writing skills and the ability to translate technical concepts into clear, accessible documentation for various stakeholders.

Having a well-rounded team with these skills ensures that the CI/CD pipeline is robust, secure, and efficient, ultimately leading to higher-quality software and faster delivery times.

Conclusion

This chapter has comprehensively explored the critical aspects of version control, configuration management, and CI in the software development process. Developers can ensure code stability, catch bugs earlier, and accelerate software releases by emphasizing disciplined code check-ins, code traceability, automated compliance checks, and rigorous unit testing. Integrating configuration management tools and version control systems facilitates efficient collaboration and project scalability. Furthermore, adopting CI practices and using automated compliance checks contribute to code quality, adherence to industry standards, and overall development productivity. By mastering these concepts and practices, project managers have the knowledge and skills to optimize their software development processes and deliver high-quality software in a fast-paced and competitive environment.

Builds will happen automatically if CI is adopted. It may fail. Gathering metrics is important to understand to improve on failures, build times, etc. Besides the overall project, metrics gathering is also important in order to make some changes. Hence, in the next chapter, the metrics that need to be gathered and the tools required to gather the metrics will be discussed.

Points to remember

- Version control is crucial for maintaining a well-structured and organized codebase, enabling efficient collaboration and code traceability.

- Disciplined code check-ins ensure code stability, minimize conflicts, and facilitate seamless collaboration within development teams.

- Automated compliance checks and rigorous unit testing help maintain code quality, adhere to industry standards, and catch potential issues early in the development cycle.

- Configuration management tools like Terraform and CloudFormation automate infrastructure provisioning and configuration, ensuring consistency and scalability across different environments.

- A robust CI process enables seamless code integration, accelerates software releases, and fosters efficient collaboration within development teams.

- Version control systems like Git, GitHub, and Bitbucket facilitate code branching, merging, and collaboration, enhancing overall development productivity.

- Integrating version control with issue-tracking systems like JIRA enhances traceability, simplifies project management, and improves team coordination.

- Static code analyzers, compliance checkers, and dependency checkers help maintain code integrity, identify potential issues, and ensure adherence to coding standards.

- Code reviews, code quality metrics, and comprehensive unit testing are essential for ensuring code stability and reliability and minimizing regression issues.

- Prioritizing version control, configuration management, and CI practices leads to enhanced code quality, faster software delivery, and increased overall productivity within development teams.

Multiple choice questions

1. **Which of the following is a popular version control system used in software development?**

   a) Subversion (SVN)

   b) Jenkins

   c) Docker

   d) Kubernetes

2. **What is the purpose of configuration management in the software development process?**

   a) Managing code branches and merges

   b) Conducting code reviews

   c) Running unit tests

   d) For documentation.

3. **Which tool is commonly used for automating infrastructure provisioning and configuration?**

   a) Git

   b) Jenkins

   c) Terraform

   d) JIRA

4. **What is the primary objective of continuous integration (CI)?**

   a) Automating infrastructure deployment

   b) Ensuring code stability and quality

   c) Managing code versions and branches

   d) Conducting end-to-end testing

5. **Which of the following is an example of a compliance check tool used in software development?**

   a) SonarQube

   b) Docker

   c) Kubernetes

   d) Jenkins

6. **What is the purpose of code reviews in the software development process?**

   a) Ensuring compliance with coding standards

   b) Automating code deployments

c) Managing infrastructure as code

d) Conducting load testing

7. **Which type of testing is typically performed during the CI/CD process to ensure code stability?**

a) Unit testing

b) compliance checks

c) Regression testing

d) all of the above

Answers

1. a
2. a
3. c
4. b
5. a
6. a
7. d

Exercises

- Create a new branch in your version control system of choice and make changes to a code file. Commit the changes and merge the branch back into the main branch.

- Using a configuration management tool like Terraform, provision a virtual machine on a cloud provider of your choice. Configure the virtual machine with specific settings and test its functionality.

- Set up a basic CI/CD pipeline using a tool like Jenkins. Configure the pipeline to trigger a build and run unit tests whenever changes are pushed to the version control repository. Ensure that the pipeline successfully deploys the application to a testing environment.

- Perform a code review on a colleague's code. Identify any potential issues, provide constructive feedback, and suggest improvements to enhance code quality and maintainability.

- Implement an automated compliance check using a tool like SonarQube. Configure the tool to analyze code for adherence to coding standards, security vulnerabilities, and potential bugs. Fix any issues identified by the tool and ensure the code passes the compliance check.

CHAPTER 17
Metrics to Gather and Tools

Introduction

In the field of software projects, metrics play a crucial role in measuring progress, quality, and efficiency. This chapter provides an overview of the various metrics used in software development, offering insights into their significance and practical applications. From requirements metrics to architecture/design, coding, QA, post-delivery, and security metrics, each category is explored to help project managers, developers, and stakeholders make informed decisions and track project success. By understanding and utilizing these metrics effectively, software projects can optimize processes, enhance quality, and drive continuous improvement.

Structure

The chapter covers the following topics:

- Requirements metrics
- Architecture/design level metrics
- Coding level metrics
- QA metrics
- Post release metrics

- Security and compliance
- Tools

Objectives

From this chapter, a project manager will gain valuable insights into the importance and practical applications of metrics in software projects. They will understand how metrics provide objective measurements of progress, quality, and efficiency, enabling data-driven decision-making. By identifying and utilizing relevant metrics, project managers can track project progress, make informed decisions, and optimize processes. Metrics also help in identifying areas for improvement, driving continuous improvement efforts. Additionally, metrics serve as a means to communicate project status to stakeholders and foster transparency. By leveraging metrics effectively, project managers can enhance project outcomes, meet stakeholder expectations, and drive successful project delivery.

Requirements metrics

The metrics capture the different requirement-related data. These data need to be projected to the senior management to show the agility of the team. The following are the metrics that need to be captured:

- **Number of requirements for the project:** Number of requirements which has been proposed by the product manager to be implemented, including both functional and non-functional requirements. These requirements outline the desired features, performance standards, and constraints that the project should adhere to, reflecting the overall goals and objectives set forth by the stakeholders.

- **Number of requirements address**: This metric reflects the total number of requirements that have been successfully implemented and validated in the software project. It includes both functional and non-functional requirements, ensuring that the project meets its intended goals and objectives. Tracking this metric allows project managers to monitor progress, assess the alignment of the project with stakeholder expectations, and ensure that the software delivers the desired features and performance standards.

- **Change requests raised on top of the requirements:** Change requests raised on top of the requirements refer to the additional features, modifications, or adjustments requested after the initial set of requirements has been established. These change requests reflect the evolving needs and priorities of stakeholders and are crucial for ensuring that the final product aligns with their expectations. The number of change requests that were implemented indicates the project's flexibility and responsiveness to stakeholders' needs, showcasing the ability of the project team to adapt and refine the software to better meet its goals.

If the requirements are stack ranked, then the change request is inserted in between and the priority of the original requirements are adjusted accordingly. For example, in the diagram below, the change request is prioritized after requirement 2 and before requirement 3. So, requirement 3s timeline is pushed to accommodate the change request. The following figure shows how the priority of the original requirements changes based on the change requests.

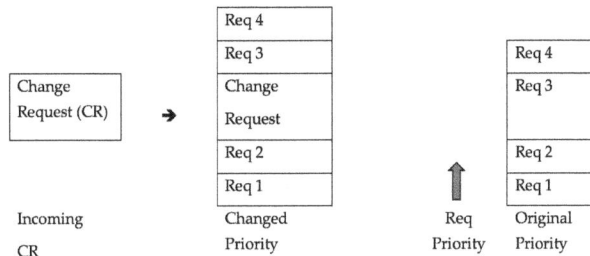

Figure 17.1: Priority changes because of change requests

The details are as follows:

- **Change requests internally raised:** These are the change requests which has been raised by the dependent teams internally. There are always changes during implementation, and dependent teams may raise change requests for these changes.

- **Change requests raised by customers:** Some change requests are also raised by customers, and these should be treated as top priority. These customer-driven change requests often reflect the end-users' evolving needs and preferences, providing valuable insights into how the product can be better aligned with their expectations.

- **Number of change requests addressed**: Addressing these requests promptly not only enhances customer satisfaction but also ensures that the final product is more user-centric and adaptable to market demands. The number of customer-raised change requests that are successfully implemented serves as a testament to the project's commitment to meeting user needs and maintaining high standards of flexibility and responsiveness.

It needs to be captured in a requirements management tool, which can be either JIRA, XCEL or any other requirements management tool. In JIRA, it is easy to manage since reports can be easily generated. Also, there may be more metrics requested; it is really easy to generate if it is in JIRA.

Architecture/design level metrics

Architecture and design level metrics can be used to measure the effectiveness of the team in architecting and designing the product. The following is the list of metrics that can be gathered from the architecture and design phase. The project manager should track these through JIRA and check how long it is taking to come up with the following. Each and every topic, like investigation, architecture, and design, can be epic in JIRA and can be tracked through JIRA. For example, the effort spent, the effort estimated, the actual timeline, etc., can be tracked through JIRA. The project manager must ensure that proper epics and tasks are created in JIRA to track these:

- **Time taken to come up with the architecture:** The time taken to come up with the architecture includes the duration from the initial brainstorming sessions to the finalization of the architectural blueprint. This phase involves extensive research, discussions with stakeholders, prototyping, and iterative refinements to ensure that the architecture is robust and aligns with the project's objectives and constraints. A well-thought-out architectural design is essential for the project's success, as it lays the foundation for all subsequent development activities, ensuring scalability, performance, and maintainability of the final product.

- **Time taken to come up with the design:** The time taken to come up with the design phase involves several critical steps. Initially, it includes brainstorming sessions where ideas are freely shared and discussed among team members and stakeholders. Following this, the team conducts extensive research to gather the necessary information and best practices that will inform the design. Prototyping is another significant component, allowing the team to visualize and test their ideas before finalizing the design. Iterative refinements are made based on feedback and testing results to ensure that the design is optimal. This thorough and thoughtful process ensures that the final design meets the project's objectives and constraints, providing a solid foundation for successful implementation.

- **What percentage of the architecture changed from the beginning to the end:** What percentage of the architecture changed from the beginning of the project to the end of the project? The end of the project is when a deployment has happened and a critical mass of customers has been reached. For example, 100 customers are using the product, where there is a mix of large, medium, and small customers. A significant percentage change in the architecture from the initial design to the final implementation indicates potential issues with the initial architectural planning. Such changes may highlight gaps in the initial understanding of the project requirements, challenges in aligning with evolving stakeholder needs, or unforeseen technical constraints. Monitoring and analyzing these changes is crucial as they provide insights into the robustness and flexibility of the architectural design process, helping to identify areas for improvement in future projects. A large % change in the architecture indicates poor architectural thinking.

Coding level metrics

Coding level metrics provide valuable insights into the development process, helping teams understand their productivity, efficiency, and code quality. By closely monitoring these metrics, development teams can identify areas for improvement, ensure adherence to best practices, and maintain a high standard of code. The following metrics can be gathered to understand various aspects of the code written:

- **Number of lines of code written:** The total number of lines of code in a project can be an important metric. This number helps estimate the amount of work done and can be used as a reference for planning and estimating future projects. By analyzing the total lines of code, teams can understand productivity levels and adjust their strategies accordingly.

- **Time taken to write the number of lines of code**: It is crucial to track the time it takes to write a certain number of lines of code. This metric provides insight into the efficiency of the development process and can help identify bottlenecks or areas where improvements are needed. Understanding the time investment helps in better project planning and resource allocation.

- **Lines of comments as a percentage of lines of code**: Comments in code are vital for maintaining clarity and understanding, especially for collaborative projects. Ideally, comments should constitute about 10% of the total lines of code. This balance ensures that the code is well-documented without being cluttered with excessive annotations. Proper commenting practices facilitate easier maintenance and updates.

- **Unit testing line coverage**: Unit tests should cover at least 85% of the lines of code. High unit test coverage ensures that the majority of the code has been tested for functionality and reliability. This metric helps maintain code quality and reduces the likelihood of bugs slipping through to production.

- **Unit testing functional coverage**: In addition to line coverage, functional coverage is also essential. It should also be around a minimum of 85%. Functional coverage measures whether the tests adequately cover all the different functionalities and scenarios in the code. High functional coverage ensures that the application behaves as expected in various situations.

- **Pass percentage of unit tests**: All unit tests should ideally pass, indicating that the code is functioning correctly according to the test cases. Even though you can have 85% unit test coverage, failing tests is not acceptable. Ensuring a 100% pass rate helps maintain the integrity and reliability of the application.

- **Total number of review comments:** Tracking the number of review comments as a percentage of lines of code can provide insights into code quality. Ideally, 100 lines of code should not generate more than 2 major comments. Regular code reviews and constructive feedback help improve coding standards and minimize errors.

- **Categorization of review comments**: Review comments can be categorized to identify their nature. For instance, some comments might be cosmetic, such as suggestions for camel casing of variable names, while others could highlight real design issues or problems stemming from slippage or forgetfulness. Categorizing comments helps teams address recurring issues and take preventive actions to enhance code quality.

- **Number of bugs fixed by an individual developer**: It is useful to track how many bugs an individual developer has fixed, including the complexity of these bugs. This metric can help differentiate developers based on their problem-solving skills and contributions to the project. It also provides valuable information for performance evaluations and identifying areas for skill development.

- **Velocity of the project**: Project velocity measures how many user stories are completed, how many bugs are fixed, and how many lines of code are written per day. The industry standard is typically between 10 to 15 lines of code per day. Monitoring project velocity helps teams assess their progress and make informed decisions about timelines and resource allocation.

- **Velocity of an engineer**: Tracking the velocity of individual engineers involves measuring how many user stories and bugs they fix. This information is useful during appraisals and helps identify top performers and areas where additional support may be needed. However, it should be an ongoing effort and not limited to appraisal periods.

- **User stories or user story points done vs the time taken to deliver**: This metric helps understand the time required to complete a user story. By analyzing this data, teams can predict the time needed for similar future stories, improving project planning and delivery timelines. It also helps in identifying any inefficiencies in the development process.

- **Number of requirements addressed:** It is important to track how many requirements, especially customer-requested ones, have been addressed. This metric ensures that the project remains aligned with client expectations and helps maintain customer satisfaction.

QA metrics

In the field of software development, the importance of **quality assurance (QA)** metrics cannot be overstated. These metrics serve as invaluable tools for evaluating, managing, and enhancing the quality of software products. By systematically gathering and analyzing QA metrics, development teams can identify strengths and weaknesses in their processes, ensure that high standards are maintained, and deliver robust, reliable software to end-users.

QA metrics encompass various aspects of the testing and development cycle, including unit test coverage, functional coverage, bug tracking, code review feedback, and project velocity. Each of these metrics provides unique insights that contribute to a comprehensive understanding of the overall quality and performance of the software.

Implementing a structured approach to gathering and analyzing QA metrics not only helps in maintaining code quality but also promotes continuous improvement. It allows teams to make data-driven decisions, optimize their workflows, and ultimately create software that meets or exceeds user expectations. In the following sections, we will delve into the key QA metrics and their significance in the software development lifecycle. The following are the different metrics that can be gathered:

- **Number of bugs:** Tracking the number of bugs as a percentage of total lines of code provides valuable insights into code quality. The industry standard is to have fewer than 3 bugs per 100 lines of code. By monitoring this metric, teams can identify areas that require improvement and ensure that the codebase remains robust and error-free. This process involves regular code reviews, comprehensive testing, and prompt bug fixing to maintain high standards of code quality and minimize the impact of bugs on the end-users.

- **Categorization of bugs:** Bugs can be categorized to understand their origins and reasons for occurrence. Categories may include developer mistakes, misunderstanding requirements, integration issues, and forgetfulness. By categorizing bugs, teams can take targeted actions to minimize recurring issues and enhance the overall quality of the software. This categorization allows teams to focus on root causes, implement corrective measures, and improve coding practices to prevent similar issues in the future.

- **Total number of test cases:** Tracking the total number of test cases for a feature helps in understanding the extent of testing required. This metric ensures that comprehensive testing is planned and executed, covering all aspects of the feature. It provides a clear picture of the testing scope and helps in identifying any gaps in test coverage that need to be addressed to ensure the feature's reliability and stability.

- **Total number of test cases executed:** Measuring the total number of test cases executed at any given point provides insights into the testing progress. This metric helps in identifying any bottlenecks in the testing process and ensures that sufficient test coverage is achieved. By keeping track of executed test cases, teams can assess the effectiveness of their testing strategies and make necessary adjustments to improve efficiency and coverage.

- **Total number of test cases not executed:** Some test cases may not be executed due to various reasons, such as dependencies on other features or being blocked by existing bugs. Tracking the number of test cases not executed helps in prioritizing bug fixes and ensuring that all critical test cases are eventually covered. This metric highlights areas that need attention and helps in planning subsequent testing efforts to ensure comprehensive test coverage.

- **Total number of test cases removed from the current release:** In some instances, certain features may not be implemented, leading to the removal of related test cases from the current release. Tracking this metric helps in understanding the scope of the release and ensuring that deferred features are accounted for in future releases. This information is crucial for maintaining an accurate and updated test plan and ensuring that all planned features are eventually tested and delivered.

- **Number of test cases passed:** Measuring the number of test cases that have passed provides a clear indication of the stability and quality of the software. A higher pass rate suggests that the feature is functioning as expected and meets the defined requirements. This metric helps build confidence in the software's performance and reliability, ensuring that it meets user expectations and performs well in real-world scenarios.

- **Number of test cases failed:** Tracking the number of failed test cases helps in identifying areas that require further attention and debugging. Each failed test case should be associated with a corresponding bug report to ensure that issues are promptly addressed and resolved. This metric provides valuable insights into the software's weaknesses and helps teams prioritize their bug-fixing efforts to enhance overall quality.

- **Total number of documentation bugs:** Documentation bugs are issues related to the accuracy and completeness of product documentation. Tracking these bugs ensures that all necessary documentation is created and maintained, providing users with clear and useful information about the product. Accurate documentation is essential for user satisfaction and helps in reducing support requests by providing users with the information they need to use the product effectively.

- **Number of bugs fixed by a verification engineer:** Measuring the number of bugs verified by a QA engineer, along with the complexity of these bugs, helps in assessing the contributions of the engineer. This metric also aids in performance evaluations and identifying areas for skill development. Tracking this information helps in recognizing the efforts of QA engineers and ensuring that they receive the necessary support and training to continue improving their skills.

- **Total number of test cases addressed by automation:** Automated testing plays a crucial role in ensuring consistent and efficient test coverage. Tracking the number of test cases addressed by automation helps in understanding the effectiveness of the automation strategy and reducing the manual testing effort during regression cycles. This metric highlights the benefits of automation in improving test efficiency and coverage, allowing teams to focus on more complex and critical testing activities.

- **Bugs filed per 1000 lines of code:** Monitoring the number of bugs filed per 1000 lines of code helps in predicting the quality of future releases. This metric provides valuable insights into the overall health of the codebase and allows teams to take proactive measures to improve code quality. By maintaining a low bug density, teams can ensure a more stable and reliable software product, enhancing user satisfaction and reducing maintenance efforts.

- **Number of documentation bugs open/fixed:** Tracking the number of open and fixed documentation bugs ensures that all required documentation is completed and up to date. This metric helps in maintaining the accuracy and usefulness of the product documentation. Ensuring that documentation is accurate and comprehensive is vital for user satisfaction and helps in reducing the learning curve for new users.

- **Fix rejects:** The number of times a user story or bug is sent back to the developer due to improper implementation is tracked as fix rejects. This metric indicates the maturity and proficiency of the development team and highlights areas that may require additional training or support. By monitoring fixed rejects, teams can identify common issues and take corrective actions to improve development practices and reduce the number of rejections.

Post release metrics

Post release metrics are gathered to understand how many defects were reported after the product was released. This is an indicator of the quality of the work done. The following are some of the metrics that can be gathered after the project is delivered:

- **Post-release defects and their categorization:** Analyzing the number of defects reported after the product's release is crucial for maintaining the quality and reliability of the software. This metric helps in identifying whether the product meets industry standards, typically aimed at 0.5 defects per 1000 lines of code. By categorizing these defects, teams can prioritize and address the most critical issues first, ensuring a systematic approach to problem-solving. Strategies to fix these defects can include code reviews, patch releases, and hotfixes, which collectively enhance the product's stability and user satisfaction.

- **Customer-reported bugs:** Tracking the number of bugs reported by customers, along with the ratio of those fixed and still open, provides essential insights into the product's performance in real-world scenarios. These metrics highlight areas where the product may be falling short of user expectations. Understanding which customers file the most bugs can also reveal patterns of product usage and highlight particularly active and engaged user segments. This feedback loop is invaluable for continuous improvement, as it helps in identifying recurring issues and developing targeted solutions that benefit the broader customer base.

- **Scalability and performance metrics:** Assessing the product's scalability and performance involves examining key metrics such as response times and the number of concurrent users the system can support. Establishing a formula or model based on these metrics allows teams to predict the product's behavior under different load conditions and prescribe actions to enhance scalability without sacrificing performance. This proactive approach ensures that the product remains robust and efficient as the user base grows, thereby avoiding potential bottlenecks and performance degradation.

- **Project delay analysis:** Analyzing project delays involves measuring the actual delay against the planned schedule and identifying the underlying causes. This analysis can reveal critical insights into project management practices, resource allocation, and risk management strategies. By understanding the reasons behind delays, teams can implement corrective measures to improve future project timelines. This might include better forecasting, streamlined workflows, and enhanced communication channels, all aimed at minimizing disruptions and ensuring timely project delivery. Retrospective needs to be done to ensure that these delays do not happen in the upcoming projects. What changes need to be done in the projects needs to be analyzed. The relevant data needs to be pulled from JIRA and other tools, and the learnings need to be incorporated into the next project.

- **Support efficiency metrics:** The efficiency and effectiveness of the support organization can be gauged by tracking the number of issues handled and resolved by Level 1 (L1) and Level 2 (L2) support teams. L1 support typically addresses basic issues and initial troubleshooting, while L2 support handles more complex problems that require specialized knowledge. By monitoring these metrics, organizations can assess the performance of their support teams, identify areas for improvement, and ensure that customer issues are resolved promptly and satisfactorily. This focus on support efficiency is key to maintaining high levels of customer satisfaction and loyalty.

Security and compliance metrics

The security and compliance metrics are as follows:

- **Number of security issues pending:** Identify the number of security issues that are still pending to be fixed. This metric indicates the total number of security vulnerabilities that are open, providing an index of the product's vulnerability. By keeping track of pending security issues, the development team can prioritize addressing these vulnerabilities to enhance the security posture of the product. Regularly reviewing and updating this metric ensures that critical security gaps are not overlooked and appropriate resources are allocated to resolve them.

- **Number of security issues fixed:** Determine the number of security issues that have been identified and successfully resolved. This metric shows the efforts made to improve the product's security and protect users from potential threats. By analyzing the trends in resolved security issues, the team can gauge the effectiveness of their security measures and identify areas for further improvement. This metric also helps in demonstrating to stakeholders the proactive steps taken to maintain a secure product environment.

- **Other compliance issues open/fixed:** Determine the number of other compliance issues that are open or closed. This includes activities like static analysis and other compliance checks that need to be looked into to ensure the product meets industry standards and regulations. By monitoring compliance issues, the team can ensure that the product adheres to relevant laws and guidelines, thereby avoiding potential legal and financial repercussions. Regular compliance audits and reviews help in maintaining a high standard of quality and trustworthiness for the product.

Tools

The following tools can be used to get different metrics, as discussed above. Many of the metrics can be obtained from JIRA or any bug-tracking tool.

Unit test	Jacoco,
Test Cases	Qtest,
Lines of code	Bitbucket, Github
Bug/User Story/Requirements/Epic Reports	JIRA
Velocity Reports	JIRA

Table 17.1 Tools for metrics gathering

Remember, some projects may succeed even without collecting these metrics. It ultimately boils down to the technical expertise of the team. Even after collecting these metrics, projects may fail. Therefore, the project manager needs to balance metrics and technical work. Being solid in technicalities, along with teamwork, is one of the main pillars of success for the team. Analysis is important for the project, and these reports will help to analyze. Not all teams will be technical experts at the beginning of the project. Over some time, these numbers can be improved, and this will help in improving the product quality.

Software process engineers are involved in getting this data on an ongoing basis. Not all reports can be developed and tracked by the project manager. Some of the important reports, as required by the project manager, can be developed by the project manager. Not all organizations have the budget for process engineers. One process engineer can span multiple product teams. That way, the budget can be optimized.

In addition, it is crucial to leverage automated tools that can help streamline the process of collecting and analyzing these metrics. Automated tools can provide real-time insights and reduce the manual effort required, allowing the team to focus more on critical development tasks. For example, a set of Python scripts can be written to collect the metrics and generate analytics. For instance, **continuous integration and continuous deployment (CI/CD)** tools like Jenkins and CircleCI can be integrated with JIRA and other tracking tools to provide a seamless flow of information and updates.

Moreover, regular training and upskilling of the team members can greatly enhance their ability to produce high-quality, secure code. This includes workshops on the latest security protocols, coding best practices, and the effective use of the tools mentioned above. Encouraging a culture of continuous learning and improvement within the team can lead to significant long-term benefits.

Lastly, fostering open communication and collaboration among all team members, including developers, testers, project managers, and process engineers, is vital. Regular meetings, clear documentation, and an open-door policy for sharing ideas and concerns can help ensure that everyone is aligned with the project's goals and working toward the same objective.

By implementing these strategies, the project can achieve a higher degree of success and security compliance, ultimately leading to the delivery of a superior product.

Conclusion

In conclusion, this chapter has provided a comprehensive exploration of metrics for software projects, highlighting their significance, applications, and benefits. Metrics serve as a powerful tool for project managers, enabling them to make data-driven decisions, track project progress, and optimize processes. By leveraging relevant metrics throughout the software development lifecycle, project managers can gain valuable insights into project performance, identify areas for improvement, and drive continuous improvement efforts. The chapter has covered various categories of metrics, including requirements metrics, architecture/design metrics, coding metrics, QA metrics, post-delivery metrics, and security metrics, equipping project managers with a wide range of metrics to utilize. Additionally, the chapter has emphasized the importance of striking a balance between metrics and technical expertise, as well as fostering teamwork and ongoing learning within the project team. By embracing metrics effectively, project managers can enhance project outcomes, meet stakeholder expectations, and deliver exceptional software products. It is essential to remember that metrics are not a guarantee of project success but rather a valuable tool to guide decision-making and process improvement. With a solid understanding of metrics and their applications, project managers can navigate the complexities of software projects with greater confidence and achieve successful project delivery.

After the project is over, post project analysis needs to be done with the metrics gathered as described above. The post project analysis to be done will be discussed in the next chapter.

Points to remember

- **Metrics provide valuable insights**: Metrics serve as a means to measure and evaluate different aspects of software projects, offering valuable insights into progress, quality, and efficiency. They enable project managers to make informed decisions and drive project success.

- **Choose relevant metrics**: It is crucial to identify and utilize metrics that are relevant to your specific project context. Different categories of metrics, such as requirements metrics, architecture/design metrics, coding metrics, QA metrics, post-delivery metrics, and security metrics, can provide insights into different aspects of the project.

- **Metrics drive data-driven decision-making**: By leveraging metrics, project managers can make data-driven decisions. Metrics provide objective and quantifiable information about project performance, enabling project managers to assess progress, identify bottlenecks, and allocate resources effectively.

- **Continuous improvement is key**: Metrics play a vital role in driving continuous improvement efforts within software projects. By analyzing metrics, project managers can identify areas for improvement, optimize processes, and enhance overall project outcomes.

- **Balance metrics with technical expertise**: While metrics are important, it is crucial to strike a balance between metrics and technical expertise. Technical proficiency and teamwork are essential pillars of success in software development, and metrics should be used as a tool to support and enhance technical work.

- **Communication is vital**: Metrics provide a tangible and measurable way to communicate project progress and performance to stakeholders. Project managers should effectively communicate metrics to stakeholders, providing regular updates, showcasing achievements, and addressing concerns or challenges.

- **Metrics are not a guarantee of success**: It is important to remember that metrics are not a guarantee of project success. They are a tool to guide decision-making and process improvement. Project managers should use metrics in conjunction with their expertise, experience, and judgment to drive successful project outcomes.

Multiple choice questions

1. **Which category of metrics evaluates the quality and characteristics of the software product?**
   a. Requirements metrics
   b. Architecture/design metrics
   c. Coding metrics
   d. Product metrics

2. **What is the recommended minimum percentage of unit test line coverage?**
   a. 50%
   b. 70%

c. 85%

d. 100%

3. **Which type of metrics measures the efficiency and effectiveness of the software development process?**

    a. Process metrics

    b. Product metrics

    c. Project metrics

    d. QA metrics.

4. **What does the number of bugs per 1000 lines of code metric indicate?**

    a. Code complexity

    b. Developer productivity

    c. Code maintainability

    d. Bug density.

5. **Which metric helps project managers assess project progress and adherence to deadlines?**

    a. Schedule metrics

    b. QA metrics

    c. Security metrics

    d. Coding metrics.

6. **Which category of metrics evaluates the progress, cost, and schedule of the software project?**

    a. Requirements metrics

    b. Architecture/design metrics

    c. Project metrics

    d. Security metrics.

7. **What is the industry standard for the number of defects per 1000 lines of code in post-release evaluation?**

    a. 1 defect

    b. 3 defects

    c. 5 defects

    d. 10 defects.

Answers

1. d

2. c

3. a

4. d

5. a

6. c

7. b

Exercises

- Consider a software project you are familiar with or imagine a hypothetical project. Identify three key metrics that would be relevant for tracking the progress and quality of the project. Explain why you chose these metrics and how they can provide valuable insights into the project's performance.

- Review a set of software requirements for a project. Based on the requirements, define two metrics that can be used to measure the completeness and stability of the requirements. Explain how these metrics can help in ensuring that the project meets the desired requirements and minimize the need for change requests.

- Assume you are a project manager overseeing a software development project. Identify three coding metrics that you would track to assess the code quality and maintainability of the project. Describe how these metrics can help in identifying potential issues, improving code quality, and facilitating future maintenance.

- Imagine you are leading a quality assurance team for a software project. Define two key metrics that you would track to assess the effectiveness of the testing process. Explain how these metrics can help in evaluating the test coverage, identifying areas of improvement, and ensuring a high level of software quality.

- Consider the post-release phase of a software project. Identify two metrics that can be used to measure customer satisfaction and identify areas for improvement in future releases. Discuss how these metrics can help in gathering feedback, addressing customer concerns, and enhancing the overall user experience.

Join our book's Discord space

Join the book's Discord Workspace for Latest updates, Offers, Tech happenings around the world, New Release and Sessions with the Authors:

https://discord.bpbonline.com

CHAPTER 18

Post Project Review

Introduction

A post-project review, also known as a project post-mortem or project retrospective, is a process that takes place after the completion of a software development project. It involves evaluating the project's overall performance, identifying lessons learned, and capturing insights to improve future projects. The primary goal of a post-project review is to assess the project's success, identify areas for improvement, and document best practices.

The post-project review is an essential part of the project management lifecycle, as it helps organizations learn from past experiences and continuously improve their software development processes.

The project completion does not mean that the entire project is completed, and then doing some of the analysis. It can be done after a couple of milestones to gauge the skills of the team and then do the analysis.

For example, in a project of 6 months, after 2 months are over, some of the analysis can be done and the feedback can be implemented in the project.

Structure

The chapter covers the following topics:

- Training

- Importance of teamwork
- Technical training
- Gradual team improvement
- Other post project tasks

Objectives

During a post-project review, the project team, stakeholders, and other relevant parties come together to reflect on the project's outcomes, processes, and challenges. It typically involves discussing the following aspects:

Evaluate whether the project met its intended goals and objectives. Identify any deviations or gaps between the initial project plan and the actual outcomes. Assess the effectiveness of project management processes, such as planning, scheduling, resource allocation, and communication. Identify any issues or bottlenecks that occurred during the project. Evaluate the performance of the project team, including their collaboration, communication, and adherence to project roles and responsibilities. Recognize individual and team achievements. Gather feedback from project stakeholders to assess their satisfaction with the project's deliverables, timelines, and overall quality. Identify areas where stakeholder expectations were not fully met. Identify key lessons learned during the project, including both positive and negative experiences. Document best practices, successful strategies, and areas for improvement to guide future projects. Based on the findings of the review, provide recommendations for process improvements, tools, methodologies, or training that can enhance future project success.

Training

Identifying training needs and opportunities is an important aspect. One does not have to wait for a full cycle to be over. The needs can be met after a few sprints in the project. Reviews can be on an ongoing basis. Here are some points to help identify training requirements:

- **Analyze project challenges**: Review the challenges faced during the project and identify areas where additional training could have mitigated or resolved those challenges. For example, if the team struggled with a specific programming language or technology, it may indicate a need for training in that area. This may help in the subsequent milestones of the project.

- **Review lessons learned**: Examine the lessons learned from the project and identify specific skills or knowledge gaps that contributed to the challenges or could have improved project outcomes. These lessons can provide insights into the areas where training would be beneficial. Holding retrospective meetings can help the team to understand what went well and what can be improved.

An example of a retrospective template for Atlassian Confluence is shown as follows:

Restrospective

⌂ Overview

Reflect on past work and identify opportunities for improvement by following the instructions for the
Retrospective Play.
  Page Properties

Date	Type // to add a date
Team	e.g., Team All-Stars
Participants	@ mention participants

Retrospective

🛈 Add your Start doing, Stop doing, and Keep doing items to the table below. We'll use these to
talk about how we can improve our process going forward.

+

Start doing	Stop doing	Keep doing
• e.g., Sparring work earlier in the development cycle	• e.g., Scheduling meetings without a clear agenda	• e.g., Sharing progress at daily standups

⌄

≛ Table options ⌄   ▢ ⌄   ▯   ⌄   ⬛   ⬛   ⋇   ▢   🗑

☑ Action items

Add 1-2 follow-up action items to help the team apply what they learned in the retrospective:

☐ Type your action, use @ to assign to someone.

Figure 18.1: Confluence retrospective template

- **Seek feedback**: Gather feedback from the project team members and stakeholders about their experience and areas where they feel additional training would have been helpful. This feedback can provide valuable insights into specific training needs.

- **Consider emerging technologies or methodologies**: If the project reveals a need to adopt new technologies or methodologies, identify training opportunities to equip the team with the necessary skills and knowledge. This will be helpful for the upcoming projects. For example, these days, **Large Language Models** (**LLMs**) have evolved rapidly. If the product manager has requested that LLM use cases be incorporated into the product, then the team needs to be trained on this new technology. It requires training, budgeting for training, and sometimes buying tools for implementation. This will require convincing senior management of the need for these tools and hence the budget allocation.

- **Collaborate with team members**: Engage in discussions with team members to understand their individual career goals and aspirations. Identify training opportunities that align with their professional development plans and can contribute to their growth.

- **Consult subject matter experts:** Seek input from **subject matter experts (SMEs)** or senior team members who can provide guidance on the skills and knowledge required for future projects. They can help identify areas where training is necessary. An SME is one who has knowledge in a particular technical area. An SME can be an internal employee or a consultant. Consultants can be hired on a need basis to provide guidance in a specialized area that the team is not aware of. For example, if the team does not have any knowledge about how to use artificial intelligence products in the project, then a consultant can be hired to impart the knowledge to the team.

- **Prioritize and plan training:** Based on the identified skill gaps and training needs, prioritize the areas that require immediate attention. Develop a training plan that outlines the specific training programs, courses, or resources needed, and allocate resources and budget accordingly.

Remember that training identification should be an ongoing process, not limited to the post-project review. Regularly assess the skill needs of the team and provide opportunities for continuous learning and development to stay up to date with industry trends and advancements.

Trainings are of two types. One is soft skills training, and the other is technical training. How do you plan for soft skills training and for technical training?

Technical training should have more investment, followed by security training, communication training, and teamwork training.

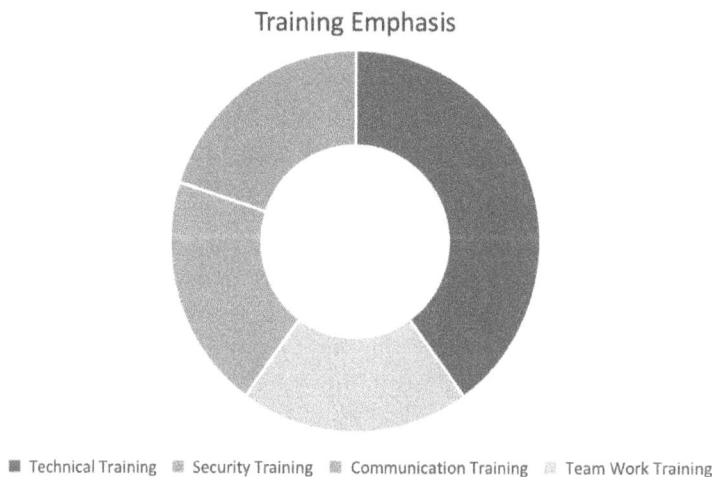

Training Emphasis

■ Technical Training ▨ Security Training ▨ Communication Training ▨ Team Work Training

Figure 18.2: Training emphasis

Soft skills training

Planning for soft skills training and technical training involves different considerations.

You must determine the soft skills that are important for the project team and align with the organization's goals. Common soft skills include communication, teamwork, leadership, problem-solving, time management, and adaptability.

Evaluate the current proficiency levels of team members in the identified soft skills. This can be done through self-assessments, surveys, or feedback from managers and peers.

The most important training for software engineers is communication. People come from different regions and different backgrounds. The way they communicate has a far-reaching effect on the project. The better the project is, if the communication is proper and correct. In the following section, we will discuss ways in which communication can be proved, not necessarily as a post-project review, but during the project too.

When planning communication training specifically for software engineers, it is important to address their unique needs and challenges. Here is a tailored approach for communication training for software engineers:

- Focus on skills such as writing concise and well-structured technical documentation, communicating complex technical concepts to non-technical stakeholders, and presenting technical information in a clear and understandable manner.

- Software engineers often work in teams and collaborate with various stakeholders. Provide training on effective collaboration, including active listening, providing and receiving constructive feedback, and resolving conflicts within a technical context. Highlight the significance of effective communication for successful teamwork and project outcomes.

- If the software engineering team follows agile methodologies, address the specific communication needs within an agile environment. Train engineers on effective communication in daily stand-ups, sprint planning, retrospectives, and other agile ceremonies. Focus on concise and transparent communication, sharing progress updates, and effectively raising and addressing technical concerns.

- **Presentation skills**: Software engineers may need to present their work or technical solutions to various audiences. Offer training on effective presentation skills, including structuring presentations, using visual aids effectively, and engaging the audience. Provide guidance on delivering technical information in a clear, concise, and engaging manner. Improve verbal communication skills, since people come from different backgrounds.

- With the increasing prevalence of remote work, focus on communication skills specific to remote collaboration. Train engineers on effective communication via emails, chats, and online meetings in remote settings.

- Remember to create a supportive environment that encourages software engineers to practice and apply their communication skills. Provide opportunities for feedback, peer review, and mentorship to foster continuous improvement. This will take time, and be patient with the engineers.

Importance of teamwork

Another important aspect is teamwork. If different team members pull projects in different directions, then the projects may not proceed well. Working as a team and pulling the project through is another soft skill that needs to be taught. There can be very talented team members in the team; however, if no teamwork is there, then the project may not succeed.

Training on teamwork is a valuable investment for organizations seeking to develop cohesive and high-performing teams. Arrange for training from external agencies that specialize in team-building activities. Breaking down groups in the team, enabling free flow of information, sharing common goals for project success, synchronization between team members as well as between teams are couple of areas which the team needs to be trained in for effective teamwork. Effective teamwork is essential for achieving shared goals, fostering innovation, and maintaining a positive work environment. Teamwork training equips individuals with the skills and knowledge to collaborate effectively, communicate openly, and build strong relationships within their teams. It covers a wide range of areas, including active listening, conflict resolution, decision-making, trust-building, effective communication, and understanding diverse perspectives.

Through interactive exercises, role-playing, and group activities, participants engage in hands-on learning experiences that simulate real-world team dynamics. They learn to recognize the strengths and contributions of team members, establish clear roles and responsibilities, and leverage individual differences to create a synergistic team environment. Teamwork training emphasizes the importance of effective communication, both verbal and non-verbal, to ensure that ideas, concerns, and feedback are shared openly and understood by all team members.

Furthermore, teamwork training focuses on conflict resolution techniques, helping individuals develop the skills to address and manage conflicts constructively. This includes fostering a culture of open dialogue, active listening, and empathy to resolve differences and find mutually beneficial solutions. Teamwork training also emphasizes the significance of collective decision-making. It equips individuals with tools and techniques to facilitate group discussions, reach consensus, and make informed decisions that consider diverse perspectives. By involving team members in the decision-making process, teamwork training empowers individuals and fosters a sense of ownership and commitment to the team's outcomes.

Overall, teamwork training promotes a culture of cooperation, encourages effective delegation, and enhances problem-solving abilities. By fostering a sense of belonging and collective responsibility, teamwork training contributes to improved team dynamics, increased productivity, and the successful achievement of project objectives. It also nurtures a positive work environment, fostering employee satisfaction, engagement, and retention. Investing in teamwork training demonstrates an organization's commitment to building strong, collaborative teams that can adapt to challenges, drive innovation, and deliver exceptional results.

Technical training

The most important aspect for the smooth execution of the project is technical training and improving the technical strength of the team. The team has to be technically good in order to do projects smoothly. Through the technical and hands-on implementation of the training obtained, the team will improve on the deliverables. However, it does not happen overnight; it requires a minimum of 1 to 2 years of grooming to get an effective team working.

To plan for the training, do the following:

- Determine the specific technical skills needed for the project. This can include programming languages, frameworks, tools, methodologies, or domain-specific knowledge.

- Evaluate the current technical proficiency of team members. This can be done through skills assessments, coding challenges, or technical interviews.

- Identify appropriate training resources for the technical skills needed. This can include online tutorials, documentation, books, video courses, instructor-led training, or specialized workshops. YouTube has a huge collection of technical training. The engineers should be encouraged to learn from YouTube and apply it in the projects.

- Emphasize practical, hands-on exercises and projects to reinforce technical skills. Provide opportunities for team members to apply their learning in real-world scenarios.

- Create a supportive environment that encourages knowledge sharing, collaboration, and mentoring among team members. Encourage experienced team members to assist and mentor those who require technical training.

- Promote a culture of continuous learning and provide resources for ongoing technical skill development. Encourage team members to explore new technologies, attend conferences, participate in webinars, and contribute to open-source projects.

- Consider evaluating the effectiveness of the technical training through assessments, tests, or certifications. This can help validate the acquired skills and provide recognition for the team members.

- Remember to tailor the training plans to the specific needs of the project and the individuals involved. Regularly assess the impact of the training and make adjustments as necessary to ensure continuous improvement.

Gradual team improvement

In an agile environment, gradual team improvement is a fundamental aspect of the iterative development process. By consistently incorporating feedback, reflecting on performance, and adapting accordingly, teams can enhance their effectiveness over time. Here are some key points to expand upon:

- **Iterative cycles**: Agile development is characterized by iterative cycles, such as sprints in Scrum. Each cycle consists of a defined timeframe where the team works on a set of prioritized tasks. At the end of each cycle, the team delivers a potentially shippable product increment.

- **Continuous feedback**: Agile teams actively seek and value feedback from stakeholders, customers, and team members. This feedback helps identify areas for improvement and guides the team in making informed decisions. Regular feedback loops ensure that the team stays aligned with project goals and customer expectations.

- **Retrospectives**: Retrospectives are an essential practice in agile methodologies. They provide a dedicated time for the team to reflect on their work, processes, and collaboration. During retrospectives, team members discuss what went well, what could be improved, and any potential actions to address identified issues. This self-assessment promotes a culture of learning and continuous improvement.

- **Identifying areas for improvement**: During retrospectives, the team analyzes their performance and identifies areas where they can improve. This may involve evaluating communication channels, identifying bottlenecks, addressing skill gaps, or refining processes. By actively seeking areas for improvement, the team can proactively address challenges and enhance their overall productivity.

- **Implementing changes**: After identifying areas for improvement, the team implements changes in the subsequent iteration or cycle. This may involve adjusting processes, refining team roles and responsibilities, adopting new tools or techniques, or enhancing communication and collaboration. The team experiments with changes and assesses their impact on productivity and quality.

- **Culture of learning and responsiveness**: Agile fosters a culture of continuous learning and responsiveness. Team members are encouraged to share knowledge, learn from mistakes, and experiment with new approaches. This culture promotes adaptability and empowers the team to respond effectively to changing requirements and challenges.

- **Incremental adjustments:** Agile teams focus on making incremental adjustments rather than large-scale changes. By taking small steps towards improvement, the team can evaluate the impact of changes and make further adjustments as needed. This iterative approach allows for a more controlled and manageable evolution of the team's processes and practices.

- **Enhanced efficiency and effectiveness**: Through gradual improvement, teams become more efficient and effective in delivering high-quality outcomes. By addressing issues early on and continuously refining their practices, teams can optimize their workflows, reduce waste, and streamline their development processes.

By embracing a dynamic and iterative approach to team improvement, agile teams can continuously evolve and deliver better results. The emphasis on feedback, reflection, and adaptation enables teams to enhance their collaboration, communication, and overall performance, leading to increased satisfaction for both the team and stakeholders.

Other post project tasks

Let us look at additional post project tasks.

Archiving of documents and artifacts

Proper archiving of documents and artifacts is essential for maintaining an organized repository of project information. This enables team members to easily refer back to past documentation, decisions, and milestones. Effective archiving practices include categorizing files systematically, ensuring metadata is accurately recorded, and utilizing reliable storage solutions. Regular audits of the archived materials can help ensure they remain accessible and relevant, enhancing the overall efficiency and knowledge management within the team. The following are some of the tasks that need to be taken care of:

- **Compliance and legal considerations**: Depending on the nature of the project and industry, there may be compliance and legal requirements regarding document retention and archiving. It is important to be aware of any specific regulations or guidelines that apply to the project and ensure that the archiving practices align with these requirements. This includes considerations such as data privacy, confidentiality, and retention periods for different types of documents. Auditing has to be done periodically to check if compliance is maintained. Auditing is critical; without it, there can be slippage in compliance. Auditing teams can be either internal or external. Bigger companies have internal auditing teams. Smaller companies can use the services of external auditing agencies.

- **Knowledge management and collaboration**: Effective archiving practices contribute to improved knowledge management and collaboration within the team.

By maintaining a well-organized archive, team members can easily access historical information, learn from past experiences, and leverage existing knowledge to make informed decisions. This promotes continuity, reduces duplication of work, and fosters a culture of learning and improvement. For example, if similar work has been done by other teams in the past, those references can be investigated for architecture or design. Some of the modules can also be reused.

Ability to pull from archives

The ability to quickly retrieve archived documents and artifacts is crucial for addressing urgent inquiries, conducting audits, or providing historical context to new team members. Implementing an efficient search and retrieval system, such as tagging, indexing, and using advanced search functionalities, can significantly reduce the time spent looking for specific documents. Additionally, training team members on best practices for document retrieval and familiarizing them with the archiving system can further streamline the process, ensuring that critical information is always within easy reach when needed.

Cross pollinating team members

Moving team members to other teams after the end of the project is a strategic approach that can enhance organizational flexibility and knowledge sharing. This practice can help distribute expertise across various projects and foster a culture of continuous learning and development. It also ensures that team members remain engaged and motivated by exposing them to new challenges and environments, thereby preventing stagnation and encouraging innovation. Furthermore, transitioning team members can facilitate cross-functional collaboration, as individuals bring their unique perspectives and skills to different teams, ultimately leading to a more dynamic and resilient organization.

Rewarding the team

Rewarding the team with outings and gifts as a mark of project success can be a valuable practice to acknowledge and celebrate the achievements of the team. Recognizing and appreciating the efforts and contributions of team members not only boosts morale but also fosters a positive and motivating work environment. Here are some key points to expand upon:

- **Celebrating achievements**: Rewarding the team with outings and gifts provides a tangible way to celebrate project success. It acknowledges the hard work, dedication, and accomplishments of the team members who have contributed to the project's achievements. By taking the time to celebrate milestones and successes, team members feel valued and motivated to continue performing at their best.

- **Morale boost**: Rewards and celebrations have a positive impact on team morale. They create a sense of camaraderie and appreciation within the team, fostering a supportive and encouraging work environment. When team members feel recognized and rewarded for their efforts, it increases job satisfaction and overall engagement, leading to higher levels of productivity and commitment.

- **Team bonding and collaboration**: Outings and team activities provide an opportunity for team members to bond and build stronger relationships. These activities can be designed to encourage teamwork, communication, and collaboration outside the project context. By engaging in social interactions and shared experiences, team members develop a deeper sense of camaraderie, which can translate into improved collaboration and communication during project work.

- **Motivation and retention**: Recognizing and rewarding the team's efforts can serve as a powerful motivator. It instills a sense of pride and accomplishment, encouraging team members to continue performing at a high level. Moreover, such rewards can contribute to employee retention by fostering a positive work culture and demonstrating that the organization values and appreciates the team's hard work.

- **Tailoring rewards**: It is important to consider individual preferences and motivations when selecting rewards. While outings and gifts can be effective, it is essential to understand the interests and preferences of team members. Some individuals may appreciate team-building activities, while others may prefer personalized gifts or recognition. By tailoring rewards to the preferences of team members, the impact and effectiveness of the rewards can be maximized.

- **Balanced approach**: It is important to strike a balance between celebrating achievements and maintaining a focus on continuous improvement. While rewards can be motivating, they should not overshadow the intrinsic satisfaction of the work itself or the long-term goals of the project. It is crucial to ensure that the team remains focused on the project's objectives and maintains a sense of continuous learning and growth.

- **Recognition and appreciation**: In addition to outings and gifts, it is equally important to provide regular recognition and appreciation for the efforts of team members. Simple gestures such as public acknowledgments, thank-you notes, or team-wide appreciation events can go a long way in fostering a culture of recognition and appreciation. These acts of recognition can be more sustainable and scalable than occasional outings and gifts.

By rewarding the team with outings and gifts as a mark of project success, organizations can create a positive work environment, boost team morale, and enhance motivation and collaboration. However, it is crucial to consider individual preferences, strike a balance, and ensure that recognition and appreciation are not solely dependent on material rewards. A holistic approach to rewards and recognition can contribute to the long-term success and satisfaction of the team.

Conclusion

In conclusion, the chapter highlights the importance of post-project reviews in the software development lifecycle. It emphasizes the need to evaluate project success, identify areas for improvement, and document best practices. The chapter also emphasizes the significance of soft skills and technical training to enhance team capabilities. Effective communication, teamwork, and technical proficiency are crucial for project success. The archiving of documents and artifacts is essential for knowledge management and efficient project management. The ability to retrieve archived materials quickly is vital for timely access to critical information. Furthermore, gradual team improvement through iterative cycles, continuous feedback, and incremental adjustments is key to enhancing efficiency and effectiveness. Finally, rewarding the team with outings and gifts as a mark of project success fosters a positive work environment and boosts morale. Overall, implementing these practices contributes to improved project outcomes and team performance.

Now, since all the major aspects of the project have been covered, the next assessment of the team members will be conducted. Ultimately, projects are run by people, and appraising the team is of utmost importance. The next chapter will discuss appraisals in more detail.

Points to remember

- Post-project reviews, also known as project post-mortems or retrospectives, are essential for evaluating project performance and capturing insights for future improvement.

- The primary goals of a post-project review are to assess project success, identify areas for improvement, and document best practices.

- Soft skills training, such as communication, teamwork, and presentation skills, is crucial for effective project collaboration and success.

- Technical training is essential for enhancing the team's technical proficiency and keeping up with emerging technologies and methodologies.

- Archiving documents and artifacts systematically ensures an organized repository of project information, facilitating easy access and reference.

- The ability to quickly retrieve archived materials is important for timely access to critical information and efficient project management.

- Gradual team improvement is achieved through iterative cycles, continuous feedback, and incremental adjustments.

- Retrospectives play a key role in team improvement by providing a dedicated time for reflection, identifying areas for enhancement, and implementing changes.

- Regular audits of archived materials help ensure their accessibility and relevance, enhancing overall knowledge management within the team.

- Rewarding the team with outings and gifts as a mark of project success boosts morale, fosters a positive work environment, and recognizes individual and team achievements.

Multiple choice questions

1. **What is the primary goal of a post-project review?**
   a. To celebrate project completion
   b. To assess project success and identify areas for improvement
   c. To document project requirements
   d. To assign blame for project failures

2. **Which of the following is an example of a soft skill?**
   a. Programming in a specific language
   b. Writing clean code
   c. Effective communication
   d. Technical troubleshooting

3. **Why is the archiving of documents and artifacts important in project management?**
   a. It helps reduce storage costs
   b. It ensures all documents are deleted
   c. It facilitates knowledge sharing and easy access to past information
   d. It is a legal requirement

4. **What is the key focus of gradual team improvement in an agile environment?**
   a. Completing projects faster
   b. Implementing large-scale changes
   c. Making incremental adjustments and addressing challenges
   d. Assigning blame for project failures

5. **What is the role of retrospectives in team improvement?**
   a. Celebrating project milestones
   b. Reflecting on project outcomes and identifying areas for improvement
   c. Assigning tasks for the next project phase
   d. Providing feedback to stakeholders

6. **What is the benefit of providing soft skills training to the team?**

    a. Improving technical proficiency

    b. Enhancing collaboration and communication

    c. Reducing project costs

    d. Increasing project scope

7. **Why is the ability to quickly retrieve archived documents important?**

    a. To increase storage capacity

    b. To impress stakeholders

    c. To address urgent inquiries and provide historical context

    d. To reduce the need for archiving

8. **How can team outings and gifts contribute to project success?**

    a. By providing financial incentives for team members

    b. By fostering a positive work environment and boosting morale

    c. By eliminating the need for training

    d. By assigning blame for project failures

9. **What is the role of technical training in team improvement?**

    a. Enhancing soft skills

    b. Fostering collaboration and communication

    c. Keeping up with emerging technologies and methodologies

    d. Eliminating the need for archiving

Answers

1. b
2. c
3. c
4. c
5. b
6. b
7. c
8. b
9. c

Exercises

- Reflect on a recent software development project you were involved in. Write a post-project review, identifying the project's successes, areas for improvement, and lessons learned. Propose specific actions to address the identified areas for improvement.

- Choose a soft skill, such as communication or teamwork. Develop a training plan to enhance that skill within your project team. Outline the key topics, activities, and resources that would be included in the training program.

- Identify three essential documents or artifacts that should be archived for a software development project. Create a categorization system and folder structure to organize these documents systematically. Write a brief description of each document and its importance for future reference.

- Imagine you need to retrieve a specific document from an archive quickly. Design a search and retrieval system that would allow you to find the document efficiently. Consider the use of metadata, tags, or indexing to facilitate the search process.

- Conduct a retrospective for a recent project or a specific phase of a project. Gather the project team and discuss what went well, what could have been improved, and any actions to address the identified areas for improvement. Document the outcomes of the retrospective and share them with the team.

- Plan a team outing or activity to celebrate a project milestone or success. Consider the preferences and interests of team members and propose a suitable activity. Outline the logistics, budget, and desired outcomes for the outing.

- Develop a technical training program for your project team. Identify a specific technical skill or technology that would benefit the team. Outline the key topics, learning resources, and hands-on exercises that would be included in the training program. Consider the duration and delivery format of the training.

Join our book's Discord space

Join the book's Discord Workspace for Latest updates, Offers, Tech happenings around the world, New Release and Sessions with the Authors:

https://discord.bpbonline.com

CHAPTER 19
Appraisals

Introduction

Appraisals in software projects are a critical component for evaluating progress, quality, and effectiveness. They provide a structured approach to measure project success and make data-driven decisions. This chapter explores the significance, methodologies, and best practices of appraisals in software projects. We will examine their integration into the software development lifecycle, key metrics used, and the role of stakeholders. Different types of appraisals, such as technical, process, and team appraisals, will be discussed, along with their benefits and challenges. By understanding appraisal principles and practices, software professionals can optimize development processes, enhance product quality, and foster a culture of continuous improvement. Join us as we unravel the world of appraisals in software projects and discover the valuable insights they provide.

Structure

The chapter covers the following topics:

- Setting goals
- Give feedback throughout the year
- Reward the best performers
- Impartiality amongst employees

- Upholding ethical principles
- Removal of personal biases
- Project managers must be technical

Setting goals

Goals should be set by the manager for the team members based on the SMART objective. The acronym SMART stands for Specific, Measurable, Achievable, Relevant, and Time-bound.

SMART goals are a widely recognized framework for setting effective and actionable goals. Let us break down each component:

- **Specific**: Goals should be clear, well-defined, and specific. They should answer the questions of who, what, where, when, and why. Specific goals provide a clear direction and help avoid ambiguity. For example, instead of a general goal like *improving coding skills,* a specific goal would be to *learn Python programming by completing an online course and building a small web application* by a certain date.

- **Measurable**: Goals should be measurable to track progress and determine when they have been achieved. They should include concrete criteria or metrics that can be used to evaluate success. Measurable goals enable objective assessment and provide a sense of accomplishment. For example, a measurable goal could be to *increase the software test coverage to 90% by the end of the quarter.*

- **Achievable**: Goals should be realistic and attainable, considering the available resources, skills, and constraints. They should stretch individuals or teams to reach their full potential, but still be within reach. Setting unattainable goals can lead to frustration and demotivation. An achievable goal takes into account the current capabilities and available support. For example, *completing the development of the core features of the application within six months* would be an achievable goal based on the project scope and available resources.

- **Relevant**: Goals should be aligned with the broader objectives of the project, team, or organization. They should have direct relevance and contribute to the desired outcomes. Relevant goals ensure that efforts are focused on what truly matters and provide a clear connection to the overall mission. For example, if the project goal is to improve user experience, a relevant goal could be to *reduce the average page load time by 20% to enhance user satisfaction,* and it should be done within a certain time frame.

- **Time-bound**: Goals should have a specific timeframe or deadline for completion. This creates a sense of urgency, helps prioritize tasks, and enables effective tracking of progress. Time-bound goals prevent procrastination and provide a clear target for achievement. For example, *launching the mobile app by the end of the second quarter* sets a specific time boundary for the goal.

By adhering to the SMART framework, software projects can set goals that are clear, measurable, attainable, relevant, and time-bound. This approach increases the likelihood of success, enhances motivation, and facilitates effective evaluation and improvement throughout the appraisal process.

Example of SMART objectives

Assuming a hypothetical project, an engineer is working on a user onboarding feature. The following are some of the SMART objectives that can be set for the engineer from January of any particular year:

- Implement the user onboarding feature by June of this year. The release is scheduled for October of this year.

- There should be fewer than five customer-reported bugs in user onboarding by December this year after the project is released.

- While coding, there should be fewer than five regressions in the code by June this year.

- 0 instances of conflict throughout the year.

- Get trained in Java Springboot by May this year. Get certification by July this year.

- File two patents by December this year.

- Review the code of two other features by December this year.

As can be seen, the objectives have measurable metrics and a defined timeline. This way, it becomes easy to measure and convey to the engineers whether the objective has been met successfully.

Give feedback throughout the year

Annual appraisals have been done away with in many organizations, however, on an ongoing basis, a feedback cycle is created, which helps to provide feedback to the employees regularly. The manager should prepare for a meeting in case of a 1:1 meeting with the reporters. It should not start with *Tell me what do we have to discuss today.* Without an agenda and research, no proper feedback can be given to the employee. A 10-minute research also helps a lot to give feedback to the employee. If 10 minutes is kept aside to prepare the agenda and research, then the meetings will be very effective.

Providing feedback throughout the year is an essential and ongoing practice in effective performance appraisals for software projects. In the fast-paced and rapidly evolving field of software development, regular and timely feedback plays a pivotal role in driving continuous improvement, addressing issues promptly, and ensuring an accurate assessment of individual and team progress. Feedback should be provided verbally as well as in written documentation. Documentation can be in emails, Word documents, or a tool. These documents should be retained as long as possible, ideally for 3-4 years. Feedback is from the manager's observations, as well as from the 360-degree feedback obtained from the team. The manager should ensure that periodic feedback is being taken from the colleagues working with the employee.

By offering feedback at various stages of the project, engineers can gain valuable insights into the strengths and weaknesses of their strengths and weaknesses. Positive feedback acknowledges and reinforces areas of strength, boosting morale and motivation. Constructive criticism, on the other hand, provides opportunities for growth and improvement by highlighting areas that require attention.

The iterative feedback process establishes a culture of open communication and collaboration within the software development team. It encourages team members to actively seek and provide feedback, fostering a supportive and learning-oriented environment. Through ongoing feedback exchanges, team members can share knowledge, best practices, and lessons learned, leading to enhanced collaboration and more effective problem-solving.

Timely feedback allows for the prompt identification and resolution of issues. By addressing concerns as they arise, potential risks can be mitigated, and necessary adjustments can be made in a timely manner. This proactive approach helps prevent minor issues from escalating into significant problems, ultimately improving the overall quality and success of the software project.

Incorporating regular feedback into the appraisal process is not only beneficial for the project but also for the growth and development of software professionals. It provides individuals with a clear understanding of their performance, areas for improvement, and specific actions they can take to enhance their skills. By receiving ongoing feedback, developers can refine their practices, expand their knowledge, and continuously strive for excellence in their work.

Furthermore, the consistent feedback loop creates a sense of accountability and ownership among team members. They become active participants in their own professional development, taking responsibility for their performance and actively seeking opportunities to learn and grow.

The mid-year or year-end appraisal should be a collation of all the feedback provided throughout the year. It should not be any different from the feedback provided consistently. Also having the recorded meeting notes throughout the year helps in collating and presenting in the mid-year or year end appraisal meeting.

Overall, integrating regular and timely feedback into the appraisal process is a powerful tool for enhancing project outcomes and fostering the growth and development of software professionals. It creates a culture of continuous improvement, collaboration, and open communication, ultimately leading to more successful and impactful software projects.

This also provides ample time for the engineers to improve in a particular area. If the feedback is provided early and the engineer is committed to improving, it helps in executing the project, too.

Reward the best performers

Rewarding the best performers is an important practice in software projects to recognize and motivate individuals who consistently demonstrate exceptional performance. By acknowledging and rewarding top performers, organizations can foster a positive work culture, encourage continued excellence, and drive overall project success.

To identify top performers using SMART goals, it is important to combine them with other performance assessment methods, such as:

- **Regular performance reviews**: The manager must conduct periodic evaluations to assess progress towards SMART goals and overall performance. These reviews provide an opportunity to discuss achievements, challenges, and areas for improvement.

- **Peer feedback**: The manager must seek input from colleagues and team members who have worked closely with the individual. Peer feedback can provide valuable insights into collaboration, teamwork, and overall performance.

- **Managerial observations**: Managers and supervisors can provide their observations and assessments based on their interactions with the individual and their overall performance.

- **Quantitative metrics**: Consider additional performance metrics such as productivity, quality of work, customer satisfaction, or impact on project outcomes. These metrics can provide a more holistic view of an individual's performance.

- **Difficult problem solving**: Top performers should be able to solve difficult problems in the project. They should be either solving the problems individually or by driving a team of engineers. If the person can solve difficult problems, by driving a team of engineers, the person must be a top performer in the team. Weight should also be given to the complexity of the problem solved.

By combining SMART goals with other performance assessment methods, organizations can identify top performers who consistently achieve their goals, demonstrate exceptional skills, contribute significantly to project success, and exhibit strong overall performance. This has to be a continuous process throughout the year. A manager needs to put in hard work to get these details to be confident in the assessment.

The employees can be arranged in order of performance and where the best performing employee in the team is ranked at the top and the worst performing employee is ranked at the bottom. The employees who end up in the top half will be rewarded more and retained for the future success of the team.

Impartiality amongst employees

Irrespective of an individual's religion, caste, creed, or any other personal characteristic, managers must uphold the principles of absolute impartiality when conducting appraisals and performance reviews. To ensure a fair and unbiased appraisal process, it is crucial to eliminate any form of bias that may be associated with an employee's religion, country of origin, skin color, or other personal characteristics. By focusing solely on an individual's professional achievements, skills, and contributions, managers can create an environment that promotes fairness, equity, and diversity within the workplace.

By removing biases related to personal characteristics, managers can more accurately assess an employee's performance and potential. This allows for a more objective evaluation that is not influenced by factors that are irrelevant to an individual's professional capabilities. Emphasizing the importance of performance and merit helps to create a work culture that values diversity and inclusion, where individuals are recognized and rewarded based on their contributions and demonstrated abilities.

Promoting fairness and equity in the appraisal process contributes to a positive work environment where all employees feel valued and respected and have equal opportunities for growth and advancement. It fosters a sense of belonging and encourages individuals to reach their full potential, knowing that their performance will be evaluated on the basis of their work rather than personal characteristics.

By maintaining a strong commitment to impartiality and focusing on professional achievements, skills, and contributions, managers can create an environment that not only upholds the principles of fairness and equity but also maximizes the potential of every individual within the organization. This approach contributes to a diverse and inclusive workplace that celebrates the unique talents and perspectives of all employees, ultimately leading to greater innovation, collaboration, and overall success

Dealing with unfair practices

The manager must notice when an employee tries to gain favor or ingratiate themselves through flattery or excessive praise of the manager. Managers should be careful about this so that during appraisals, there should not be any bias for this kind of employee. While some employees may engage in this behavior in an attempt to improve their standing or gain certain benefits, it is generally not a recommended or effective approach in a professional setting.

It is important to foster genuine and respectful professional relationships based on merit, open communication, and mutual respect. Employees should focus on demonstrating their skills, performance, and contributions through their work and maintain professionalism in their interactions with their superiors.

Building a healthy and positive working relationship with managers is best achieved through open and honest communication, proactive collaboration, and consistent delivery of high-quality work. Employees should strive to be reliable and accountable and demonstrate their value through their expertise and dedication to their responsibilities.

While it is natural to seek recognition and advancement, it is important to do so in a genuine and authentic manner based on one's abilities and accomplishments. Anything done by unfair means should be avoided. Anything done through unethical means eventually gets caught. Managers and systems in place in an organization are pretty strong these days to determine unethical behavior. For example, let us say a task has been given to someone. This person, instead of doing the work by themselves, gets it done by someone else. This is unethical behavior and should be avoided. Eventually, this kind of behavior gets caught. By focusing on professional growth, maintaining a strong work ethic, and fostering positive working relationships, employees can create a solid foundation for career development and success.

Upholding ethical principles

Being ethical in gathering feedback is essential to maintain trust, respect, and fairness within the workplace. Here are some key principles to guide ethical feedback collection:

- **Informed consent**: Obtain the informed consent of individuals before collecting feedback. Clearly communicate the purpose, process, and potential outcomes of the feedback collection, ensuring that participants understand how their feedback will be used.

- **Confidentiality and anonymity**: Protect the confidentiality and anonymity of individuals providing feedback. Assure participants that their responses will be kept confidential and that their identities will not be disclosed without their explicit permission.

- **Voluntary participation**: Ensure that participation in feedback collection is voluntary. Employees should not be coerced or pressured to provide feedback. Respect their autonomy and allow them to choose whether or not to participate.

- **Objectivity and fairness**: Strive for objectivity and fairness in the feedback collection process. Use standardized and unbiased methods to gather feedback, avoiding leading or manipulative questions. Treat all feedback with equal consideration and avoid favoritism or bias.

- **Avoid retaliation**: Assure employees that providing honest feedback will not result in any form of retaliation. Create a safe environment where individuals feel comfortable expressing their opinions and concerns without fear of negative consequences.

By adhering to these ethical principles, organizations can foster a culture of trust, openness, and respect. Ethical feedback collection promotes employee engagement, supports personal and professional growth, and contributes to the overall improvement of the work environment.

An example of gathering feedback is shown as follows. The feedback providers will be asked to put a ranking between 1-5 against each of these criteria. The points will be totaled. Whoever scores the most will be the best performer on the team.

The different points against which the engineers are judged can be listed as follows:

- Name of the engineer

- Scope (focused to broad)
- Decision-making impact (limited to moderate)
- Task focus (is able to focus on broader tasks)
- Task complexity
- Leadership and influencing skills
- Communication skills
- Team skills
- Self sufficient
- Completes tasks on time
- Quality of tasks completed
- Goto person
- Technical competency
- **TOTAL** of all the points

Removal of personal biases

Personal liking of an individual can also be an unconscious bias, which may affect the appraisal. The manager may like one individual over others, and the rest of the team may assume that the appraisal process is just paperwork. The manager will anyway promote the people whom the manager likes. This will have a detrimental impact on the team. Managers should remove this unconscious bias and do an unbiased appraisal. The methodologies that have been discussed in the previous sections are followed, and then, to a large extent, the appraisals will be fair to most people.

Manager should attend trainings to know how to remove biasness from their minds. There is always an unconscious bias, which also needs to be removed. The only way is to attend training regarding the subject. Region, religion, political opinions, gender bias, vendetta, etc., should be kept aside while appraising a person.

Subjective good performance

Some employees show a lot of work just before the appraisal, which means they significantly increase their effort and productivity right before their performance review is due, often to make a positive impression on their manager and potentially secure a better raise or promotion rather than consistently performing at that level throughout the evaluation period. The manager needs to understand this from the monthly feedback and compare it with other engineers. Appraisals are always relative.

Non-performing and deceptive employees should be removed from the team. They create negativity in the team and demotivate the performers in the team. This kind of employee should be put in a performance improvement plan and removed from the team. Each and every company has a performance improvement plan process. The manager needs to work with human resources staff to put an employee in the performance improvement plan.

Project managers must be technical

Having technical proficiency as a project manager can indeed contribute to earning the respect of team members. When a project manager possesses strong technical knowledge and skills, it can lead to several positive outcomes.

Technical proficiency enables project managers to communicate effectively with team members about project requirements, challenges, and potential solutions. This fosters clear and meaningful communication, as team members feel understood and confident in the project manager's ability to grasp technical complexities.

A project manager with technical expertise can provide valuable guidance and direction to team members. They can offer insights, advice, and problem-solving strategies, which team members appreciate and respect. This expertise helps build trust and confidence in the project manager's leadership.

Technical proficiency allows project managers to make informed decisions based on a solid understanding of the project's technical aspects. This helps in assessing risks, evaluating trade-offs, and making sound choices, which team members recognize and respect.

A technically skilled project manager can better understand the challenges and constraints faced by team members. This understanding fosters empathy and enables the project manager to provide appropriate support, resources, and guidance, which earns the respect and appreciation of the team.

Technical expertise equips project managers with the ability to identify and address technical issues effectively. By contributing to problem-solving efforts, project managers demonstrate their value and earn the respect of team members who rely on their guidance.

However, it is important to note that technical proficiency alone may not be sufficient to earn the complete respect of team members. It is equally crucial for project managers to possess strong leadership, communication, and interpersonal skills. Building positive relationships, demonstrating integrity, and fostering a collaborative and supportive environment are equally important factors in earning the respect of team members.

By combining technical expertise with effective leadership and interpersonal skills, project managers can create an environment where team members feel valued, supported, and respected, ultimately leading to more successful project outcomes.

Conclusion

Appraisals play a significant role in software projects, providing a structured approach to evaluate progress, quality, and effectiveness. By incorporating regular feedback, setting SMART goals, and maintaining ethical practices, organizations can optimize the appraisal process and create a positive work environment. Recognizing and rewarding top performers based on merit, while ensuring fairness and removing biases, fosters a culture of equity and motivation. Additionally, project managers who possess technical proficiency can earn the respect of team members through effective communication, expert guidance, and problem-solving skills. By adhering to these principles and practices, software projects can drive continuous improvement, enhance performance, and foster a culture of excellence and inclusivity. With a focus on fairness, objectivity, and growth, appraisals become a valuable tool for maximizing the potential of individuals and teams, ultimately leading to successful software project outcomes.

Points to remember

- Appraisals in software projects are crucial for evaluating progress, quality, and effectiveness.

- Set **Specific, Measurable, Achievable, Relevant, Time-bound** (**SMART**) goals to provide clear and actionable objectives.

- Regular and ongoing feedback throughout the year is essential for continuous improvement and addressing performance concerns.

- Rewards should be based on merit and aligned with performance, not influenced by personal characteristics.

- Conduct appraisals irrespective of religion, caste, creed, or any other personal characteristic.

- Ethical practices are vital when gathering feedback, including informed consent, confidentiality, and fairness.

- Be aware of employees who intensify their efforts just before the appraisal and address the issue through consistent evaluation and ongoing feedback.

- Technical proficiency in project management can contribute to earning the respect of team members, but strong leadership and interpersonal skills are also important.

- Mitigate unconscious biases in the appraisal process to ensure fairness and accurate evaluations.

- Address non-performing employees through performance improvement plans, training, and support, with termination as a last resort.

Multiple choice questions

1. **Which of the following is a key principle of setting goals for appraisals?**
    a. Ambiguity
    b. Vagueness

    c.   Specificity

    d.   Inconsistency

2. **What does the SMART acronym stand for in the context of goal setting?**

    a.   Specific, Measurable, Achievable, Relevant, Timely

    b.   Standard, Measurable, Achievable, Relevant, Timely

    c.   Specific, Measurable, Ambitious, Relevant, Timely

    d.   Standard, Measurable, Ambitious, Relevant, Timely

3. **What is the benefit of providing feedback throughout the year?**

    a.   It helps maintain employee morale

    b.   It is a requirement for annual appraisals

    c.   It ensures consistent performance

    d.   It allows managers to manipulate the appraisal process

4. **Why is it important to remove biases during the appraisal process?**

    a.   To create a toxic work environment

    b.   To ensure fairness and objectivity

    c.   To favor specific employees

    d.   To promote personal preferences

5. **How can project managers earn the respect of team members?**

    a.   Through technical proficiency

    b.   Through effective communication

    c.   Through strong leadership skills

    d.   All of the above

6. **What is the purpose of ethical feedback collection?**

    a.   To manipulate employees

    b.   To ensure confidentiality and fairness

    c.   To create bias in appraisals

    d.   To favor specific individuals

7. **How should non-performing employees be addressed?**

    a.   Terminate them immediately

    b.   Provide ongoing feedback and support

    c.   Ignore their performance issues

    d.   Promote them to a higher position

8. **What is the role of continuous improvement in the appraisal process?**

    a. To maintain the status quo

    b. To encourage employee growth and development

    c. To create a toxic work environment

    d. To promote biases in evaluations

Answer

1. c
2. a
3. c
4. b
5. d
6. b
7. b
8. b

Exercises

- **Exercise: Setting SMART goals task**: Choose a specific software development goal and write it using the SMART framework. Include the specific, measurable, achievable, relevant, and time-bound elements.

- **Exercise: Providing constructive feedback task**: Imagine you are a project manager providing feedback to a team member on their performance. Write a constructive feedback message highlighting their strengths and areas for improvement. Focus on specific examples and provide actionable suggestions for growth.

- **Exercise: Identifying biases task**: Reflect on your own potential biases in the appraisal process. Identify any unconscious biases you may have and consider how they could impact your evaluations. Write down strategies you can employ to mitigate these biases.

- **Exercise: Conducting a mock appraisal task**: Role-play a mock appraisal scenario with a colleague or friend. Take turns being the appraiser and the employee. Practice providing feedback, discussing performance goals, and addressing areas for improvement. Provide constructive feedback and suggestions for growth.

- **Exercise: Appraisal process improvement task**: Evaluate your organization's current appraisal process. Identify one area for improvement and propose a specific change or enhancement that could make the process more effective, fair, or inclusive. Justify your proposed change and outline the potential benefits it could bring.

Index